CAMBRIDGE LIBRARY COLLECTION

Books of enduring scholarly value

Archaeology

The discovery of material remains from the recent or the ancient past has always been a source of fascination, but the development of archaeology as an academic discipline which interpreted such finds is relatively recent. It was the work of Winckelmann at Pompeii in the 1760s which first revealed the potential of systematic excavation to scholars and the wider public. Pioneering figures of the nineteenth century such as Schliemann, Layard and Petrie transformed archaeology from a search for ancient artifacts, by means as crude as using gunpowder to break into a tomb, to a science which drew from a wide range of disciplines - ancient languages and literature, geology, chemistry, social history - to increase our understanding of human life and society in the remote past.

The Care of Ancient Monuments

The eminent art historian Gerard Baldwin Brown (1849–1932) held, for fifty years, the first Chair in the History of Art in Britain at the University of Edinburgh. He published on a wide range of art and architecture; his major work was the six-volume *Arts in Early England* (1903–37). His interest in the wider social context of art was reflected in his concern for the preservation of ancient monuments for the public. It was after the publication of the present book in 1906 that Brown was appointed member of a Royal Commission to compile an inventory of ancient Scottish monuments. The first half of the book outlines best practice for the preservation of monuments and architectural and natural beauty. The second part, based on extensive secondary literature and official documentation, demonstrates how other countries managed their historic monuments: in Europe, India, the Middle East and the United States.

Cambridge University Press has long been a pioneer in the reissuing of out-of-print titles from its own backlist, producing digital reprints of books that are still sought after by scholars and students but could not be reprinted economically using traditional technology. The Cambridge Library Collection extends this activity to a wider range of books which are still of importance to researchers and professionals, either for the source material they contain, or as landmarks in the history of their academic discipline.

Drawing from the world-renowned collections in the Cambridge University Library, and guided by the advice of experts in each subject area, Cambridge University Press is using state-of-the-art scanning machines in its own Printing House to capture the content of each book selected for inclusion. The files are processed to give a consistently clear, crisp image, and the books finished to the high quality standard for which the Press is recognised around the world. The latest print-on-demand technology ensures that the books will remain available indefinitely, and that orders for single or multiple copies can quickly be supplied.

The Cambridge Library Collection will bring back to life books of enduring scholarly value (including out-of-copyright works originally issued by other publishers) across a wide range of disciplines in the humanities and social sciences and in science and technology.

The Care of
Ancient Monuments

*An Account of the Legislative and Other
Measures Adopted in European Countries
for Protecting Ancient Monuments and
Objects and Scenes of Natural Beauty, and for
Preserving the Aspect of Historical Cities*

G. BALDWIN BROWN

CAMBRIDGE
UNIVERSITY PRESS

CAMBRIDGE UNIVERSITY PRESS

Cambridge, New York, Melbourne, Madrid, Cape Town, Singapore,
São Paolo, Delhi, Dubai, Tokyo, Mexico City

Published in the United States of America by Cambridge University Press, New York

www.cambridge.org
Information on this title: www.cambridge.org/9781108016063

© in this compilation Cambridge University Press 2010

This edition first published 1905
This digitally printed version 2010

ISBN 978-1-108-01606-3 Paperback

THE CARE OF ANCIENT
MONUMENTS

CAMBRIDGE UNIVERSITY PRESS WAREHOUSE,

C. F. CLAY, Manager.

London: FETTER LANE, E.C.

Glasgow: 50, WELLINGTON STREET.

Leipzig: F. A. BROCKHAUS.

New York: THE MACMILLAN COMPANY.

Bombay and Calcutta: MACMILLAN AND CO., Ltd.

THE CARE OF ANCIENT MONUMENTS

AN ACCOUNT OF THE LEGISLATIVE AND OTHER MEASURES
ADOPTED IN EUROPEAN COUNTRIES FOR PROTECTING
ANCIENT MONUMENTS AND OBJECTS AND SCENES
OF NATURAL BEAUTY, AND FOR PRESERVING
THE ASPECT OF HISTORICAL CITIES

BY

G. BALDWIN BROWN, M.A.

WATSON GORDON PROFESSOR OF FINE ART IN THE
UNIVERSITY OF EDINBURGH.

'Les longs souvenirs font les grands peuples'
MONTALEMBERT

CAMBRIDGE:
at the University Press
1905

𝕮𝖆𝖒𝖇𝖗𝖎𝖉𝖌𝖊:

PRINTED BY JOHN CLAY, M.A.
AT THE UNIVERSITY PRESS.

TO

CANON RAWNSLEY

HONORARY SECRETARY TO THE NATIONAL TRUST

IN REMEMBRANCE OF LIFE-LONG FRIENDSHIP

PREFACE.

THE purpose and scope of the present work are explained in the Introduction. It is an attempt to convey in a succinct form information as to measures in force for the safeguarding of ancient buildings and other objects of historical and artistic interest ; for the maintenance of a fitting aesthetic standard in the architecture of towns ; and for the preservation of the natural beauties of rural districts. The method pursued is to state in the various sections of the first part of the book the problems connected with monument administration, and then in the second part to convey some idea of the treatment of such problems in the past in the different countries of Europe, and of the solutions which at the present time are being essayed.

For well-nigh a century past some of these countries have been taking stock of their national assets in this department, and devising the best measures they could think of for their protection ; while within the last few years in Germany, France, Austria, Belgium, Holland, Italy, Spain, Portugal, and other lands, there has been a renewed activity in all the agencies of preservation, of which we in this country would do well to take account. In the year 1902 alone, no fewer than four Monument Acts were passed in European legislatures, and at this moment in Austria, Bavaria, Prussia, Spain, and some other countries, laws on the subject are under consideration. In Germany, which is now taking the lead, there has been held for the last five years an annual congress exclusively devoted to monument questions, and to these meetings the various German states have sent official representatives. There is a special organ in the press of the fatherland, reserved for the discussion of these topics, and, in a word, our neighbours across the North Sea are exhibiting in their whole treatment of the subject their national spirit of thoroughness. France also has possessed, since 1887, her own monument periodical, and an international congress for the protection of works of art and of monuments was held in Paris in connection with the exhibition of 1889. The international congresses of architects have also busied themselves with the subject, and that held at Madrid in April 1904, called upon all countries to form fresh associations for the defence of monuments of history and of art. In Austria, the great Technical High School at Vienna is establishing a special chair or lectureship in ' The Care of Monuments'.

The attention excited in our own country by this activity of foreign governments and peoples has not been great. A move of some importance was made in 1897, when, on the initiative of the Society of Antiquaries, the British government obtained through its representatives abroad reports on the statutory provisions for the care of historical monuments in force in the various European kingdoms. The information thus obtained was embodied in a Parliamentary paper, and in the same year the chairman of council of the National Trust, Sir Robert Hunter, added to that society's current report a memorandum on these same agencies. These papers were not however complete, no notice, for example, being taken in either case of the elaborate Prussian arrangements for the care of monuments, which occupy nearly three hundred pages in the standard work on monument preservation of von Wussow. Since the above date no report on the subject has appeared in English, though the last five years have witnessed many interesting developments in foreign countries. On the Continent the two chief works that deal with the whole subject, the *Preservation of Monuments* of von Wussow, and the *Care of Monuments* of Freiherr von Helfert, were published, the one in 1885 the other in 1897, and though more recently valuable sketches of contemporary activity on the subject have been given by Dr Clemen and others, yet it is believed that nothing so complete as the present work has yet appeared abroad. Hence there seemed to be a place, and even a prospective demand, for a narrative of what has been accomplished and is still in progress in this department, in the European kingdoms whose monuments travellers are wont to visit and admire.

The information thus presented has been partly derived from printed works mentioned in the bibliographical paragraphs, and partly from official papers, reports, etc. ; but very much has been owed also to the kindness of correspondents in various parts of Europe, who have, with a courtesy and patience for which the writer cannot be sufficiently grateful, replied to queries addressed to them, and have in many cases sent copies of official documents which otherwise he could hardly have procured. The chapters dealing with the separate countries, in the second part of the volume, are preceded in each case by a note indicating the sources of information from which the account has been drawn, and an opportunity is there afforded of mentioning the names and recognizing the friendliness of the many correspondents to whom the writer is thus indebted. He desires in this place to convey generally to all who have helped him an expression of his sincere thanks.

In some cases official documents, or portions of them, are translated in the text in full. These parts of the text are not distinguished by difference of type, but attention is called to them by the use of the inverted comma at the left hand of every line of such quotations. In other cases a résumé of the provisions of the document in question has been found sufficient. Many of the clauses in such instruments are purely administrative, or are merely intended to safeguard the application in practice of the general principle, which is the only point of interest to the enquirer ; they occur in much the same forms in all documents of the class concerned. It would unduly have increased the bulk of the volume to have given these clauses in extenso.

There has been no attempt to institute comparisons among the different countries with regard to the sums officially

expended on behalf of ancient monuments. The financial
and administrative systems of the countries differ so widely
that accurate comparisons would be very difficult, even to one
practically familiar with these systems, but there is another
reason why the sums thus disbursed have not been detailed.
A comparatively lavish expenditure on monuments is not
always wholly to the credit of a country, for much of the
money is possibly spent on works of so-called restoration,
many of which had better have been left unattempted.
Restoration for the sake of restoration is the worst possible
way of spending money voted for the care of ancient monuments; and it is to be feared that a good part of the resources
lavished on monuments in England, France, Italy, and some
other countries, has been wasted on needless and inartistic
renewals. A better way to use funds set aside for these
purposes in national or civic budgets, is to spend them first
on preventive works and necessary repairs, and next on the
purchase for the general good, either by arrangement or
compulsion, of public and domestic buildings of artistic or
historical value, or of scenes and sites of natural beauty. It
is not, in a word, the mere amount that a country spends on
its monuments that is of importance, but rather the judicious
distribution of the sums available.

In the survey of what is done abroad the design of the
book is to take account only of the countries of Europe, but
there has been added a chapter on monument legislation in
certain non-European lands of old renown, such as India and
Egypt, the abundant monuments of which are largely under
European care. The inclusion of the United States would
on many grounds have been advisable, but would have
logically involved a great and undue extension of the limits
of the work. A few paragraphs on the interesting subject of
American care for monuments and for scenes of natural
beauty are however subjoined as an Appendix.

UNIVERSITY OF EDINBURGH.
July 1905.

TABLE OF CONTENTS.

PART I.

THE PRINCIPLES AND PRACTICE OF MONUMENT ADMINISTRATION.

SECT.   PAGE

Introduction   3

1. The Significance and History of the Care of Monuments.   11

2. The Meaning of the Term 'Monument'   16

3. The Limit of Age for Monuments   18

4. The different Kinds of Monuments   20

5. Why should Monuments be Preserved?   24

6. Quis Custodiet Ipsos Custodes? The Function of Public
   Opinion   31

7. Means for the Preservation of Monuments: A. Private
   Societies and Publications   34

8. Means for the Preservation of Monuments: B. Official and
   semi-official Agencies, Museums   41

9. Means for the Preservation of Monuments: C. Legislation,
   National and Local   44

10. Restoration and Anti-Restoration   46

11. 'Classement', Inventorization, and Official Publications .   57

12. Superintendence of Excavations and Disposal of 'Finds':
    Treasure-trove   61

13. Prohibition of Sale or Exportation   66

14. Expropriation or Compulsory Purchase   67

PART II.

MONUMENT ADMINISTRATION IN THE VARIOUS EUROPEAN COUNTRIES.

CHAP. PAGE

I. FRANCE 73

II. GERMANY 97

III. ITALY 126

IV. GREAT BRITAIN AND IRELAND 148

V. THE AUSTRIAN EMPIRE 166

VI. BELGIUM, HOLLAND, AND SWITZERLAND . . . 172

VII. DENMARK, NORWAY, AND SWEDEN 184

VIII. RUSSIA AND FINLAND 200

IX. SPAIN AND PORTUGAL 208

X. GREECE AND TURKEY 216

XI. THE DANUBIAN PROVINCES 225

XII. INDIA, EGYPT, ALGERIA, TUNIS 230

APPENDIX, a note on the Care of Monuments in the United States 243

INDEX 249

GENERAL BIBLIOGRAPHY.

*Only general works and collections of documents are mentioned below.
The special works dealing with each country, with the other sources of
information from which the notice of each country has been compiled,
are indicated at the heads of the chapters in the second part of the book.*

Von Wussow, *Die Erhaltung der Denkmäler in den Kulturstaaten der
Gegenwart*, Berlin, 1885.

Freiherr von Helfert, *Denkmalpflege*, Wien u. Leipzig, 1897.

Annuaire de Législation Étrangère, Paris, Société de Législation
Comparée, 1872 f.

l

*Only general works and collections of documents are mentioned below.
The special works dealing with each country, with the other sources of
information from which the notice of each country has been compiled,
are indicated at the heads of the chapters in the second part of the book.*

l

Erster Tag jur Denkmalpflege, Sonder-Abdruck aus dem Korrespondenzblatt des Gesamtvereins der deutschen Geschichts- und Altertumsvereine, Berlin, 1900. Report of Monument Congress.

Zweiter, Dritter, Vierter, Fünfter, Tag für Denkmalpflege, Steno-
graphische Berichte, Karlsruhe-Berlin, 1901, 1902, 1903, 1904.

*Reports from Her Majesty's Representatives abroad as to the Statutory
Provisions existing in Foreign Countries for the Preservation of
Historical Buildings*, Accounts and Papers, Miscellaneous, No. 2
(1897) [c—8443], London, 1897.

*Memorandum as to the Steps taken in various Countries for the Preser-
vation of Historic Monuments and Places of Beauty*, Appendix by
Sir Robert Hunter to the Report for 1896-7 of the National Trust
for Places of Historic Interest and Natural Beauty, London, 1897.

Congrès International pour la Protection des Œuvres d'Art et des
Monuments, tenu à Paris du 24 au 29 Juin 1889. *Procès-verbaux
Sommaires*, Paris, Impr. Nat., 1889.

PART I

THE PRINCIPLES AND PRACTICE OF MONUMENT ADMINISTRATION

PART I

THE PRINCIPLES AND PRACTICE OF MONUMENT ADMINISTRATION

INTRODUCTION.

THE subject of this book is the Care of Ancient Monuments, and the term 'monument' embraces all old buildings and other memorials of bygone days. These are heirlooms from the past and appeal to the piety and patriotism of the present. Their number can never be increased, but on the contrary as time goes on they must necessarily become fewer. As the decay or destruction of any one of them involves an increase of value in those that endure, so the care of them will become every year a matter of more and more urgent duty.

In our own country coming developments in public life may give to the historic monument a worth we can hardly now realize. Whatever may be the future in other respects of Great Britain in relation to the Empire at large, it must always remain the soil in which are rooted all the traditional memories of the race. In the tangible evidences of a storied past, this island possesses what is necessarily wanting to our colonies and to the offshoots from those colonies. Britain is the land of the castle and the country seat and the gabled cottage, of the town hall and burgher's tenement, of the market cross, of the cathedral and the country church, institutions which have behind them a continuous history of a thousand years, and around which the nation has grown strong enough to flourish itself and to send forth branches that are spread over the earth. The interest which these memorials excite in the minds of our kinsfolk from across the seas is very great, and will probably increase as the generations advance. The feelings thus kindled help to keep alive throughout the Empire the sense of the unity of the stock, while anyone who has taken American acquaintances round one of our older cities, such as York or Edinburgh, knows how the consciousness of a still ampler solidarity is evoked by the antique historic scenes. These streets and houses, as well as the more conspicuous monuments of which they are the setting, are imperial assets, and on economic, almost on political, grounds, the duty of safeguarding them might well be recognized even by the least artistic and least antiquarian of the population.

Yet it is a fact that in this country the care of these ancestral possessions is not made a matter of imperial, or even of national, concern. Though we can boast an Ancient Monuments Act, it covers very little and affords even to that little only a limited protection, while we are almost wholly destitute of the elaborate official and semi-official machinery of Conservators, of Commissions, and of Inventories, available in almost every European country. Our owners of monuments, whether corporate bodies or private individuals, are as a rule unhampered by any law or central authority in the exercise of their powers over their property. There are in our own country monuments of national and even of world-wide importance, that are legally speaking at the absolute disposal of a single individual. The case of Stonehenge, which has recently been before the public, may be freely referred to, because the present owner of the monument is the last person in the world to fail in care for it. It is not for a moment pretended that such private owners are in general indifferent to the treasures under their charge. On the contrary, it is gladly recognized that both individuals and public bodies are often as jealous for the safe keeping and proper treatment of their artistic possessions as any outsiders could possibly be; but provision unfortunately has to be made for cases in which owners may neglect, injure, or actually destroy, monuments of great aesthetic or historical value of which they have the disposal. In such cases control is only attempted by private societies and individuals, who appeal to the community and give a public turn to what the parties implicated would fain keep a private transaction. Unless there be ceaseless vigilance on the part of these unofficial watch-dogs, acts of waste and vandalism may at any moment be committed.

In a country like our own, redolent of ancient memories, but at the same time astir with restless movement, the interests at stake in this matter are too great for the British system of 'laissez-faire' to be satisfactory. The considerations (1) that these monuments when once destroyed can never by any possibility be replaced, (2) that in the minds of many they are of extreme value, and (3) that their character and history give them in many cases a place in the common and even in the national life, should be quite sufficient to lead anyone interested in public economy to doubt whether we are right to leave the care of them in irresponsible hands. The question at issue is the question whether national possessions should remain in the absolute control of private individuals or corporations, and on this continental opinion is pretty well unanimous in the negative. Our insular way of thinking however, and our methods of action and inaction, differ from those in vogue on the Continent, and to the British mind the' matter presents itself in another light.

It may be of use here briefly to indicate what are, broadly speaking, the opposing principles that underlie all discussions as to the care of ancient monuments. On the one side then, there may be asserted as indefeasible the right of the community over monuments in which is written the common history, and which in centuries past have been the centres of the common life. On the other side there may be asserted, as equally indefeasible, the right of private or corporate owners to do as they will with their own. We may find a classic expression of the former principle in some phrases used in 1872 by an Italian Minister of Public Instruction when introducing before the Senate a draft Act for the protection of ancient monuments. 'The State has a supreme interest in using all vigilance and care for the proper custody of the precious monuments of art and of antiquity: its intervention is accordingly justified in all that concerns this great patrimony of the nation. From this exalted interest is derived the principle that the State alone can give permission for restorations, removals, or works of repair; that the State in the same way has not only the duty of preserving the monuments so that they shall be of service to the progress in education of the studious, but also the duty of repressing and punishing all attempts at vandalism; and, as regards excavations, of exacting in every case previous notice so that these may never be undertaken without its leave. The same principle gives to the State the right to interdict, save by its previous permission, the exportation from the kingdom and the sale of artistic works by authors no longer living, of collections of coins, and of rare manuscripts and documents; and finally the right of precedence in the acquisition of objects found in excavations, and other articles of value whenever their proprietor desires to sell them or send them out of the country.'

The draft Act thus introduced had for its intention 'absolutely to prevent the monuments of antique civilization and the masterpieces of Italian art, in whosesoever possession they might be, being in any way injured or destroyed', and amongst its provisions it contained one according to which any remains of ancient public buildings, such as temples or city walls, that might come to light in excavations on private grounds, passed at once ipso facto into the possession of the state, the proprietor of the soil receiving an indemnity. By another provision it was rigidly forbidden, under penalty, to destroy or alter objects of art and antiquity, even when these were in private proprietorship[1]. A member of the Committee of the Italian Senate that reported on this draft Act used the argument that there was an essential difference between the inexhaustible productions of nature and of human industry, which can be renewed at any moment, and the rare creations of the higher intelligence that when once lost can never be repeated or restored; and that in the case of objects of this

---

[1] Mariotti, *La Legislazione delle Belle Arti*, Roma, 1892, pp. 317, 334, 331.

unique character, absolute possession, the 'jus utendi et abu-
tendi' should not be conceded to irresponsible persons or
bodies[1].

With such uncompromising assertions of the public interest
in all national treasures of art and antiquity, assertions which
as we shall see can be paralleled from French writers, we
may contrast the expressions of the opposite view that were
heard in the British Parliament from opponents of our
extremely mild and unpretentious Monument Act of 1882.
As originally drawn, this Act contained a clause under which
a private owner, who possessed an ancient monument and
wished to destroy it, was bound to offer it first for purchase
at a valuation by the Treasury. This limitation on the freedom
of an owner to destroy what might be a unique work of genius
and a priceless national possession the British Parliament
refused to accept, and the Act as carried contains no compulsory provisions at all. Yet this innocuous measure, with
all its teeth drawn, was protested against to the last in the
House of Commons (postea, p. 153 f.) as an 'invasion of the
rights of property...in order to gratify the antiquarian tastes
of the few at the public expense'!

It should be pointed out that this cry of the 'invasion of
the rights of property' has been raised over and over again
in opposition to measures brought forward in the public
interest, and that such measures, limiting private rights, are
in beneficent operation all about us. Private rights in
property are being invaded every day in connection with
public works, and the principle that the community is justified
on proper grounds in interfering with these rights is in every
civilized society fully established. The practical question
concerns the propriety of these grounds, and this is a matter
in each case for consideration and argument. The Italian
speakers and writers just quoted claim a very extensive right
of interference for reasons of an aesthetic and historical kind;
whereas the opponents of the British Ancient Monuments
Act would deny that these reasons have any validity at all.

[1] ibid., p. 318.

It seems pretty obvious that what we should in our own circumstances aim at is something between the absolute control of the state over ancient monuments even in private hands, and the system of almost complete 'laissez-faire', which at present prevails among ourselves. How much it would be practicable in the present state of public opinion to demand is a matter for consideration, and the main purpose of what follows is to help those interested to form an opinion on the various issues involved.

It will conduce to clearness if a little space be occupied here with a note on the general scheme of monument legislation and administration, as we find it at work on the Continent. In all foreign countries official attention is given to the subject, and one of the Ministers[1] is in charge of the interests of monument preservation and of amenity in general. He has as his council a Commission of experts, and there is generally a staff of official Conservators, Inspectors, and Architects who carry on the active part of the work. In some countries this consists primarily in the supervision, upkeep, and, if need be, repair or restoration, of public buildings under state care ; in other countries in the control of excavations and the proper safeguarding and disposal of immovable and movable objects found in them. A certain pecuniary provision, generally grumbled at as too small, is placed at the disposal of the department.

The work, whatever its exact form, is comparatively easy when state property only is dealt with, but when the monument, or the ground under excavation, belongs to a corporate body or a private individual, a conflict of interests at once

---

[1] ' Foreign countries are often supposed to rejoice in Ministers of the Fine Arts, but as a fact no Minister of the Fine Arts pure and simple exists anywhere.... Abroad, the interests of art engage part of the attention of the head of a more extensive department, such as Public Instruction and the Fine Arts (France), Public Instruction (Italy), the Interior (Belgium, Bavaria), Home Affairs (Holland), Religion and Education (Austria), Religious, Educational, and Medical Affairs (Prussia), or Public Works (Prussia). The Ministers representing these departments are in each case charged officially with the care of artistic interests, but they have to fight for the place of art in their annual budgets, and have to play the benevolent despot with powers often sadly restricted.'—*Journal of the Royal Institute of British Architects*, third series, vol. XII, p. 73.

arises, and the main purpose of monument legislation is to obtain in such cases for the authorities of the department effective control over the objects involved. The case of corporate ownership presents different features in different countries. In some, as in France, the state has considerable power over corporations such as municipal councils, railway companies, hospitals, colleges, and the like; while in other countries, of which Britain is one, these bodies are more independent, and tend to become recalcitrant on the slightest suspicion of unauthorized pressure from the side of government. Monument Acts will of course be drafted in accordance with these varying conditions, but it will generally be found that public opinion is in favour of government as against corporations, and it should not be difficult for any state to secure proper public control in the case of objects of national value in the hands of town-councils and secular or ecclesiastical corporations.

The case of monuments, or land holding concealed treasures, in the possession of private proprietors is a more difficult one, for the cry 'the rights of private property are in danger' rouses the ordinary citizen to alertness, and public opinion will as a rule incline towards the side of the individual. It is true that, as has been pointed out, the principle of interference with private rights is universally conceded, for almost daily land is compulsorily purchased to facilitate railways, roads, or other public works, but it is a different matter to use the same compulsion on grounds that many regard as sentimental, and in all discussions on draft Monument Acts the question of questions has been How far is this compulsion possible or advisable? In the three most important recent Monument Acts, those of France, 1887, and of Italy and Hesse-Darmstadt, 1902[1], compulsion is actually allowed, though there are differences in the manner and measure of its application. In all these Acts, expropriation, or compulsory purchase on the part of the state, is permitted as a last resort for the purpose of rescuing a monument in danger;

---

[1] These Acts are analysed, postea, pp. 85 f., 133 f., 108 f.

but independently of this, all the Acts favour an arrangement between the private (or corporate) owners of a monument of value and the state, according to which the object is entered on a schedule of protected monuments, and the owner is bound under the Act not to injure or alter it without official leave.   An owner cannot be directly compelled to enter into an arrangement of the kind, but the existence of the right of expropriation enables the state to put on him a certain pressure in the required direction.   When the undertaking is once given, if he offend against it, the French Act subjects him to an action for damages from the side of the government, while those of Italy and Hesse prescribe fines, and in some cases even imprisonment.   To sum up then, in foreign schemes of monument legislation the state has the right of expropriating private or corporate property on artistic and historical grounds, while it has also the power of punishing an owner if he have entered into an arrangement with the state and fail to keep his pledges.   In our own country artistic and historical grounds are not held a sufficient basis for expropriation of private or corporate property, while the absence of this right deprives the state of any means of exercising pressure on a proprietor to induce him to enter into an arrangement for protection.

It has just been said that the main purpose of the present book is to enable those interested in our ancient monuments to form an opinion for themselves on the proper way in which to deal with them.   The book is not a ' Tendenzschrift ', designed to inculcate any special views that the writer of it may hold.   At the same time the reader may not be sorry to possess at the outset the writer's general opinion as to the objects at which friends of monuments in Britain should aim. To establish the principle that private or corporate property may be expropriated on aesthetic or historical grounds should be the first of these objects, but it is one that will not be secured without some considerable delay and difficulty.   Much less resistance would be offered to a less formidable proposal, which would commit government to the Care of Monuments without rousing the spectre of 'interference with the rights of private property'. The proposal in question is one for the appointment of a Royal Commission, on the lines of the Historical Manuscripts Commission, but with powers extending over the wider field of ancient monuments in general. Such a Royal Commission would have in view in the first instance Inventorization, and would coordinate the various agencies which, as will be shown in § 11, are already at work in this direction. After inventorization, which would secure to us definite information as to the artistic and historical treasures we at present possess, would come measures of protection; and, as the example of Austria shows, a strong Commission can do much, even without legal powers of compulsion, to bring owners to a proper sense of the value of monuments under their control. Finally, the Report of such a Commission would form the proper basis for a new and extended Monument Act on the lines of those recently passed, or still under discussion, on the Continent.

§ 1. The Significance and History of the Care of Monuments.

It has been said that the history of the Care of Monuments began on the day when Leo X gave to Raphael the control over the remains of ancient art at Rome. The Pope desired to exploit the ruined buildings for the sake of obtaining spoils of marble for the work on St Peter's, and little credit is due to him for his action. It led however to the compilation of a Report on ancient Rome, inspired if not written by Raphael, and in this we read the utterances of a cultured and feeling mind. The writer of the report had 'studied the ruins minutely and measured them with diligence'; had read about them in ancient authors and compared with these notices the remains themselves, and great was his grief, he tells us, to see 'the corpse of this noble city, that was once the queen of the world, so grievously torn and disfigured'. If each man owed the duty of piety to his parents and to his country, how much the more would he (the writer) spend all his little strength to save what remained of 'the common fatherland of all Christian men [1]'!

But the interest in ancient monuments is far older than Raphael or the Renaissance. The ideas which underlie it are indeed a part of the mental equipment of rational humanity. From the first hour when the conceptions of a past and a future became clear to the human intelligence, the monument has had its place and function. If man, as Johnson remarked, rises in the scale of being when the past and the future are more important to him than the present, the monument, which sets past and future asunder and makes them distinct to thought, has helped the race toward civilization. When the earliest of monument-makers reared the gigantic menhir to its standing-place, they had in their minds some past event, some death or pact or victory ; and were conscious too of the times to come when successive generations would gaze back on their achievement. Whatever else the ancient monument may have meant to man, it has been at all times eloquent in this witness to the continuity of the race. The life of humanity takes upon itself a new value when, measured by the eternal monument, it stretches backward to remotest aeons, and forward through a corresponding track of time. Apart from any special associations of a historical kind, or any aesthetic value, which an ancient monument may possess, it has this universal, this secular, interest, and this must underlie all our relations with it.

And if the care of monuments has existed from the time when the earliest memorials were reared, so through all the epochs of human history there have been men whose thoughts have fastened with interest of an intimate kind upon these witnesses of the past. They have read in the monuments the record not of time alone, but of events of which time has been the scene. To these memorials they have attached

---

[1] This report or letter was first ascribed to Baldassare Castiglione, but was vindicated for Raphael by a writer of the 18th century, Daniele Francesconi. Raphael's authorship has been accepted by Passavant, Müntz, and others, but Crowe and Cavalcaselle think that he cannot have actually indited the document. Mariotti, *La Legislazione delle Belle Arti*, Roma, 1892, p. xxxvi, prints the more important passages.

pious reminiscences and aspirations, which from the association have themselves acquired strength and vividness.   The Hebrews, with their moralizing instinct, clothed the rude stone monuments of the earlier races of Canaan with patriotic significance, and when their children asked them What mean these stones? they answered with tales of national deliverance and with lessons of the fear of Jehovah.   In the modern world, one of the most striking testimonies which history affords to the principle that underlies the care of monuments is seen in the Crusades.   Never was there afforded more convincing proof of the vitality lent to ideas by their attachment to tangible monuments than the centering of so much of the religious activity of the twelfth and thirteenth centuries in the stones of the Holy Sepulchre.

From an early date moreover, practical measures have been adopted to give effect to the feelings of piety which these time-honoured memorials have evoked.   In ancient Egypt and Babylonia there was a care of monuments, not of course always in evidence, but showing itself from time to time in archaeological study and restoration.   In the classical world, no sooner had the fresh impulse of the formative arts of Greece died down, than we find the older Hellenic monuments preserved in honour, and Augustus, and still more, Hadrian, represent a reverence for this form of 'exemplaria Graeca' to which no cultured Roman was altogether strange.   Of nearer kinship to the modern care of monuments is the conservation of the relics of Roman Antiquity by the more enlightened Teutonic chieftains.   Cassiodorus served in this department Theodoric of Rome and Ravenna, and may be claimed as, in the sense of to-day, the first official custodian of ancient monuments.   Charles the Great was assisted in a similar capacity by the famous Eginhard.   Petrarch wrote to Cola di Rienzi to protest against any destruction or exportation from Rome of the artistic adornments of the city, and some of the Popes of the fifteenth century prohibited by edict any injury to ancient buildings or their remains either within the walls of Rome or in the neighbouring country.   The report by Raphael or his spokesman on the condition of Roman monuments in

his day has a thoroughly modern sound ; but Raphael was
born into evil times, and during the next half century the
most appalling acts of vandalism were perpetrated at Rome
by men who had succeeded Raphael's Pope as bishops, and
Raphael himself as chief papal architects. 'No pen can
describe', writes Lanciani, 'the ravages committed by the
Fabbrica di San Pietro in the course of the last sixty years
of the sixteenth century', and Roman edifices, that might
have come down to us almost intact, were literally torn to
pieces to supply materials for the modern basilica.

Towards the middle of the eighteenth century however,
the discovery of Herculaneum and Pompeii, and a little later
the publication of Winckelmann's treatise on classical art,
paved the way for the intelligent study in the modern spirit
of the monuments of antiquity ; while in 1762 Stuart and
Revett began in their epoch-making work the scientific
publication of the surviving buildings of ancient Athens.
Meanwhile, in the far north, as early as the first half of the
seventeenth century, Gustavus Adolphus, and after him
Charles XI, of Sweden issued ordinances for the protection
of the national monuments, of which a decree of the latter in
1666 enumerates castles and ramparts, cairns, standing stones,
tumuli and barrows[1]. In 1721 a rescript of King John V of
Portugal laments the destruction of so many artistic objects
that had come down from Phoenician, Greek, Carthaginian,
Roman, and Arab sources, and gives directions for conservation, which were to have been followed by a law, that never
seems to have seen the light[2]. In 1780 a Markgraf of Bayreuth
sent out an elaborate rescript enjoining on his people a proper
care for the examples of mediaeval art in his domains[3]. In
England, during a good part of the eighteenth century, the
Gentleman's Magazine had been sounding notes of warning
about the destruction, actual and threatened, of mediaeval
artistic treasures, and the Society of Antiquaries had published
Archaeologia since 1770.

[1] von Wussow, *Die Erhaltung der Denkmäler*, Berlin, 1885, I, 215 f.
[2] ibid., p. 210.
[3] *Die Denkmalpflege* (Zeitschrift), Berlin, 1901, p. 66.

For practical purposes we may begin the story of the modern care of monuments with the early part of the nineteenth century, and we find it then connected with the so-called Romantic movement, a reaction against the neo-classicism of the preceding hundred years. This appears in the attitude of Victor Hugo, who was not only foremost in the ranks of French literary Romanticists, but opened a crusade for the rescue and protection of the mediaeval monuments of his own country. In Germany the movement began when the national consciousness had been roused in the struggle of the Wars of Liberation, and it found at once a classic expression in a report to the Prussian government submitted in 1815 by the architect Schinkel[1]. Schinkel who had been asked to inspect the church at Wittenberg, injured in the French wars, made his report the occasion of a forcible appeal to his countrymen to save the glorious relics of their mediaeval art. In England, the so-called Gothic revival was a phase of the same romantic movement, and this brought with it vigorous, though not always well-advised, measures for the care of our Gothic and Romanesque monuments. In Italy and Greece, and to some extent also in the Austrian Empire, attention was first given to movable objects of artistic and historical interest, which might be already known or might come to light in excavations; but in Austria the aegis of the state was soon thrown over mediaeval as well as antique treasures. In Denmark and the other Scandinavian kingdoms pre-historic antiquities first attracted notice. At the early date of 1807 a Royal Commission was appointed in the first named country for the conservation of antiquities[2].

In almost all cases we may take the turn of the first and the second quarters of the nineteenth century, as the period from which a continuous and growing interest has been shown in all continental countries in the safeguarding of the national assets in the form of artistic and historical monuments. In the second part of this book an attempt is made to give in the case of each European country a succinct account of the history of its official or private activity in the care of monu-

---

[1] *Die Denkmalpflege*, 1901, p. 6.   [2] von Wussow, I, 136.

ments, with especial reference to existing conditions; countries
such as France, Germany, and Italy, with which we are most
familiar, and from which we can learn the most practical
lessons, being treated with proportionate fulness. Before however this part of our task be reached, it will be advisable to
offer some preliminary explanations of the problems involved
in monument administration, and the different solutions which
in various regions are being essayed.

§ 2. THE MEANING OF THE TERM 'MONUMENT'.

In the first place what is the meaning of the term ' Monument'? We must of course dissociate the word from its
common use as applied to public memorials of departed
worthies, such as the Nelson Monument in Trafalgar Square,
or the Scott Monument at Edinburgh. The care of such
monuments is invested in officials responsible for public order,
and no special private effort or statutory enactment is needed
to prevent the heads being knocked off the decorative statues
on the latter, or the backs of Landseer's lions being polished
smooth by sliding urchins. These are matters for the police.
It is not injuries of these kinds that are provided against in
what is known as monument legislation. Penal codes only
punish offences committed with malicious intention or with
culpable carelessness of the property of others; whereas the
offences against ancient monuments which people of good
taste and piety are always trying to prevent, are perpetrated
by people on their own property, and without any criminal
intent that the ordinary law can recognize. When we speak
of ' monuments' and the ' care of monuments' in the sense in
which the words are used in these pages, a far more extensive
collection of objects is in contemplation than the public monuments noticed in the guide books. Roughly speaking all old
structures, and all the objects we preserve in museums, are
included for the present purpose under the term, and attempts
have often been made to find some logical definition of the
word when used in this wider sense. The attempts have not

succeeded, and in the absence of a definition we must fall back on general descriptions, some of the best of which are given in certain recent German Acts and rescripts. Thus in a draft of a monument law for the Grand-Duchy of Baden, prepared in 1883-4 but not carried into effect, the term is taken to include 'all immovable and movable objects which have been handed down from a bygone period of civilization, and as characteristic productions of their time have a special significance for the comprehension of art and art-industry and their development, for the knowledge of antiquity and for historical investigation in general, as well as for keeping alive the remembrance of events of outstanding interest[1]'.

Still fuller is the description of what is meant by 'monument' contained in a joint minute issued in May 1904 by the Prussian Ministers of Religion, Education etc., and of Public Works[2]. 'Monument' is here made to include 'all remains of bygone artistic periods, be they purely historical, as for example inscriptions; or of importance for the understanding of past phases of civilization and art (pre-historic tombs, weapons and the like); or again of picturesque significance for the general effect of a scene or a landscape, as towers, gates, etc.; or of value as a model for the present time in the domain of the formative arts or of handicraft. The worth of a monument' the minute goes on 'does not always reside in its importance for the art or the history of the whole land, but not seldom in its value for a much smaller area, or for the actual place where it stands (walls, ramparts, etc.).' It will be noted here that the description includes not only buildings and other immovable objects but also movable objects of an artistic kind as small as examples of goldsmiths' work, and historical relics equally portable, such as manuscripts.

Why all these things should be called 'monuments', by the same term that we apply to the Fire-of-London Column or the Lion of Thorvaldsen, will be seen if we consider for a moment the meaning of the word. 'Monument', in French

---

[1] See postea, p. 106 f.
[2] *Die Denkmalpflege*, 1904, p. 77.

'monument', in Italian and Spanish 'monumento', is connected with the Latin 'moneo', 'I remind', while the German
term 'Denkmal' is associated with 'denken', 'to think'. The
monument is something that gives us pause, that bids us
reflect, and is a reminder of past or absent things. In this
sense the extended use of the word is as justifiable as the
narrower. The Wellington Monument in St Paul's brings
before us the thought of 'the man who fought a hundred
fights' and who sleeps below in the vaults, but equally does
the Roman milestone or the Gothic cathedral make us think
of the men who marked their irresistible march by the former,
or breathed their religion into stone in the other's majestic
pile. These relics of old time are monuments because they
recall, not this or that named and famous personage or group,
but the whole life with all its associations of some period or
place of which the interest is in the past. The questions why
it is good so to recall the past, and how this recollection can
best be kept alive, will occupy us a little later ; all that has
to be done here is to explain and justify the use of the word
'monument' or 'Denkmal' when we speak of 'the Care of
Monuments' or 'die Denkmalpflege'.

§ 3. THE LIMIT OF AGE FOR MONUMENTS.

The monument, we have just seen, belongs to the past.
The question may be asked What degree of remoteness
from the present must a production possess for it to come
within the description of a monument? Different codes and
rescripts give different answers, but the tendency is now to
bring the limit of time pretty near to our own day. The
shyness of the British parliamentary mind in presence of
monuments is so great, that in our Ancient Monuments Act
of 1882 the legislature could hardly contemplate anything
nearer in date than pre-historic standing stones or tumuli[1].
The Greek law of 1834, the first in time of modern monument
Acts[2], was framed almost entirely with a view to the remains
of Hellenic antiquity, and only noted in Art. CXI that Early-

---

[1] postea, p. 155.   [2] postea, p. 216 f.

Christian and mediaeval remains were not excluded from the scope of the Act, but quite recently in 1902 a ministerial decree extended the protection of the Hellenic state to all historical monuments whatever their period[1]. When the Austrian Central-Commission was established in 1850 it had to deal with works up to about 1800, but in 1899 by imperial decree, the first half of the nineteenth century has been included in its view[2]. In Prussia the report by Schinkel of 1815, mentioned on page 15, did not contemplate anything more recent than the middle of the seventeenth century, but the ministerial minute of 1904, just referred to, states that 'the protection of monuments is extended to the works of all periods of culture that are closed. The last of these epochs reaches about to the year 1870'. Article 1 of the Italian monument law of 1902[3] excludes from the application of the Act works by living artists and all productions not more than fifty years old. The Hessian law of the same date leaves the limit to be fixed by a subsequent ordinance, and a limit of about thirty years has since been agreed on[4]. In general it will be enough to say that any work representing a distinct style that is no longer in vogue may have an artistic and historical interest justifying its inclusion in a list of 'monuments'. Thus for example St Pancras' Church London, or Archibald Elliot's neo-classic building similarly adapted from the Erechtheion, that was erected in 1817 opposite the western end of St Giles' Edinburgh, and was demolished in 1900, might be, or might have been, scheduled as monuments on the ground that over and above their excellent workmanship and the purity of their details, they had a historical value as marking a distinct phase of modern British architecture. Similarly any portable product of an artistic industry that has quite died out may be worthy of preservation in a museum, and so come under the term in question. If the potter's wheel be entirely superseded by the stamping or moulding processes, then a piece of thrown work, though made only the other day, would for Britain at any rate become an artistic monument.

---

[1] *Die Denkmalpflege*, 1902, p. 47.   [2] ibid., p. 64.
[3] postea, p. 133 f.   [4] postea, p. 113.

§ 4. THE DIFFERENT KINDS OF MONUMENTS.

It will be noticed in monument legislation that protected objects are sometimes called 'monuments of art' (Hungarian law of 1881) and at other times 'historical monuments', which is the term commonly used in France. Although however the objects contemplated by the French protective law of 1887 are called officially 'Monuments Historiques[1]', yet in the title of the Act itself they are called 'Monuments et objets d'Art ayant un intérêt historique et artistique'. The truth is that in the vast majority of cases the objects with which we are dealing have an interest that is both historical and artistic, historical because they carry us back into the midst of the life of older times, and artistic because almost everything made by man under earlier conditions of production possesses an artistic interest. There are of course exceptions, for a round barrow can hardly be called an artistic object, while a deftly wrought piece of peasant silver-work is only in a somewhat forced sense 'historical'. Still the broad fact is indubitable, that the objects contemplated in monument legislation have in most cases the right to be termed both historical and artistic, though in the case of some the historical, in the case of others the artistic, interest may be more prominent.

There is a third use of the word 'monument' or 'Denkmal' coming now into vogue that from the point of view of language can hardly be justified. It is now made to apply to natural objects of beauty and interest. The Monument Law of the Grand-Duchy of Hesse, passed in 1902[2], states in its Article 33 that 'Natural phenomena of the earth's surface, such as watercourses, rocks, trees, and the like' ('Naturdenkmäler', natural monuments)[3], can be placed under the protection of the Act.

---

[1] This is the title of the list published by the Ministry of Public Instruction and of the Fine Arts in 1889. See postea, p. 73.

[2] postea, p. 111.

[3] Quite recently it has been suggested in Germany to use the term 'Naturmale' for these natural objects of interest. There is no convenient equivalent term in English.

Of course in cases where the natural scene or object has historical associations, as for example Runnymede, the term monument is strictly accurate, but its application to the Falls of Foyers or Burnham Beeches is not so logical. The convenience of the extended application is undoubted, because these natural objects are now included, as we have just seen, in the protection given by Monument Acts, and a society like the National Trust, which in Germany would be called a Monument Society (Denkmäler-Verein), contemplates protection alike for buildings of historic interest, and for places of natural beauty. There is too a more solid justification for the extended use, for the effect on the mind of a scene of natural sublimity is similar to the effect of one of the grand monuments of antiquity. We have seen already that the monument, in the strict meaning of the term, appeals to our sense of the immensity of time. In like manner the sublime objects of nature touch the imagination with an awe-inspiring apprehension of the vastness of the material universe, or the irresistible forces which are in motion when the powers of earth and air are unchained,

> ' Und Stürme brausen um die Wette
> Vom Meer auf's Land, vom Land auf's Meer,
> Und bilden wüthend eine Kette
> Der tiefsten Wirkung rings umher.'

On this ground Niagara Falls or the Yellowstone Park, both in their ways as sublime as Stonehenge or the Great Pyramid, may fitly be termed ' monuments ', and the safeguarding of scenes of the kind is as much a duty of the monument legislator as preventing the demolition of Notre Dame.

When the natural scenes and objects are rather pretty and pleasant than inspiring, we may still bring them under the same category as the beautiful object of art or the old-fashioned homely domestic building or implement. These things all nourish the quiet ideal life of contemplation and enjoyment, which is as precious in its way for man as the strenuous life of action and acquisition. The whole movement, for which the Germans have the convenient term

'Denkmalpflege', represents a reaction against the tendency to become too much absorbed in practical affairs and in the pursuit of worldly advantage. The citizens of the United States, it has been observed, are at once the most practical and the most ideal of men, the fact being that the idealism of the American character is an inevitable recoil of the healthy human intelligence from the over-insistent claims of the material. So in the older European lands men are turning in the same spirit to nature and to art and to the memorials of simpler and quieter periods of human civilization. For this reason it is as important to preserve unsullied the fields and streams in the neighbourhood of growing cities, as it is to safeguard the older domestic buildings in which the past history of the civic community is enshrined.

The word monument may accordingly be fitly used in a general popular sense to cover natural scenes and objects, as well as those productions of past generations in which we discern a historical or artistic value.

Besides the distinction of historical, artistic, and natural monuments, there is the further division between movable and immovable objects, while the French Monument Act of 1887 subdivides the last into 'immovables by nature' such as buildings or tumuli, and 'immovables by destination' such as altars in churches, which might be, but are never meant to be, shifted from their places. Movable objects may be of historical interest, like documents, or of artistic interest, like cameos, or may be, like illuminated manuscripts or Greek coins, at once historical and artistic. Movable natural objects may be caught in the net of the monument legislator, for it is as important to prevent all the primrose roots being extirpated from a wood, as it is for the trees of the wood to be left standing.

The chief immovable objects are buildings, including the rude stone monuments of pre-historic times. The interest of these again may be historical or artistic, or may partake of the nature of both, but apart from this there is a practical distinction between two classes of architectural monuments that plays an important part in monument legislation. There are on the one side, in every district and in every ancient town, certain outstanding buildings or other structures of which every inhabitant could give off-hand a general list, and which would be included in any limited inventory of the chief historical and artistic treasures of a state.   But there are also on the other side a much larger number of humbler domestic relics of the older days, in the shape of town houses, country cottages, street fountains, rustic bridges, sign boards, and the like, which would never find a place in any state inventory, but which combine to give their picturesque charm to our more ancient towns and hamlets.   The preservation of these is a matter of local rather than of national importance, but there is no part of the care of monuments that needs more earnest attention ; and it will have been noticed that the Prussian ministerial minute of 1904[1] expressly contemplates such objects.   With all this domestic apparatus may be grouped the remains of ancient military works such as ramparts, walls, fosses, gates, which, though in themselves perhaps reduced to mere fragments, are of the utmost moment as aids to the reconstruction of the older history of our towns.   The Germans have a convenient term ' das Stadtbild', which they use in this connection in the sense of the characteristic aspect of a city.   This aspect is the creation of centuries during which the urban community has been fashioning for itself a material environment.   The habitations, the places of meeting, the arrangements for internal convenience and for security, have come gradually into being as suited the situation and needs of the body politic, and the result is a complete and harmonious picture, the preservation of which is an object to all people of sense and feeling.   This ' Stadtbild ' does not depend on the few outstanding monuments but on the general physiognomy of the place.   Venice is still Venice though the most conspicuous of its monuments has been overthrown, but it would cease to be Venice were all the smaller canals, the network of which gives the place its cachet, filled in and macadamized !

---

[1] ante, p. 17.

§ 5. Why should Monuments be Preserved?

The abstract value to the community of the objects or scenes under consideration will as a matter of theory be generally admitted. Every one likes the country and is open to the impressions of beauty and sublimity from natural scenery, while few will deny that they are interested in a historic memorial and are sensible to the charm of a picturesque mediaeval building. Manuscripts all will agree are in their place in national or civic record-chambers, while museums cannot be too full of good pictures and statues, and of all the thousand productions of the decorative and industrial arts of olden time. There is indeed no call for argument in favour of the safeguarding of such movable objects as fill our museums. If the nation or town be fortunate enough to possess these, there is every reason why they should be preserved, while when they are in private hands it is easy to see a reason why they should if possible be kept in the country, and not suffered to pass into the hands of a foreign purchaser.

The case is different when the saving of these objects from the foreigner, or their transference from private ownership to that of the community, involves a demand upon the public purse. For the taxpayer to be willing to furnish funds for these purposes, implies on his part a sense of the value of such possessions which is not inherent in the taxpayer's mind as such. There will be a difference among countries or communities in respect to the sacrifices they will make to acquire or retain exceptional treasures of a movable kind. Our own country is tolerably rich in monuments of this order, and public opinion acquiesces in the alienation of objects which many foreign countries would never suffer to cross the frontier. The Botticelli illustrations to Dante, purchased by the German government at the Hamilton sale, is a case in point. The British intelligence is hardly enough instructed in art to recognize the immense value of unique possessions of the kind, and in this matter a good deal may be done for the education of the public.

It is still more important for a right state of feeling to be induced in the public mind in regard to scenes and objects of natural beauty and to time-honoured buildings and other antique structures of historical or artistic interest. When these are within, or in the neighbourhood of, growing modern towns, they are subjected to a very real and pressing danger. They are not like objects in a museum, out of everybody's way, but are often to the eye of the hasty observer very much in the way, and need in his view to be demolished, or, in the case of the natural scene, built over or utilized for a factory or a railway line. The question Why should these things be preserved, is accordingly one of the utmost moment, and all interested in the care of monuments have addressed themselves to it.

In our own country the task of the apologist is particularly difficult, for it is generally looked upon as sentimentality or weakness to put the interests of preservation higher than some utilitarian consideration of the moment, and it is held in some quarters as an article of faith that any practical demand may claim priority over the ideal plea of the lover of monuments or of nature. To some extent this attitude on the part of the English public is to be explained by the perfervid zeal of some eloquent lovers of monuments and of nature of our own time. The ordinary citizen, held up to obloquy as a utilitarian, has stiffened his back and tries to keep the champion of amenity at a distance. He will justify to his own mind this attitude of resistance on the plea that lovers of nature and art are unreasonable in their demands and deaf to appeals from the side of sanitation or business or convenience. It is well therefore to make it clear that those who are working most effectually to-day in the service of monuments and of scenery are persons of moderate demands, who recognize that in growing modern communities these considerations of health and business and convenience are of the highest importance, and must necessarily sometimes override questions of amenity. These persons however, that is to say the reasonable modern monument-lovers, maintain on the other hand, that with patience and goodwill it will often be found possible to reconcile these conflicting claims from the sides of utility and amenity, and to save what at first sight would seem irrevocably doomed. London has afforded in recent years a valuable object-lesson bearing on this point. The two well-known churches in the Strand, St Mary-le-Strand and St Clement Danes, used to block that thoroughfare to a very considerable extent, and again and again have the practical people demonstrated that they must in the interests of convenience and business be removed. They are not monuments of the first rank, but good specimens of a characteristic English style, carried out in the Portland stone to which London architecture is so much indebted. On this ground they were resolutely and successfully defended by the lovers of amenity. The result has been that in the extensive scheme now being carried out by the London County Council they are not only preserved but become foci of a large architectural composition. They have now not only ceased to be obstructions but have become ornaments, and at the same time serve to point a warning against hasty demolition of the older features of our cities.

Some of the most urgent pleas for protection come now not from professed amateurs of the beautiful but from men of affairs, and from active civic officials, who are alarmed at the sacrifices which are being made on every side to the exigencies of the present. This is markedly the case in Germany. No European country indeed offers such instructive material for the study of the question at issue as Germany. The internal union which resulted from the war of 1870–1 was followed by an immense development of commercial activity. The greater German towns began rapidly to enlarge their limits and modernize their outward appearance. Anyone who remembers Cologne when the city was still confined within its mediaeval enceinte, and who spends a few hours to-day in its electric tramcars, receives an object-lesson in city expansion of a most striking kind. Thoughtful and patriotic citizens, who saw the traditional aspect of the cities of the fatherland dissolving before their eyes, were wounded in their historic sense and in their affection for home. From this has arisen a powerful movement, dating from about six years ago, the tendency of which may be summed up in the word recently adopted as the title of a patriotic society—'Heimatschutz' or 'The Defence of Home'. As our Teutonic neighbours are nothing if not systematic, they have taken up and discussed these questions with characteristic thoroughness. An annual Congress, under the title 'Tag für Denkmalpflege' or 'Meeting for the Care of Monuments', is held in different towns of the Empire, and a special journal, the organ of the movement, gives every month a chronicle of all that is tried or accomplished for the cause, in Germany or abroad, either by legislation or by private agency.

This movement in Germany is by no means under the direction of extremists, but is led by practical men who are familiar with the exigencies of modern life and whose desire is not to sacrifice the new to the old, but, as the burgomaster of a historical city put it the other day 'to reverence the old, and then on the basis of what has been handed down to go on and deal in the best manner possible with modern needs'. The preservation of natural scenes and objects, especially in the vicinity of growing towns, is also being discussed by statesmen and men of affairs, and is being seriously considered with a view to legislation by the Ministers of more than one European country.

Various reasons may be urged for the preservation of natural and artistic beauties. To those who love these as Wordsworth loved nature, or Ruskin the monuments of mediaeval art, their worth is beyond estimate. To share such a feeling as is breathed through the poet's lines at Tintern Abbey is an experience which to an impressionable spirit is better than wealth or luxury, and to such an one the natural scene that stirs the poetic thought will be a thing to be preserved at any cost. An enjoyment equally intense is the privilege of those who are sensitive to the nameless charm of poetic association that plays about the old cathedral or Rathhaus or castle. How finely Ruskin puts this into words

when he writes of the old steps that once gave access to the
West Front of Amiens—'the great old foundation-steps, open,
sweeping broad from side to side for all who came; unwalled,
undivided, sunned all along by the westering day, lighted
only by the moon and the stars at night; falling steep and
many down the hillside—ceasing one by one, at last wide
and few towards the level—and worn by pilgrim feet for six
hundred years[1]'!

These experiences are however personal ones. If we be
sensible of the charm, the question of preservation is for us
settled—we would sacrifice anything rather than let these
scenes and monuments be lost to modern life, but we cannot
make others sensible of the charm. To the mass of mankind

'A primrose by a river's brim'

will be a yellow primrose and nothing more, and we cannot
expect from them very active sympathy in this ideal pre-
sentment of the case. On the other hand there are arguments
tending to the same end which are of a more practical kind.
The preservation of open spaces can be urged on pleas of
health, and the country as a recreation ground can be safely
appealed for to the most prosaic ratepayer. What has been
accomplished in this matter of recent years by the London
County Council has been done in the name of an enlightened
utilitarianism. The preservation of the Yellowstone Park in
America is the most magnificent outcome of this policy in
modern times, just as the safeguarding of the Falls of Niagara
is a proof of enlightened care for a single outstanding
natural monument. The efforts of the National Trust to
secure similar reserves on a smaller scale in our own country
are meeting with satisfactory support from the public.

It is not so easy to make the public see the importance of
preserving the older features of our towns, on which the
'Stadtbild' or general physiognomy of the place so largely
depends. To this point many continental speakers and writers
on this subject have addressed themselves, and the appeal
has been urged on the modern citizen that he should realize

[1] *The Bible of Amiens.*

with pride the inheritance which has in this way come down to him from the past. At the beginning of the movement for the care of monuments in France, about 1830, Montalembert condensed this appeal into the pregnant phrase quoted on the title page of this book, and one of his countrymen at a later time thus expressed the idea of the work of the French protective 'Commission des Monuments Historiques' —'To preserve the fabrics which testify to the glory of the land, is to make its past live again for the profit of its present and of its future'. The question really comes to this—What is it to imply in the coming time to be 'a citizen of no mean city'? Is it to imply only that one's city is big and growing and busy, handsome and well-groomed and fully equipped, and easy to get about in? or will it carry with it a sense of the dignity of a civic life that has developed through twenty generations, and a pride in the streets and buildings which were the scene of doings, the haunts of personalities, that may have made the city famous throughout the civilized world? This view was urged not long ago at a care-of-monuments congress at Düsseldorf by the burgomaster of Hildesheim, and the speech is accepted in Germany as a classic expression of the principles of the movement in regard to this matter[1]. 'Does a civic administration' he asked 'exist merely for the sake of enabling the people to fulfil the needs of daily life as well, as cheaply, and as completely as possible? Is the City Council there for this alone? Certainly it is one of its most important tasks to consider questions of health and all connected with them, but, gentlemen, does man live by bread alone? Does the well-being of men consist only in bodily things, or is there not something far higher, the spiritual well-being of men, and does it not contribute greatly to this when they feel in close relation to the past, and take delight in realizing how the city has gradually built itself up, and how not only the streets, but every single public building, each individual house, even each piece of carved ornament, has grown in the course of time to be what it is. To make this feeling real is the task of the civic authorities....It is

[1] *Dritter Tag für Denkmalpflege*, Karlsruhe, 1902, p. 97 f.

a matter of intimate duty, of conscience, on the part of city governors to care for the older monuments, not in amateur fashion as a by-work, but of set purpose as one of the most important objects of civic administration.'

Such care as the good burgomaster of Hildesheim claims for the older buildings of a city is their due on two grounds. They are worth preservation both for their artistic charm and their historical interest. Most educated people feel, or at any rate admit, the beauty of conspicuous monuments of architecture such as a fine mediaeval church or a Jacobean town hall, but the charm of varied outline and detail and texture, which clings about the unpretending domestic structures of the three centuries before the Victorian era, is not so readily recognized. To the cultured sense however these simple examples of the traditional art of old time are of priceless value, because they can never be replaced. They grew up naturally under conditions of work that have passed away for ever. The spirit of the craftsmen who put them together, the methods by which their materials were prepared and worked, have alike become things of the past. There is a variety, a play of life, a human interest, about these old structures that the house built under modern conditions can never possess. Hence there is no part of the care of monuments that is of more moment than the preservation for their aesthetic charm of good specimens of the antique domestic architecture of our streets. The eye never falls on them but it dwells there for a while delighted and refreshed, and each time one is destroyed a source of pure and healthful pleasure is taken from us.

The historical value of these domestic structures is more obvious. They are a link with the past, and when that past is redolent of social, intellectual, and romantic memories, to recall it adds richness and interest to the present. We must never forget too, that, in preserving the monuments to which these memories cling, we are doing a work for which those who are now far away, and those who will come after—our children and theirs—will show us gratitude. This consideration was well urged by one of the speakers in a debate on the

British Ancient Monuments Act in 1875. 'There was an ever-increasing stream of visitors to this country from across the Atlantic, who came here, not to inspect our railways, our warehouses, or our docks, but to seek out in quiet nooks our ancient monuments, which were the landmarks of our common history. In times to come, when the English-speaking race should have spread itself over the greater part of the globe, and should have acquired wealth and power, the culture that wealth and civilization gave would lead it to seek for that which wealth could not purchase nor civilization create, namely, the monuments over which it could affectionately linger as the existing records of the old home in England. He thought that such a feeling was likely to conduce to the peace, security, and happiness of the world[1].'

§ 6. QUIS CUSTODIET IPSOS CUSTODES? THE FUNCTION OF PUBLIC OPINION.

It has been already pointed out that the ultimate authority in monument preservation is public opinion. In all constitutional countries, and to a growing extent in those autocratically governed, public opinion prepares the way for legislation, and no Acts for the defence of monuments can be passed, and no funds voted for the proper carrying out of these Acts, unless there be in the background in the mind of the people a certain force of intelligent belief in the need for agency of the kind. Everywhere, on the Continent as among ourselves, public opinion is really the final arbiter of all these questions. On the Continent official agencies are in full operation, but these official agencies are in fact the creation of public opinion, and their action to be really fruitful must be sustained by the same force. This fundamental fact is recognized to the full by the friends of ancient monuments abroad, and in all the active propaganda on the subject, of which Germany is now

---

[1] *Hansard's Debates*, CCXXV, 906. Speech by Mr Ferguson.

the scene, speakers and writers have insisted that the movement must carry the public with it, or it will have no real staying-power. It is not the case that state machinery is expected on the Continent to do all the work required. Its value is recognized as a sort of crystallization of public opinion, and it is in this aspect that we should do well to establish it among ourselves. Public opinion, when left to itself, is in its very nature an unorganized force, acting spasmodically upon stimulus supplied by some striking event, or by the initiative of individuals who can magnetize their fellows. What is required is some permanent agency representing the public mind at its best and always kept in working order. Such permanent agencies, in the form of laws and of official or semi-official organizations must be established by the general sense of the community, and if this be their sanction, they will soon cease to appear oppressive to the individual whose rights they may seem to curtail. In any case, independently of the actual extent of the legal powers assumed, whether a government does much or little, the fact that it takes official action at all gives a general trend to public opinion and makes it easier for individuals or societies, working in harmony with the official agency, to bring a healthy influence to bear in individual cases.

The permanent agencies, always in working order, that are here referred to, are of three kinds, private, official, and legislative. The private agencies are voluntary associations with an artistic, archaeological, or historical aim, which swarm in all the more civilized countries of Europe, and make it a part of their work to influence public opinion in the direction of a proper respect for monuments. The official agencies are state-appointed Conservators and Commissioners, who have the authority of government at their back though they may not be possessed of actual legal powers for constraining others to do their will. Lastly there is the agency of the law, embodied in definite Acts and decrees, which people are obliged under penalties to obey. Behind all these agencies there is still public opinion, which is at once the prime mover

and the court of final appeal. The official bodies, which are
made trustees for the public in the interests of monument
preservation, receive their mandate from the people, and if
they fail, or appear to fail, in their duty, they can be arraigned
at the bar of public opinion.

An instance occurred quite recently in France. There is
no one of the historical monuments under the protection of
the law in that country that is better known or more interesting than the fortifications of Avignon. Any traveller who
has visited that city within the last year or two will have been
shocked and amazed to see long sections of that noble and
well-preserved enceinte under demolition. Enquiry will have
revealed to him the fact that the Minister of Public Instruction
and of the Fine Arts, acting as in duty bound under the
advice of the Commission on Historic Monuments, has agreed
with the municipal authorities of Avignon that they may
break down some half-mile of the ancient wall, on condition
that they accept as incontestable the right of the state in the
rest of the enceinte! Experience unfortunately shows, as in
the case of the admission of the railway into Princes Street
Gardens at Edinburgh, that to introduce the thin end of the
wedge, under the condition 'that it is not to go in any further',
is a most hazardous policy, and representatives of the public
in France have been right in doing all they could to rouse
public attention to the threatening situation thus created[1].
Again, in our own country, in 1904 the Town Council of
Berwick-on-Tweed was actually itself demolishing the last
remains of the fortified enceinte formed by Edward I when
Berwick was one of the most important places in the two
kingdoms. There were no legal means of safeguarding this
exceptionally interesting relic, so an appeal had to be made
to public opinion which was ultimately sufficiently aroused
to arrest the scheme. This same question Quis custodiet
ipsos custodes? will from time to time force itself to the
front, and on these occasions there is nothing for it but to
appeal to the general sense of the community as final arbiter.

---

[1] *L'Ami des Monuments*, vol. XV, p. 113, 'Vandalism at Avignon'.

§ 7. Means for the Preservation of Monuments: A. Private Societies and Publications.

The private societies, which form the first of the means for preservation under notice, may, as we have seen, in respect to monument conservation, be regarded as a sort of crystallization of public opinion, representing this at its best and keeping its machinery always in working order. It will be sufficient to glance at the associations in question in one or two of the most important European countries besides our own, and we may divide them into three classes, (1) societies of a national scope, (2) local archaeological associations, (3) societies recently founded with a special view to the monument questions of the day.

Taking our own country first, in class 1, we find the Society of Antiquaries of London, Burlington House, W., incorporated by Royal Charter in 1751, but with a record going back far beyond this date[1]; the Royal Archaeological Institute of Great Britain and Ireland, 20 Hanover Square, London, founded 1844[2]; the British Archaeological Association, 32 Sackville Street, London, of the same date[3]; the Society of Antiquaries of Scotland, Museum of Antiquities, Edinburgh[4]; the Royal Society of Antiquaries of Ireland, 6 Stephens Green, Dublin (begun in 1849 as a Kilkenny Society)[5], and the Cambrian Archaeological Association, London, founded 1846[6]. These are all of national scope. Their chief publications are indicated below, and information about them may be found in the *Year Book of the Scientific and Learned Societies of Great Britain and Ireland*[7].

Local societies are numerous. There is one in almost every county, and England especially is fairly covered by

---

[1] Chief publication, *Archaeologia*, yearly volumes from 1770.
[2] *The Archaeological Journal*, from 1845.
[3] *Journal of the Archaeological Association*, from 1845.
[4] *Proceedings*, annually from 1851.
[5] *Journal*, yearly.
[6] *Archaeologia Cambrensis*, from 1846.
[7] London, yearly from 1884.

them. Only one or two English ones are mentioned here as specimens, and there are many others as worthy of reference as the few that are adduced. There are for example the Kent Archaeological Society, Museum, Maidstone, founded 1857[1]; the Wiltshire Archaeological and Natural History Society, Museum, Devizes, 1853[2]; the Bristol and Gloucestershire Archaeological Society, Gloucester, 1876[3]; the Associated Architectural Societies, a number of local associations covering Lincolnshire, Yorkshire, and parts of the Midlands (publications at Williamson, High Street, Lincoln)[4]; the Newcastle-on-Tyne Society of Antiquaries, The Castle, Newcastle-on-Tyne, 1813[5]; and the Cumberland and Westmoreland Antiquarian and Archaeological Society, Tullie House, Carlisle, 1866[6]. Of town societies may be mentioned the St Paul's Ecclesiological Society, London, founded 1879[7]; the Chester Archaeological and Historic Society, Chester[8]; the Oxford Architectural and Historical Society, Ashmolean Museum, Oxford, 1839; the Thoresby Society, Leeds, 1889[9]; while almost all the larger towns have their own Architectural Associations, many of which issue *Transactions* and *Sketch Books*, and take an active interest in the preservation of the ancient monuments of their districts. Many a needful work of repair, and improvement in arrangements for custody, has been owed to a visit paid to an old building by the local architectural society. A large body of valuable plans and drawings has been brought into existence by the private labours of members of these societies. All this is material for a future work of inventorization. See § 11.

Societies of the third class have a practical aim in view, and are less concerned with archaeological study than with an active propaganda in favour of monument protection. These will be noticed a little later in connection with the societies of similar character on the Continent.

---

[1] *Archaeologia Cantiana*, from 1858.
[2] *The Wiltshire Magazine*, from 1854.   [3] *Transactions* from 1878.
[4] *Associated Societies Reports*, from 1851.   [5] *Archaeologia Aeliana*, from 1822.
[6] *Transactions* from 1866.   [7] *Transactions* from 1881.
[8] *Journal* from 1850.   [9] *Publications* from 1889.

Casting our eyes across the Channel we find France fully supplied with local associations which cover the country as with a network. Of these there is a complete and scientific bibliography in course of publication by the 'Comité de Travaux Historiques et Scientifiques' under the editorship of M.M. R. de Lasteyrie and E. Lefèvre Pontalis[1]. This bibliography includes all learned societies, and not those only that are concerned with monuments. Of the latter a few of the most important may be selected. The 'Société Nationale des Antiquaires de France' was founded, under the name 'Académie Celtique', in 1804 and has just celebrated its centenary, but most of the French antiquarian societies were founded after about 1830, largely in consequence of the impulse given at that time to the study of ancient monuments by the genius of the erudite and enthusiastic Norman, Arcisse de Caumont. In 1834 de Caumont founded the 'Société Française d'Archéologie pour la Conservation et la Description des Monuments Historiques', with its headquarters at Caen, as a national association concerned with the whole country, and the organ of this society the well known *Bulletin Monumental*[2] is one of the most important publications of the kind in existence. The 'Institut des Provinces', which he started in 1845, was intended to assist the Society in spreading over France a reticulation of organized agencies for the safeguarding of the national monuments. Among the more important district associations are the 'Société des Antiquaires de Normandie', Caen, 1823, another creation of de Caumont[3]; the 'Société des Antiquaires de Picardie', Amiens, 1836[4]; the 'Société Archéologique et historique des Côtes-du-Nord', Saint Brieuc, 1842[5]; the 'Société des Antiquaires de l'Ouest', Poitiers, 1834[6]; the 'Société Archéologique de Touraine', Tours, 1840[7]; the 'Société Historique et Archéologique du Maine', le Mans, 1875[8]; the 'Société Archéologique

---

[1] *Bibliographie générale des Travaux Historiques et Scientifiques publiés par les Socié és Savantes de la France*, Paris, 1888 etc.

[2] Yearly from 1835.   [3] *Mémoires*, from 1825.

[4] *Mémoires, Bulletins*, etc.   [5] *Mémoires*.

[6] *Mémoires, Bulletins*.   [7] *Mémoires*, etc.

[8] Various publications.

du Midi de la France', Toulouse, 1831[1]; the 'Société Éduenne des Lettres, Sciences et Arts', Autun, 1836[2]; the 'Société d'Archéologie Lorraine', Nancy, 1848[3]; while as specimens of societies more locally limited there may be mentioned the 'Académie Nationale de Reims', Reims, 1841[4]; the 'Académie des Sciences, Belles Lettres, et Arts de Clermont Ferrand', Clermont, 1747[5]. More recent societies of the third class indicated above will be noticed presently.

In Germany there exists a General Association of German Historical and Antiquarian Societies, 'Gesamtverein der deutschen Geschichts- und Altertumsvereine', founded 1852, which represents the whole country, and embraces one hundred and sixty two local societies[6]. A notice of all these is given in the official *Kunsthandbuch für Deutschland* published by the Administration of the Royal Museums in Berlin[7]. A few may be mentioned, such as the ' Verein von Altertumsfreunden im Rheinlande', Bonn, 1841[8]; the 'Historischer Verein für das Grossherzogtum Hessen', Darmstadt, 1834[9]; the 'Königlicher Sächsischer Altertumsverein', Dresden, 1824[10]; the Munich 'Altertumsverein', München, 1864[11]; the 'Württembergischer Geschichts- und Altertumsverein', Stuttgart, 1843[12]; the 'Harzverein für Geschichte und Altertumskunde', Wernigerode, 1868[13]; etc. etc. There are also town historical societies, such as the 'Verein für Geschichte der Stadt Nürnberg', 1878, and the 'Verein für Geschichte der Stadt Hannover', 1893, etc.

All the societies which have been now mentioned in the three countries under notice are mainly historical and antiquarian in intent; though their members are always ready from time to time to throw their influence into the right scale

[1] *Mémoires, Album des Monuments de l'Art dans le Midi de la France*, etc.
[2] Various publications.   [3] *Mémoires*, etc.
[4] Various publications.   [5] *Annales, Mémoires*, etc.
[6] Publication, *Korrespondenzblatt d. G.-V. d. d. G. u. A.-V.*
[7] Berlin, Reimer, 1904.   [8] *Jahrbücher* from 1842.
[9] *Archiv für Hessische Gesch. und Altertumskunde*, from 1835.
[10] Various publications.   [11] *Sitzungsberichte*, etc.
[12] *Jahreshefte* from 1844, etc.
[13] *Zeitschrift d. H.-V.* from 1868.

in all monument discussions. The third class of societies
mentioned above are those that have in the first instance a
practical object, and have been in most cases founded with a
definite aim for the furtherance of the cause of monument
preservation. One that has had a great influence abroad is
our own Society for the Protection of Ancient Buildings,
20 Buckingham Street, Strand, founded in 1877 largely through
the agency of the late William Morris. The personality of
Morris was more imposing than that of any one who has
busied himself in our own time with the care of monuments,
and Morris and his Society are held on the Continent in high
esteem. The National Trust for Places of Historic Interest
and Natural Beauty, 25 Victoria Street, London, founded in
1894, is an important English society, the aim of which is to
achieve by organized public opinion and by the efforts of
individuals, what is done abroad by official agencies and
government interference. It can hold and administer monuments and properties, and raises funds for the purchase of
sites of interest and beauty which thereby become perpetual
possessions of the people. The National Society for Checking
the Abuses of Public Advertising was founded in 1893[1].

In France M. Charles Normand founded in 1887 a 'Comité
des Monuments Français', with a special organ in the form of
a well illustrated periodical called *L'Ami des Monuments*[2],
which announces itself as 'founded with the aim of watching
over the monuments of Art of France, and the general
appearance of her Towns, and of defending the Picturesque
and the Beautiful'. On all monument questions relating to
France this publication is worth consulting, and is of especial
value as a protest against the centralized bureaucracy which
has held in its hands for so long the monument administration
in France. A German periodical founded more recently in
the same interests is of much greater worth as giving a wider
outlook on the whole field of the care of monuments in every
civilized land. The periodical in question is called '*Die
Denkmalpflege*' '*The Care of Monuments*' and was started in

---

[1] Hon. Sec. Richardson Evans, Camp View, Wimbledon.
[2] From 1887. Published in Paris, Rue Miromesnil 98. 25—30 francs yearly.

1899[1], as the organ of the movement for the defence of the older monuments of the Fatherland which has enlisted so much public sympathy in Germany for the last five years. The league called 'Heimatschutz[2]', 'the Defence of Home', which has been recently formed, carries out the propaganda to which the periodical gives literary expression. Many local societies both in Germany and France are at work on the same lines. The numerous historical towns are being supplied with protective associations, that have the same aims as the older Cockburn Association of Edinburgh[3]. Such exist in Hildesheim, Bremen, Trier, Dresden, Magdeburg, Danzig, Rothenburg a. d. Tauber, Hannover, in Germany; in Austria, Vienna has her 'Verein zum Schutze und zur Erhaltung der Kunstdenkmäler Wiens und Niederösterreichs'. In France, in 1897 there was formed in the Prefecture of the Seine a 'Commission du Vieux Paris', the object of which is to 'search out the vestiges of the older city, to record their present condition, and as far as is practicable to supervise their maintenance; to follow day by day any excavations undertaken, and inspect carefully and record all alterations that have become unavoidable'. A 'Société des Amis des Monuments Parisiens' does the same work in more independent fashion. There is a similar 'Société des Amis des Monuments Rouennais' and a 'Commission Municipale du Vieux Lyon' was established on the lines of that of Paris in 1898. In Belgium there has been great activity on the part of private societies which will be noticed in the chapter on that country in the sequel. An energetic local 'Société pour la Protection des Sites et des Monuments de la Province de Namur' has lately sprung into existence, and will probably lead to the foundation of others of the same kind. In Italy there is the same sort of awakening of personal interest in the protection of the national monuments which is the best and healthiest form which the movement for the care of monuments can

[1] Published by Ernst und Sohn, Berlin. 8—12 marks yearly.
[2] Secretary Dr R. Mielke, 18 Rönnestrasse, Charlottenburg.
[3] Founded in 1875 with the aim of 'The Preservation of the Amenity of Edinburgh and its Neighbourhood'.

take. In various towns of the peninsula societies are formed
by 'Amici dei Monumenti', the object of which is to watch
carefully the official proceedings of the government authorities
who deal with monuments, and to keep the public interested in
the subject through the medium of the press. The 'Riunione
Artistica' of Perugia recently formed a special committee of
its members for this purpose. At Rome the 'Associazione
Artistica fra i Cultori di Architettura' has been doing good
work in a city that needs intelligent treatment perhaps more
than any other.

The private societies here noticed do not publish elaborate
memoirs like the older antiquarian associations, but content
themselves with annual reports, which however contain useful
facts for the lover of monuments. The subject of private or
non-official publications should not be left without a word on
antiquarian and artistic journals not connected with any
society. Across the channel the *Revue des deux Mondes*,
perhaps the leading review of the world, lent itself in the
'thirties as the mouthpiece of the first protests against modern
vandalism uttered by Montalembert and by Victor Hugo, and
Didron's *Annales Archéologiques*[1], the *Gazette Archéologique*[2]
and *Revue Archéologique*[3], with the more recent *Revue de l'Art
Chrétien*[4], devote themselves to the serious study of the
monuments the preservation of which we are discussing.
Germany is not rich in independent periodicals of the kind,
though the recent *Denkmalpflege* is the most useful of all
such publications. In our own country the architectural
papers, such as *The Builder*, break a lance from time to time
for some threatened monument, and try to keep up the tone of
public opinion on the subject. Many of the most influential and
active champions of ancient monuments are found in the ranks
of the architectural profession, and the Council of the Royal
Institute of British Architects is a body that, like the Council
of the Society of Antiquaries, represents in this matter the view
of all sane and pious lovers of monuments. At the same time
the fact cannot be concealed that the architect differs from

[1] Paris, 1844–1881.
[2] Paris, 1875–1889.
[3] Paris, 1844, in progress.
[4] Lille, Paris, 1857, in progress.

the antiquary in that his interest, *qua* architect, is directed rather to the substitution for antique buildings of new ones, than to the safeguarding of the old; and experience has shown that the architect is not always on the side of preservation when a fine monument is threatened. Architecture is thus sometimes wounded in the house of its friends, and some of the most pronounced opponents of the Society for the Protection of Ancient Buildings are to be found in the ranks of the profession. *The Antiquary* and *The Reliquary and Illustrated Archaeologist* are periodicals devoted to the cause of ancient monuments. The numerous and well-illustrated artistic periodicals in which England is so rich, though occupied largely with the artistic productions of the hour, are generally ready with a word in season on all important monument questions, and journals such as *The Burlington Magazine* and *The Connoisseur* give scholarly attention to the things of old time.

§ 8. MEANS FOR THE PRESERVATION OF MONUMENTS:
B. OFFICIAL AND SEMI-OFFICIAL AGENCIES, MUSEUMS.

The principal private agencies, in the form of antiquarian and other societies, that are at work in some of the chief European countries, have been noticed in the preceding section. This has been done because these societies are not dealt with subsequently under the various countries. The case is different with the official and semi-official agencies, an account of which will be found in the second part of this book. In this place accordingly it is only necessary to note that the official agencies are as a rule state-appointed Conservators of monuments, and Monument-Commissions the members of which form a council attached to the Minister, whether of the Interior, of Education, or of Religion, who has in charge the department of the Fine Arts. The commissions are generally served by Inspectors of monuments, and it is their business to make themselves acquainted with the statistics of the buildings and works of art within their country or district, to form an opinion as to their condition and as to the need of repairs or restoration, and especially to gain timely notice when any monument is threatened with danger.   In the case of monuments belonging to the state, or more strictly to that department of state over which the Minister has actual control, the Minister of the Fine Arts can take the necessary measures, but in all other cases, he, or the commission in his name, can only give advice or exercise moral pressure on the owners of the monument.   This applies to the numerous states which possess official monument-commissions, but no monument-law which gives them legal powers over objects not under their immediate hand.   The work of these conservators and commissions is described in the sequel under the different countries.

In some cases the state, without appointing a commission of its own, will support and subsidize well-established private societies, whose operations acquire in this way a semi-official character.   This is the case for example in Switzerland and in Norway.   See postea, pp. 178, 191.

The installation and management of state or state-subsidized museums is part of the official care of monuments.   Upon this theme much has been written of late years and the whole subject of Museums has been recently treated with ample fulness in the work by Dr David Murray entitled *Museums: their History and their Use*[1].   Great Britain possesses moreover a Museums Association which holds annual conferences on museum administration.   The questions discussed in these works and at the conferences do not specially concern the subject in hand, and there is only one point connected with museums on which it is necessary to say a word.   This is the question of national against local museums, which is of importance as connected with the still larger problem of centralization or decentralization in monument administration generally.   It will be seen later on that France pursues in general, as would be expected, a centralizing policy, while the care of monuments in Germany and in Italy is delegated largely to district administrators.   In France however, magnificent as are the national museums of the capital and

---

[1] Three vols., Glasgow, MacLehose, 1904.

its neighbourhood, there is a splendid apparatus of local collections in the provinces, generally housed in fine ancient buildings the preservation of which is thus secured, and specially notable for their wealth in sculptured stones of both classical and mediaeval date. There are about one hundred and thirty of these good provincial museums in France[1]. Germany is still richer, but there the collections are not provincial, but are state collections of the kingdoms and duchies now grouped together under the Empire.

Britain also possesses excellent local museums some of which are in their way as well arranged and supervised as the British Museum or those of the Society of Antiquaries of Scotland or the Royal Irish Academy in Dublin. Now though there is something imposing in the idea of a single central collection gathering together for comparison all important available specimens, yet the balance of evidence seems in favour of the encouragement of local collections side by side with the central one. The local museum acts favourably, by way of stimulus and instruction, upon those persons in a district who are of an antiquarian turn of mind, while donors are encouraged to liberality when the local museum records the names of those who have enriched the collection from their own stores. A possessor of some antiquarian treasure may not feel particularly tempted to present it to a huge collection at a distance, where the object itself and the name of the donor will be practically lost ; but may feel proud to know it displayed on the shelves of the museum of his native town, where his fellow citizens will see and recognize it. The activity of local societies should by all means be encouraged, and the district museum focusses the society's work, and often gives it a local habitation. The connection between the Society of Antiquaries of Newcastle and the museum in the Black Gate is close and fruitful, and many of the private societies mentioned on page 35 meet in the museums of their towns.

---

[1] Clemen, *Die Denkmalpflege in Frankreich*, Berlin, 1898, ch. VIII.

§ 9. MEANS FOR THE PRESERVATION OF MONUMENTS:
C. .LEGISLATION, NATIONAL AND LOCAL.

There is a distinction between formal Monument Acts on
the one hand, and, on the other, royal rescripts, ministerial
circulars, and the like, which have official authority but not
the force of law.   Most states even to-day carry on their care
of monuments by the latter process, and have not yet legislated
directly for the purpose, and among these states are some of
the most advanced of all, such as Prussia.   In Germany
monument legislation is not imperial business but is left to
the separate states, and of these only the Grand-Duchy of
Hesse-Darmstadt has as yet achieved a Monument Act.   The
Austrian empire is also destitute of an Act, though there is
one that applies to the Kingdom of Hungary.   It has been
remarked that the larger and more advanced the state the
less easy is it to frame and to pass a satisfactory monument
law.   One reason of this is that the law, to be effective in its
protection of monuments, has to interfere to a greater or less
extent with the rights of private proprietors, and in advanced
communities the individual has considerable self-assertive-
ness, and actively contests such proposed interference.   The
British Ancient Monuments Protection Act of 1882, though its
tampering with the rights of private property is infinitesimal,
was resisted for ten years on this very ground by the Parliamentary landowners.   Most Acts that have been passed within
the last few years were more severe on the private proprietor
in their earlier drafts than in their final form.   For really
drastic enactments we have to go to countries that are more
or less orientally governed, and where the personal rights of
the highly civilized man are almost unknown.   The monument
law for example of Tunis is a far more severe one than could
ever be passed in France, and the law in Turkey makes
summary demands of which in Italy it dares not whisper.

The following European countries possess formal Monument Acts, and they are arranged according to the dates of
the legislation.   Greece, 1834 and 1899; Hungary, 1881;

Great Britain, 1882 ; Turkey, 1884 ; France, 1887 ; Bulgaria, 1889; Roumania, 1892 ; Canton de Vaud, 1898 ; Portugal, 1901 ; Italy, Hesse, Cantons of Bern and Neufchâtel, 1902. A notice of these is given under the various countries in the sequel. It should be added that other countries and these some of the most important in Europe have state Monument Acts at this moment under discussion. This is the case in Prussia, in the Austrian empire, in Spain, in Bavaria ; while Baden in 1883–4 had an excellent draft of a similar measure before the legislature. It should be noted that several states possess elaborate royal decrees and ministerial rescripts that have the practical force of laws though they are not actual statutes. Spain, Sweden, Russia, Belgium and other countries are in this condition.

Distinct from these Acts, which are pieces of state or cantonal legislation, are certain local by-laws and regulations affecting monuments and applying only to single towns. These exist chiefly in Germany, where certain towns have passed them on the strength of general Acts which allow local legislative action within fixed limits. Some of the provisions of these municipal by-laws, if carried out, are more effective for preservation than even the state Acts. The latter naturally contemplate the comparatively few outstanding monuments of a national kind, whereas the former, the local regulations, have for their aim the maintenance of the general appearance of an old city, or its ' Stadtbild '. Germany presents us with many examples of this local legislation which we shall find in force at towns like Hildesheim, Nürnberg, Rothenburg, Lübeck, Frankfurt, etc. Outside Germany Italy may be quoted as a country where there is municipal legislation with an aesthetic purpose, and something equivalent is to be found elsewhere. Even in our own country, where respect for private property is so punctiliously observed, we are not wholly without regulations of the kind. Thus the Corporation of Chester can prevent any new structures being placed so as to abut against the city walls[1], and the Town Council of Edinburgh some few years ago gained powers to

---

[1] Chester Improvement Act, 1884.

check any flagrant abuses in the matter of advertisements[1]. It seems obvious that in the case of cities like these, parts of which still possess their old 'Stadtbild' in its antique aspect, some further powers should be placed in the hands of the authorities to prevent injury to this by the thoughtless action, of private owners of property. All this subject will however be fully treated in the sequel.

§ 10.   RESTORATION AND ANTI-RESTORATION.

There is no subject connected with the care of ancient monuments more important than the one indicated in the title of this section, and there is none on which opinions are more divided. The advocates of restoration have a plausible and consistent theory, on which a vast amount of work of the kind has been carried out during the last half century in most of the countries of Europe. To the anti-restorationists this theory is pedantic and futile, and the work which it has guided had better have been left undone[2].

The motto of the anti-restorationist is 'Preserve and do not Restore'. The advice is unexceptionable, but it comes in many cases too late. If works of protection were all that was required there would be no problem to solve, for all will agree that ancient buildings which are still sound should never be allowed to fall into disrepair. Restoration in the strict sense

[1] Edinburgh Corporation Act, 1899. Clauses 45 f.

[2] The article 'Restauration' in vol. VIII of Viollet-le-Duc's *Dictionnaire de l'Architecture Française* is a classical expression of the orthodox theory of restoration. This may be studied also in some articles by M. L. Cloquet in the *Revue de l'Art Chrétien* for 1901–2, entitled 'La Restauration des Monuments Anciens'. The subject, introduced by M. Cloquet, was discussed at the sixth International Congress of Architects held at Madrid in 1904; and formed the subject of a discussion and elaborate deliverance at the first German Congress for the Care of Monuments held at Dresden in 1900.

The views of the Anti-restorationists are clearly conveyed in a series of small brochures and leaflets issued by the Society for the Protection of Ancient Buildings, 20 Buckingham Street, Strand, London, and in the periodical *L'Ami des Monuments* published at 98 Rue Miromesnil, Paris.

The whole subject has been well reviewed by M. Charles Buls, of Brussels, in a pamphlet called *La Restauration des Monuments Anciens*, published by Weissenbruch, Bruxelles, 1903.

means putting back or reproducing what has fallen or been lost, and if by careful supervision such accidents can be prevented the restorer need never be called in. The real problem presents itself when a time-worn monument has unfortunately passed beyond the stage when merely protective works suffice to render it fit for modern uses; or when a monument, which may be in itself still sound, needs enlargement to meet the needs of its modern users. The alternative then is no longer between protection and restoration, but between restoration or enlargement and the practical abandonment of the structure for modern purposes, and it may easily be seen that there is matter here for considerable controversy.

It is no part of the present purpose to take a side in this controversy. The writer is in this matter an opportunist, whose general sympathy with the opponents of restoration does not go so far as to lead him to condemn indiscriminately all undertakings of the kind. It appears indeed that no one general principle can be laid down to meet all cases, and that each case as it presents itself must be dealt with on its own merits. Restoration or addition, which at best must mean the placing of new work in juxtaposition with old, necessarily involves a certain aesthetic loss, while this loss may become a most serious and even fatal one when, as too often has happened, the old work is itself tampered with to bring it into accord with the new. Yet there are occasions when a loss of the minor kind must be borne for the sake of other interests of a social or religious order which are involved. The case for restoration is a strong one when there is a demand on the part of a community for accommodation in an ancient building that in its original or its impaired condition cannot supply what is needed. Let us suppose the building to be the mediaeval church of a town or village. To erect a new edifice on another site would not answer the purpose in view, for the old one is consecrated in the minds of the people by immemorial prescription, and where their fathers worshipped there they too would fain assemble still for the common service. To re-erect a ruined portion of the structure,

or build an addition such as a new aisle, is an obvious way of
meeting a desire on the part of the community with which all
must be in sympathy.

The case however is different when the ruined structure
serves no actual purpose in the life of to-day, and when
restoration, if undertaken, would be, so to say, forced on the
building merely for restoration's sake. An attempt has been
recently made to bring this distinction out more clearly by
dividing ancient monuments into two classes, '*dead monuments*,
i.e. those belonging to a past civilization or serving obsolete
purposes, and *living monuments*, i.e. those which continue to
serve the purposes for which they were originally intended[1]'.
The idea is a sound one in so far as it emphasizes the fact
that buildings must be treated with due regard to the place
they hold in modern life, but on the whole such classification
is to be deprecated. For one thing it opposes aesthetic and
social interests. The dead monument is only to be preserved,
so that the aesthetic loss already referred to caused by the
addition of new work to old is in its case avoided; whereas
the living monument may suffer this addition, to our aesthetic
loss but social gain. Hence might arise in some minds a
tendency to turn all our monuments over to the dead side,
and to withdraw from them the present interest they have for
us as things of use. The contrary should really be the case.
The tendency should be to make our ancient monuments as
far as possible all living ones, and so to link the present to
the past by imperishable bonds. To secure this, it may again
be said, one must be prepared for some sacrifice on the
aesthetic side.

For this reason it is not possible cordially to subscribe
to the advice of the Society for the Protection of Ancient
Buildings, contained in its original manifesto of 1877 and
re-issued without alteration in 1902. The advice is 'to put
Protection in the place of Restoration, to stave off decay by

[1] Resolution passed by the Madrid Congress of Architects, 1904. Reported
R. I. B. A. Journal, April 23, 1904. The Congress resolved that only in the
case of the *living monument* was restoration to be allowed. The *dead monument*
was only to be carefully preserved.

daily care, to prop a perilous wall or mend a leaky roof by such means as are obviously meant for support or covering, and show no pretence of other art, and otherwise to resist all tampering with either the fabric or ornament of the building as it stands ; if it has become inconvenient for its present use, to raise another building rather than alter or enlarge the old one ; in fine to treat our ancient buildings as monuments of a byegone art, created by byegone manners, that modern art cannot meddle with without destroying.' Such an austere method of dealing with structures, which may be still the foci of much of our religious and social life, will not and should not satisfy the intelligent public of to-day. Our British cathedrals and country churches are not yet 'dead' 'monuments of a byegone art' (though it is possible that such a fate may now be in store for some churches of France) but are still capable of those changes and modifications and bursts of fresh growth which are the signs of enduring vitality.

A reference to one or two examples will make clear what is here meant.

Some twenty years ago the ruined nave of Dunblane Abbey in Scotland was re-roofed and restored to serve the purposes of public worship for the increasing population of the town. Though the work was carried out with admirable taste, and no attempt was made to renew the weather-worn stonework where it was still structurally sound, yet it would be idle to conceal the fact that much of the artistic charm of the old building has been lost in the process. Again, the Abbey Church of Hexham in Northumberland possesses a beautiful Early English choir and transepts of the same style that in their architectural forms, their fittings, and still more the nameless charm of poetic association that haunts their ample spaces, are among the most beautiful of English monuments. There has been no nave since the thirteenth century when the Scots burned down the venerable Saxon one of the seventh century, and the restoration or rebuilding of the nave has been resolved on for some time past and is now in progress. Hexham is in very safe hands and the necessary work will be carried out in a spirit of piety, yet to one who has loved the place it can never be the same again. Still the loss must be accepted, for the sake of feeling that the life of the building, in its relation to the growing town of which it is the centre, will be quickened and made more real, and its extended spaces will promise accommodation to generations of citizens yet unborn.

On the other hand, there are ruined structures which can serve no practical use, or structures which, though they have felt the touch of time, can still fulfil their original purposes, and in neither of these cases is restoration called for. The first case may be illustrated from the monastic church on the island of Iona. The structure so far as it remained was of great interest and beauty, and the associations of the spot so sacred that any disturbance of the *genius loci* was on every ground to be avoided. Yet through a chain of untoward circumstances the hand of the restorer has come to be laid on a fabric that only asked to be properly supervised and then let alone with its romantic memories about it. The restored building has no useful purpose that it can serve. The restoration is for restoration's sake, and is in every way to be deplored. An illustration of the second case is furnished by the Chapter House at Canterbury. This was a building in full use, and structurally complete; in no sense a ruin, though it was timeworn and in its decorative features decayed. The effect of this dilapidation was not really to injure the artistic effect of the interior but rather to increase it. The eye dwelt contentedly on the mellow harmony of the broken hues and felt no desire for the mechanical neatness of a new 'job'. Proper structural supervision was all the graceful fabric needed, yet it has now been put into a state of 'decorative repair' which has robbed it of almost all its aesthetic charm. It is now a place to avoid rather than seek, and is a monumental example of the evils of restoration for restoration's sake.

The history of restoration, and of the anti-restoration movement, may be briefly indicated. Almost all ancient buildings, and especially mediaeval churches, have been altered and added to at various times to suit the changing needs of those who used them. The alterations at each epoch were generally carried out in the special architectural style of that epoch, though there are not wanting examples of deliberate efforts made by the older builders to reproduce the style of still earlier times[1]. In the first half of the nineteenth century the Romantic movement, and the High Church religious revival which in this country was contemporary with it, drew special attention to our mediaeval churches, which were found to be in a dilapidated and encumbered condition highly unsatisfactory to the newly awakened zeal of the times. Work on the fabrics and fittings was clearly necessary, but the age possessed no architectural style of its own, and it was a matter for consideration what form this work should take. Then was developed the orthodox theory of restoration, the principle of which was 'to bring an ancient building back to its original condition and appearance by faithfully and minutely reproducing all that had been lost or destroyed, and by making the new work resemble the old as closely as possible[2]'. The buildings, as we have just noticed, were carried out at different times and in different styles, and were full of fittings showing the styles of all the successive periods of architecture from the twelfth century downwards. It seemed good to the leading spirits of the restoration epoch in France and England, men like Viollet-le-Duc and Sir Gilbert Scott, to attempt to bring back the buildings in architecture and arrangements to something like a unity of style. The style of the thirteenth century was commonly taken as a standard of perfection, and the restorer effaced as far as possible the evidences of later work, while all the new masonry and fittings were studiously carried out in this same fashion. The result of this process in too many cases was a wholesale clearance of interiors which has left them painfully bare and unfurnished. Viollet-le-Duc treated Notre Dame at Paris in this fashion, and Salisbury Cathedral in England (before the

---

[1] M. Anthyme Saint-Paul, *Viollet-le-Duc*, Paris, 1881, Chapitre III, gives a good many French examples of such reproduction. The western towers of Westminster, the production of a classical epoch, are the most conspicuous English example.

[2] *Notes on the Repair of Ancient Buildings*, issued by the Protection Society, London, Batsford, 1903, p. 11.

time of Gilbert Scott) was similarly denuded. The new work carried out in exact accordance with the model gave an air of consistency to the edifice, but took from it the play of life and the variety which it possessed in its former miscellaneous condition.

It is now generally acknowledged that this procedure was a mistake. The appearance together in an ancient building of so many different kinds of work, each characteristic of its own period, though it may scandalize the purist, is a phenomenon of historical interest which should by no means be effaced. The orthodox modern restorer is not allowed now to select some one style from among those represented in an edifice, and to suppress the others in its favour. He must be prepared to reproduce work of the fifteenth or the seventeenth centuries as faithfully as that of the fourteenth or the twelfth, and must adapt the style of his new work to the style of that part of the building with which it should most suitably harmonize[1].

With this modification the orthodox theory of restoration remains much what it was in the early days of the restoration epoch, and in its present form it was clearly and fully enunciated and discussed on the occasion of the first German Congress for the Care of Monuments held in Dresden in 1900. It was there laid down that the ruling principle in all works, either of repair, restoration, or addition, should be the most scrupulous piety towards the ancient fabric in all its parts. The forms, the materials, the methods of technical treatment and of construction, must follow as exactly as possible the old models, and it was expressly stated that in any new portions there was to be avoided even the very slightest expression of the artistic individuality of the architect in charge, who was on the contrary to confine himself with

---

[1] 'Ancient buildings will generally be found to have been altered at various periods; when this is the case the whole of the old work should be preserved and exposed to view, so as to show the history of the fabric, with its successive alterations, as distinctly as possible.' From *General Advice on the Conservation of Ancient Monuments*, issued by the Royal Institute of British Architects, 9 Conduit Street, London.

the most jealous care within the strict limits of the style and character of the original monument[1].

This theory of restoration by the exact copying of the older work, like other orthodox theories, has been subjected to unsparing criticism on the part of a minority, whose valour and persistence have made a serious breach in the bulwarks behind which the obnoxious doctrine has been so long entrenched. The assault was led by Mr Ruskin, whose 'Lamp of Memory' in the *Seven Lamps of Architecture* contains in its latter pages an eloquent protest against the whole idea of 'faithful restoration' then in vogue. William Morris followed upon the same side, and in the tracts issued by the Society for the Protection of Ancient Buildings, founded by Morris and others in 1877, as well as in the French periodical *L'Ami des Monuments*, we have clear and accessible statements of the anti-restoration argument.

Condensing this into the narrowest possible limits it may be reduced to the two propositions, first, that the theoretically faithful reproduction of old work is impossible; and, second, that even if it were possible it would not be desirable. It is impracticable because in the nature of things old work cannot be reproduced. This is true both as regards its form and its spirit. Materials, processes, appliances, tools, the training and the habits of workmen, are in modern times unlike what they were of old, and still more dissimilar is the present relation of designer and craftsman to that prevailing in mediaeval days, with the result that the whole spirit of the work of the two periods must necessarily be different. 'It must be remembered that the mediaeval builders were themselves artists, and the mere skill of tooling shewn on an ancient stone gives us pleasure. Any art which is found in the modern work is the art of the designer and not of the workman. The two periods differ so widely, in conditions and methods, that it is impossible that they should both

---

[1] 'Ein jedes, auch nur leisestes Hervortreten der künstlerischen Eigenart des herstellenden Architekten über den den Baustil und die Eigenart des Denkmals umfassenden Rahmen hinaus ist bei solchen Neuschöpfungen auf das peinlichste zu vermeiden.' Report of Congress in *Die Denkmalpflege*, 1900, p. 115.

produce similar work. A man who knows exactly what he
wants to make, works in a much freer way and will meet
with better success than the man who is only copying something he does not fully understand, and who consequently
cannot put into his work the human quality which gives such
an interest and charm to all spontaneous work [1].'

Again, were such exact reproduction in itself possible, it
would be inadvisable, because by imposing this conscientious,
nay, slavish, copying upon designer and craftsman alike, we
should be starving their creative faculty, and condemning
them to forego their artistic birthright, their prerogative of
freedom. Furthermore, the result when achieved would to
the ordinary spectator have the effect of a deceit or forgery.
No doubt the sensitive eye could always detect these great
though subtle differences between old work and new, but the
intelligent though inexpert student of architecture might
often be led astray in the matter of dating. The danger of
this has presented itself to the minds of those who have
worked out the orthodox theory. The resolutions of the
Dresden Congress forbade the use of artificial colouring-
matter to assimilate the hue of new stonework to that of the
old, and an elaborate system has been devised for indicating
by conventional marks or inscriptions those parts of a building
which are modern additions or restorations. There is something ridiculous in the idea of labouring anxiously to make
one thing exactly like another, and then labelling them with
equal care to show that they are different, while in practice, in
our own country certainly, the proposed system would be too
troublesome to be carried out.

It was noticed above that the protest of the minority has
now really shaken in the public mind the orthodox theory.
Though the Dresden Congress adhered to the latter, yet
there were not wanting voices which protested against its
pedantry and futility, and it was significant that Dr Clemen,
who, as chief conservator of monuments for the Rhine-
land, has more fine mediaeval buildings under his care than

---

[1] From *Objections to so-called Restoration*, a leaflet issued by the Society for
the Protection of Ancient Buildings.

any other man in Europe, admitted that 'As a rule all representatives of the care of monuments in Germany now agree
in this, that restoration work properly so called must everywhere be confinèd within narrower and narrower limits, so
that the Germans are coming to occupy the same position
in this matter as the English anti-restorationists and the
French Friends of monuments[1].'

There can be no question that the protests of the minority
have had a most salutary effect, first, in reducing, though
only to some small extent, the general area of operations of
the restorer; and, next, in checking some of the subsidiary
operations of the orthodox practitioner, which were all the
more deplorable in that they were quite needless. That the
practice of purging an unfortunate interior of its historical
apparatus in fittings and details is now discredited, has been
already noticed. Another evil of the first magnitude has
been the habit of the restorer to work over the old parts of
his building—which he need not touch at all—in such a way
as to take off the *cachet* of age and reduce the surface to the
commonplace evenness of new work. Considering how very
much of the charm of ancient structures consists in the varied
and sensitive texture and colour of the parts, which they owe
alike to time and to old methods of manipulation, it is almost
inconceivable that men who count themselves artists should
deliberately efface the charm, and give us exteriors pared
away to dismal flatness like those of Durham or St Giles'
Edinburgh, or should of set purpose level up the quaint
undulations of the pavement of St Mark's at Venice. We
may wish full potency to the voices of the few who have
all along protested against these and other wanton offences
which the term 'restoration' is allowed to cover.

It is a different matter when we are asked to accept the
alternatives which the protestors offer to the orthodox theory
of restoration. To set our churches aside as dead monuments
to be preserved but not used; or to confine all new work
upon them to what is strictly plain and utilitarian, are un-

---

[1] *Korrespondenzblatt des Gesamtvereins der deutschen Geschichts- und Altertumsvereine*, 1900, p. 54.

satisfactory solutions of the difficulty.   Equally open to doubt
is the method advocated by an influential minority at the
Dresden Congress, according to which the designer of the
new work is not to copy the old, but to express his own
artistic genius in what he produces, offering it frankly in
technique and in form as something new.   If this imply that
the designer is to give free play to his own individuality, so
that the new nave at Hexham migh conceivably become an
ebullition of 'l'Art nouveau', then in the name of piety and
common sense we must raise a protest.   There is surely however a *via media* to be found.   The international gathering of
architects at Madrid in 1904 resolved that what they called
'living' monuments might be restored, and that 'such restoration should be effected in the original style of the monument'.
The common sense of the situation seems to require us to
acquiesce in this dictum.   This need not however involve such
lifeless 'peinlich' copying of old forms as the orthodox theory
demands.   Though the present generation of architects may
have no common distinctive style, like the styles that have
prevailed in the successive epochs of the past, yet our artists
have learned to express their own individuality in forms,
which, though belonging properly to the past, they have yet
been able to make in a real sense their own.   When there is a
demand for new work on a building the main fabric of which
is in a certain style, it is surely possible to secure an architect
who has made that style his own special study.   Such an one
may be trusted to express himself with freedom in the new
work while preserving a harmonious relation between the new
and the old.   He will make a work of art and not a mechanical
copy, and add a new generation to the long existence of a still
living monument.

   Though, as was said above, no general principle can be
laid down for all cases, and each must be judged on its own
merits, yet it would seem possible to find in the direction
indicated a solution of the difficult problems which this subject offers.

§ 11. 'CLASSEMENT', INVENTORIZATION, AND OFFICIAL PUBLICATIONS.

The word ' classement' and the operation it represents are characteristically French. 'Classer' is practically equivalent to our English verb 'to schedule' and to 'class' in this sense means to place upon a list of limited scope, so as to mark off the object thus dealt with from others of the same kind. French monument administration concerns itself mainly though not exclusively with a limited number of monuments placed thus upon a list apart. In its origin the term 'classer' seems to have had a rather more special meaning, for in the earliest ministerial circulars of 1837, in which M. Guizot, then Minister of the Interior, gives directions for the formation of such a list, the phrases occur 'you will classify the monuments in the order of their importance' (vous les classerez dans leur ordre d'importance) and 'to classify each monument according to the degree of interest which it presents (pour classer chaque monument selon le degré d'intérêt qu'il présente) and this would seem to imply that a gradation of 'Class I', 'Class II', etc., had been contemplated[1]. If this were the original idea it was soon given up, and no distinction of importance is now recognized, the only difference being between the 'monument classé' and the 'monument non-classé'. This distinction operates very favourably in the case of the scheduled object, upon which is set the official stamp of merit and importance, but the monuments that remain below the line, as it were, suffer proportionately in esteem. The difference between 'classé' and 'non-classé' is necessarily very great, whereas monuments shade off very gradually in artistic value and historical significance, and many judges of these things might place some of the unclassed monuments above others which are on the list. The fact indeed that a monument is excluded from the schedule may seem to the heedless an official hint that it is fair game for the spoiler.

---

[1] Wolff, *Handbuch der staatlichen Denkmalpflege in Elsass-Lothringen*, Strassburg, 1903, pp. 58, 60, gives the texts.

Hence the principle of 'classement' is by no means universally approved by those most interested in the care of monuments, and the sixth international Congress for Art History held at Lübeck in 1900 decided that 'the limitation of the protection of the state only to a few classified monuments cannot be entirely approved of either from the point of view of art or of that of history[1]'. Dr Gurlitt, who is in official charge of the task of drawing up an inventory of the whole of the artistic treasures of the kingdom of Saxony, stated at the monument-congress at Dresden in 1900 that the French system in his opinion might be positively harmful. 'When the scheduling goes no further than it does in France it is of no use,' he says, and notes that in the South of France it had worked injuriously[2]. We should remember however that those states which have adopted 'classement' as the foundation of their system of monument administration take care to provide for additions to be made to the schedules when necessary. This is the case in France and England, while in Roumania there is the valuable provision that the schedule is to be gone over and revised every five years[3]. In the monument law passed by Canton Bern in Switzerland in 1902 there is provision for a revision of the list every three years.

Inventorization means something different from 'classement'. In theory it implies a complete list of all objects of artistic or historical interest within a certain district, and not merely a selection made with a view to ulterior legislation. In the case of countries at all rich in such objects a complete inventory is an extensive affair, and the task of drawing one up, say, for Italy, is one of appalling magnitude. Both in Italy and in France projects of this kind were started and came after a while to a standstill, but the work in Italy at any rate is again in active operation. Only the other day a State Commission was appointed in Holland to draw up 'a summary inventory of all monuments movable and immov-

---

[1] *Die Denkmalpflege*, 1900, p. 104.
[2] *Korrespondenzblatt des Gesamtvereins der deutschen Geschichts- und Altertumsvereine*, 1900.
[3] postea, p. 226.

able of the country[1]'.   It may be said in general that official
inventories of artistic and historical treasures are everywhere
on the Continent in progress, though they are on different
schemes and in various stages of advance. As regards Germany
it was officially reported in 1901 that in the last thirty years,
in all the states of the German Empire, descriptive lists (inventories) of the architectural and artistic monuments have
been undertaken, and to a very considerable extent have been
already completed....The inventories of the separate German
states form already a row of more than a hundred and thirty
volumes, and by the completion of parts that are still wanting
the number will soon rise to two hundred volumes[2].' The
official *Kunsthandbuch für Deutschland* of 1904[3] gives a list of
these publications up to date.   Only those versed in the dark
secrets of German serial publication would venture to say
how many volumes these make, but the number of separate
works is nearly fifty.   Some of the works, embracing ' Bau-
und Kunstdenkmäler', are on a monumental scale, and they
are practically all subsidized by the state or public corporations.   It needs hardly to be said that no state inventory will
be likely to contain all the older domestic buildings and
picturesque details to be found in the towns and villages of
the dominions : local inventories however, of narrower scope,
may enter more closely into detail.   Some towns have inventories of their own.   Thus there is a list of all the old
houses in Cologne, that is said to be used effectively for
purposes of preservation.   The same has been done at
Hildesheim and other ancient German cities.   One of the
functions of the Commission du Vieux Paris ' mentioned
ante, p. 39, has been the scheduling of older monuments,
and at Vienna the ' Society for the protection and preservation of the artistic monuments of Vienna and Lower Austria '
has in hand an inventory of all artistic monuments.   In 1903
there was published at Lyons an illustrated *Inventaire Général
du Vieux Lyon*, which contains a list of existing houses that

---

[1] postea, p. 176.
[2] *Zweiter Tag für Denkmalpflege*, Karlsruhe, 1901, p. 119.
[3] Berlin, Reimer.

have a value from the point of view of Lyonnaise history and art. Lübeck began in 1903 to print an inventory and description of her public and private monuments.

It is recognized everywhere that this inventorization is a necessary first step in any scheme for the care and protection of monuments. A country, a district, a town, must know what it possesses before it can effectively concert measures for safeguarding its treasures. In our own country, save in the one matter of historical manuscripts (see postea, p. 150 f.), how little has been accomplished in regard to these essential preliminaries to an organized Denkmalpflege! Our official schedule of Ancient Monuments connected with the working of the Ancient Monuments Acts of 1882 and 1892 embraces less than a hundred items and these are nearly all of the prehistoric class. Dr David Murray, in his *Archaeological Survey of the United Kingdom*[1], notes what has been done in this connection by the Society of Antiquaries and other agencies, but deals only with monuments of archaeological interest. 'Bau- und Kunstdenkmäler' in the German sense mean something far more extensive than this. All parts of the United Kingdom have of course received attention in publications dealing with the monuments of various kinds of which they are the habitat, but these publications, whether of societies or of individual authors, are of an accidental kind, without connection one with another. They may be best described as a body of material by the aid of which a systematic catalogue raisonné of our artistic treasures might be compiled. For example, the catalogues of the Winter Exhibitions of the works of Old Masters at Burlington House for the last thirty years would give a very good idea of the wealth of artistic treasures in the single department of pictures contained in private collections in this country. Michaelis's *Ancient Marbles in Great Britain*[2] does the same for fragments of antique sculpture. The material prepared in this manner by various independent agencies would probably be found to be most complete in the case of Scotland, for which country a fairly satisfactory inventory of monuments of architecture and art

---

[1] Glasgow, 1896.   [2] Cambridge, 1882.

might with comparatively little difficulty be compiled. Thanks to the recent publication by the Society of Antiquaries of Scotland of the Sculptured Stones of the country[1]; to the eight fully illustrated volumes by Messrs McGibbon and Ross dealing with the religious, military and domestic architecture of Scotland[2]; to the reports on local museums published in the *Proceedings* of the Society of Antiquaries of Scotland[3]; and to the attention now paid to the contents of private picture galleries, archaeological and artistic Scotland is fairly well mapped out, and if ever a national work of inventorization were set on foot, it is in Scotland that it might be started with the best promise of a satisfactory result.

§ 12. SUPERINTENDENCE OF EXCAVATIONS AND DISPOSAL OF 'FINDS': TREASURE-TROVE.

In all countries where the state occupies itself in any way with the subject of ancient monuments, attention is paid to the possible existence under the surface of the ground of remains of old buildings and of movable works of art that may be of the highest interest and value. There are accordingly in most lands regulations which control excavations made in quest of such remains or objects even on private ground, and provide for the proper disposal of all that may be found either accidentally or as the result of deliberate search. It so happens that some of the countries, where the soil conceals artistic treasures of the rarest and most precious kind, are inhabited by a population at a low level of civilization and culture. Such countries are Turkey, Egypt, Tunis, Algeria. In these and similar regions somewhat severe measures are in operation for preserving in the public interest anything of value that may come to light. The more advanced countries differ in their procedure, but the Acts and rescripts of all of them contain clauses which give to the state certain

---

[1] *The Early Christian Monuments of Scotland*, Edin. 1903.

[2] *Castellated and Domestic Architecture of Scotland*, 5 vols., Edin. 1887–92. *Ecclesiastical Architecture of Scotland*, 3 vols., Edin. 1896–7.

[3] Vol. x New Series, 1887–8, p. 331 f.

milder rights over excavations and 'finds'. Even in our own realm of freedom, where anyone can excavate on his own land without leave or notice, and as a rule dispose of what he finds at his own sweet will, the Crown in right of so-called 'Treasure-trove' has a lien on a certain class of the resultant discoveries.

The case of Great Britain, where state interference with excavations and discoveries is at its minimum, may be noticed first. By English law the finder of any object has a good title to it as against anyone but the owner. An object picked up on the land of another is not held necessarily to belong to the owner of the soil; it may have been dropped accidentally by a third person, and belongs to the finder till that person be produced, but if on the other hand the object be pulled out from the ground, it is held to have been part of the ground and hence the property of the land-owner. A land-owner accordingly has absolute property in all objects of artistic or historical interest that may be unearthed from the soil of his estate, but this right is subject to the limitation connected with treasure-trove. By an ancient English statute precious objects in gold or silver coined or uncoined, that appear to have been at some time in the past hidden in the ground, and of which the proprietor is unknown, are, wherever they come to light, the property of the Crown[1]. If they do not seem to have been at the beginning purposely hidden, but only to have become accidentally covered over and so concealed from view, then they are not treasure-trove; the Crown has no claim to them, and they become the property of the land-owner.

In Scotland, which possesses its own legal system independent of that of England, the representative of the Crown advances claims upon 'finds' of antiquarian value far more extensive than the claims authorized by the English statutes. In a case argued there in 1889 the Crown claimed the possession of certain ornaments in jet discovered in a burial cist or coffin on the estate of the Earl of Home. This was not 'treasure' in the sense of the English law of treasure-trove,

---

[1] Or of a lord of the manor who has grant of treasure-trove.

but the claim of the Crown was recognized by the Scottish Courts though the case actually ended in a compromise[1].

The whole subject of treasure-trove, both in England and in Scotland, is somewhat complicated, and has given rise to considerable discussion. It is claimed for it on one side that the institution may be worked so as to serve the cause of monument preservation. If the Crown make good its claim to a 'find' of this order, it is the custom for the object to be placed in a national museum, and for the finder to be paid the bullion value of the treasure with something over. On the other side various objections have been raised against the institution from the archaeological standpoint, on which information is furnished in Dr David Murray's book[2]. It is not easy to see the reason of these objections. The Crown acts in the matter solely as trustee for the public, and archaeologists have reason to wish its power of appropriation rather extended than limited. Some of those who have watched most closely the operations of the Crown in this department in Scotland are strongly in favour of the present system. In England there exists of course the obvious legal difficulty of proving whether e.g a hoard upturned by the plough was originally hidden on purpose, or placed under the public eye in a tomb as part of its furniture. Only a year or two ago, in the great treasure-trove case of 1903 with regard to certain golden objects found in Ireland and sold to the British Museum, a game of archaeological high-jinks was played in endeavours to prove or disprove in court an ingenious theory that the objects had once been thrown openly into the waves as offerings to a Hibernian god of the sea! As some expert witnesses denied the existence of any such Irish marine deity, and others doubted whether on the spot in question there had been any sea, it is not surprising that the Crown made good its claim, so that the objects now repose amidst others of their kind in the collection of the Irish Academy in Dublin[3].

[1] *The Scotsman*, Oct. 21, 23, 1889.

[2] *An Archaeological Survey*, etc., p. 57 f.

[3] *The Juridical Review*, Edinburgh and London, Sept. 1903.

Another recent case of treasure-trove that was tried at law is so typical that it is worth a word. In November 1904 an earthenware jug containing some 400 gold and silver coins of the reigns of Elizabeth, James I, and Charles I, was discovered by some navvies who were making a road in the neighbourhood of Oswestry in Shropshire. With the insouciance of the British working man they disposed of their treasure for fills of tobacco and threepenny pieces, but the authorities hearing of the find recovered most of the coins, on which the Coroner of the district proceeded to hold an enquiry for the sake of determining their legal owner. The Crown claimed them as treasure-trove, the owner of the soil as objects abandoned but not purposely concealed. Expert opinion was locally available, and it was made clear that the hoard was in all probability purposely hidden on the occasion of the siege of Oswestry in the Civil War in 1643. Hence the Crown was held to have made good its claim, but not before one of the rustic witnesses had enunciated the principle 'findings keepings'—the oldest and best law of treasure-trove, and one in full force in earlier days along the marches of Wales[1]!

It is often stated that a law of treasure-trove of this kind exists in Denmark. Ordinances of the seventeenth and eighteenth centuries gave to the Crown all treasure in gold, silver, or other precious material, and in 1752 it was decreed that the finder should be paid the bullion worth of the discovery, though the owner of the land had nothing. The distinction however, so vital to the English system, between treasure purposely hidden and treasure only abandoned, does not seem to be recognized in the Danish enactments, nor in similar rules in force in Sweden and other countries[2].

At the opposite pole to English legislation, where the law of treasure-trove represents the only legal restriction of private rights in excavation and 'finds,' we note those of Bulgaria, of 1889, and of Roumania and Bosnia, of 1892, which declare

---

[1] *The Border Counties Advertizer*, Oswestry, Nov. 30, Dec. 7, and Dec. 21, 1904.
[2] For authorities see the chapters in the second part relating to the several countries concerned.

that all objects of antique art unearthed or yet to be discovered are the absolute property of the state. A Turkish
Imperial Iradé of 1884 also declares (Art. 3) that 'all objects
of antiquity existing in the Ottoman Empire, which have
been discovered or will in the future be brought to light
through excavations...belong in full possession to the
state.' No one may excavate without leave (Art. 7) and if
leave be given all that is discovered is state property. Only
in the case of an accidental discovery made by a proprietor
on his own land is he legally entitled to a half-share in
what is found. The Greek laws of 1834 and 1899 declare
as a general principle that 'all antiquities found in Greece,
as the legacy of Hellenic forefathers, are to be considered the
common national possession of all Hellenes', but in practice
the state only claims a half-share in antiques which come to
light in private land. Anything however thus found must be
at once declared, and the state has the right of pre-emption
should the owner wish to turn into money the half-share in
the discovery which the code allows.

In Austria, by the older legislation anything of value that
was discovered belonged one-third to the finder, one-third to
the owner of the soil and the remaining third to the state.
In 1846 however the state gave up its share, allowing the
other two participants to divide the value between them.
The reason for this is significant. The state surrendered its
claim on the ground that the assertion of it led to the concealment of finds on the part of discoverers, and on these
same grounds the general principle of state claims to archaeological finds has been often deprecated. In practice states
which make absolute claim to property in finds yet pay a
part, or the whole, or more than the whole, of the bullion
value to the finder. It is obvious that if this be not done
the find will be concealed and sold to the best advantage by
its discoverer. In Bulgaria the peasant who lights upon an
antique coin as likely as not sells it to a Macedonian trader
from the other side of the mountain frontier. Under the old
English law there was a penalty of death for concealing
treasure-trove, but it is found that better results are secured

by the opposite method of rewarding those who exhibit what they have found. In the Italian monument law of 1902 it is laid down that foreigners who obtain leave to excavate must present all they find to an Italian public museum, while natives must admit the claim of the state to a fourth part of what they discover. The French law of 1887 and the Hessian of 1902 make no claim on the part of the state to a share in finds in private ground. The disposition of what is discovered is regulated in France by the 'Code Civil', which in § 716 gives the whole treasure to one who finds it on his own property, but when it is discovered on another's land it goes half to the finder and half to the owner of the soil. The Prussian civil code has a corresponding provision.

Most continental Monument Acts however regulate excavations in so far that notice must be given of their inception and of any discoveries made as their result, while in Italy they must be under the supervision of the state authorities. Ground in private possession may be expropriated by the state for the sake of carrying out excavations. It is thus expressly provided in the Hungarian law of 1881, in that of France, 1887, of Hesse, 1902, etc. In Great Britain and Ireland, as has been already noticed, there is no restriction, no provision for supervision, and no duty of announcement.

§ 13. PROHIBITION OF SALE OR EXPORTATION.

This is not a matter that specially concerns our own country. We are buyers rather than sellers, and though we occasionally lose by our indifference some treasure of priceless value, the scandal thus created does not affect the public mind so deeply that legislation on the subject would stand much chance of being carried. It is true that the British public is periodically startled by the rumour that the proprietor of Stonehenge is going to sell the monument for exportation to America, and is reminded thereby that there exists no law for the prevention of such an act; but it relies on the common sense of owners to preserve them from unpopular proceedings of the kind, and goes to sleep contentedly till aroused by the next scare.

The countries specially affected are those in which heir-looms of great value have been handed down in families whose worldly fortunes have sunk in modern days to a low ebb. This occurs not seldom in Italy, and Italy is accordingly the classic land of regulations prohibiting the sale or exportation of private treasures, that have from their unique character a national importance. Such prohibitions to be effective must be enforced by the law. Public opinion and private societies do not here come into view. The subject may therefore be passed over here as it will be noticed in connection with the legislation of the different countries.

§ 14. EXPROPRIATION OR COMPULSORY PURCHASE.

The crux of all Monument Acts is the difficulty of safe-guarding structures and other objects in private hands. The state can deal as it likes with its own property, and has a certain hold on the property of public bodies that are officially connected with the state, but private individuals and private corporations, where there is no dependence on government, claim the right to dispose of their property at their own will. The problem of the monument legislator is to prevent these independent entities from injuring monuments that may be of national interest, either by neglect, by alteration, or by in-judicious repair; or from destroying them, or alienating them for gain. In despotic countries this may be effectively pre-vented by convenient summary processes, but the more civilized the community the less feasible is direct interference with the rights of private property. Indemnification of the owner for any such interference is held in most legislatures to be a sine qua non, and this is best secured by the state purchasing the property the treatment of which is in dispute. The purchase may of course be by agreement, and then no question of compulsion arises, but a monument in the hands of a proprietor who will not sell it, and yet threatens it with deleterious treatment, can only be saved when purchase is allowed to be compulsory. The process in itself is a familiar one. Few works of public utility, such as a railway, could be carried out unless proprietors unwilling to sell the land needed for the project could be expropriated. All civilized communities have this power over the property of individual citizens, and unless it were from time to time exercised public works on a large scale would be impracticable. In the case of Great Britain and Ireland the Lands Clauses Consolidation Acts of 1845 confirm the power and give directions how the somewhat cumbrous process is to be carried out. In France a law of May 3, 1841, does the same for that country, and lays it down that expropriation is allowable 'à cause d'utilité publique'. In Italy a law of June 25, 1865, allows 'espropriazione in causa di pubblica utilità', and in Prussia a law of June 11, 1874, allows expropriation or compulsory purchase of private property (Enteignung) but 'nur aus Gründen des öffentlichen Wohles'. Similar provisions exist in other codes, so that the process is a perfectly familiar one.

The use of the process, on the other hand, in favour of monument preservation is not quite so clear. Its applicability depends on whether or not this monument preservation be regarded as a matter of public utility. In our own country it would be an innovation so to regard it, and in our Ancient Monuments Act of 1882 it is expressly laid down that the compulsory clauses of the Lands Clauses Consolidation Acts are *not* to be employed for the purchase of a monument in the interest of its safe preservation. Any purchase of the kind can only be by agreement. In France on the other hand the law of 1841 has been actually put in force several times in the interests of monuments even before the passing of the formal Monument Act of 1887, and in this last Act its employment for the purpose is expressly authorized. In Prussia jurists have affirmed that a similar application to monument preservation of the general law of 'Enteignung' would be legal[1], and it has actually been put in force for the purpose[2].

It needs hardly to be said that almost all Monument Acts give this power of expropriation. The exercise of it has however always remained a function of the central government, and the process has been somewhat long and complicated. A beginning has been made in the Hessian law of 1902[3] with the principle of the delegation of this power by the central government to local bodies such as town councils. It is obvious that the exercise of this power must be carefully safeguarded, as its too frequent employment would lead to difficulties and discontent. The whole subject of expropriation in the interests of amenity is one for careful consideration, but in continental countries the principle is fully established.

[1] Dr Jur. F. W. Bredt, *Die Denkmalpflege und ihre Gestaltung in Preussen*, Berlin, 1904, p. 50.

[2] *Vierter Tag für Denkmalpflege*, Berlin, 1903, p. 11.

[3] See postea, pp. 110, 118.

PART II

MONUMENT ADMINISTRATION IN THE
VARIOUS EUROPEAN COUNTRIES

PART II

MONUMENT ADMINISTRATION IN THE VARIOUS EUROPEAN COUNTRIES

CHAPTER I.

FRANCE.

BIBLIOGRAPHY AND SOURCES OF INFORMATION.

Ministère de l'Instruction Publique et des Beaux-Arts. Direction des Beaux-Arts. *Monuments Historiques, Loi et Décrets relatifs à la Conservation des Monuments Historiques. Liste des Monuments Classés.* Paris, Imprimerie Nationale, 1889.

Législation Relative aux Monuments et Objets d'Art, par L. Tétreau, Paris, 1896.

Die Denkmalpflege in Frankreich, von Dr Paul Clemen, Berlin, 1898.

Handbuch der Staatlichen Denkmalpflege in Elsass-Lothringen, von F. Wolff, Strassburg, 1903.

Inventaire Général du Vieux Lyon, par C. Jamot, Lyon, 1903.

L'Ami des Monuments et des Arts, quarterly periodical from 1887, Paris, Rue Miromesnil, 98.

Congrès International pour la Protection des Œuvres d'Art et des Monuments. ' *Procès-verbaux Sommaires*, Paris, Imprimerie Nationale, 1889.

Communication, of March 1905, from the 'Direction Administrative des Services d'Architecture et des Promenades et Plantations', in the Prefecture of the Department of the Seine, kindly sent with enclosed documents such as the *Règlement Sanitaire de la Ville de Paris*, 1904.

Letter from M. le Comte R. de Lasteyrie, member of the Commission des Monuments Historiques.

FRANCE has been called the 'classic land' of monument-lore, and her Historical Monuments Act of 1887 is generally regarded as the most important contribution yet made to legislation for the care of these relics of the past. In some respects the title of 'classic land' would apply more fitly still to Italy, where the Care of Monuments has from time to time occupied public attention from the days of Augustus downwards, and where Raphael himself filled a post equivalent to that of Inspector of Ancient Monuments in the high days of the Renaissance. The French have however distinguished themselves by the truly classic expression they have given, through the pens of some of their greatest writers, to the principles and sentiments that underlie the modern interest in these memorials of the past. The Monument Act of 1887 is of comparatively recent date but has a history behind it. It was really in preparation for fifty years, and during this period writers like Montalembert, Chateaubriand, Guizot, Victor Hugo, and others inspired by them, were moulding the thought of the times, and furnishing mottoes for future workers in this field in every land. The phrase of the first-named writer, 'Les longs souvenirs font les grands peuples'—'long memories make great peoples'—a terse and noble epigram, will be found on the title page of more than one work consecrated to this subject. In Victor Hugo's impassioned protest entitled 'Guerre aux Démolisseurs', he writes of 'a universal cry that summons the new France to the rescue of the old'. 'Better than all books', exclaims M. Antonin Proust, Minister of Fine Arts in 1881-2, 'the keeps of Coucy and of Gisors, the ramparts of Carcassonne and Avignon instruct us about the power of the feudal régime. In these books of stone we find what Augustin Thierry has called the soul of history.' An official declaration delivered in the Chamber of Deputies in 1841 by M. Martin, the Keeper of the Seal, may serve as a sort of charter for workers at monument defence. 'Public utility', he asserted, 'is not a purely material thing; national traditions, history, art itself, are they not in truth matters of public utility, just as much as bridges and arsenals and roads?'

The history which has culminated in the Act of 1887 is briefly traced in the following paragraphs[1].

The first movement for the care of monuments in the modern sense in France was due to a reaction against the

[1] P. Clemen, *Die Denkmalpflege in Frankreich*, Berlin, 1898, is the best book on the whole subject.

destruction wrought in the land at the outbreak of the French Revolution. It affected however at first only movable works of art, a great collection of which was got together by Alexandre Lenoir under the name of 'Musée des Monuments Francais'. This was 'the earliest national museum known to modern history, richer in national monuments of the middle ages and the Renaissance than any collection now existing in Europe[1]'. It was broken up at the Restoration, but the Musée Cluny may be regarded as its offspring. Political conditions however prevented a like care being shown for architectural monuments, for decrees of 1792 ordained 'the destruction of all monuments of a kind to recall the memory of feudalism, and the obliteration of everything liable to revive the remembrance of despotic rule[2]'. That the destruction of architectural monuments was not merely due to the first excesses of the Revolution is proved by the fact that the worst act of Vandalism in modern times, the demolition of the stupendous Abbey Church of Cluny, the grandest monument of Romanesque architecture, was only actually carried out in the year 1811.

The mania for destruction seems to have had freest course during the period of the restored monarchy, on which Montalembert makes the grave statement that 'la Restauration, à qui son nom seul semblait imposer la mission spéciale de réparer et de conserver les monuments du passé, a été, tout au contraire, une époque de destruction sans limite. Il n'y a pas un département, en France, où il ne se soit consommé, pendant les quinze années de la Restauration, plus d'irrémédiables dévastations que pendant toute la durée de la République et de l'Empire.' It was after the July Revolution of 1830 that the movement really began which had its final outcome in the legislation of 1887. Victor Hugo had given a fine literary expression to the feeling of the best men of the time in his *Guerre aux Démolisseurs*, which was first

---

[1] Clemen, loc. cit. p. 3.

[2] An account of the measures relating to monuments proposed or put in force at the time of the French Revolution is given in some articles published in vols. XI and XII of *L'Ami des Monuments et des Arts*.

published in 1825, and this was followed by a second protest
under the same title in the *Revue des Deux Mondes* in 1832,
while Montalembert strengthened the cause by his tract 'du
Vandalisme en France' in the same Journal for 1833. Guizot,
made Minister of Instruction after the Revolution of July,
took the first official steps to give effect to the reaction by appointing in 1830 a General Inspector of Historical Monuments
in the person of Louis Vitet, whose work it was to lay the
foundation for future measures for the care of monuments
in France. Vitet was succeeded by Prosper Mérimée, whose
magnetic. personality inspired and animated the work his
predecessor had set on foot. Decisive acts followed from the
side of the government. In 1830 the Minister of the Interior
obtained for the first time a credit of £3,200 for the upkeep of
national monuments, and from that time onwards there has
been always entered in the French Budget for this purpose
a yearly sum, which in 1896 had grown to the stately figure
of £120,000[1]. 1837 saw the establishment of the 'Commission
des Monuments Historiques', which since that time has been
the chief organ of the care of monuments for the whole of
France, while by its side was set, also in 1837, the 'Comité
des Travaux Historiques', a section of which called the
'Comité historique des Arts et Monuments' was intended
to support the executive 'Commission' by supplying the
historical, documentary, and archaeological lore required for
a scientific treatment of the matter in hand. As a specimen
of the sort of work which falls to this comité, there may be
quoted a 'Questionnaire' or set of inquiries as to the pre-
historic, classical, and mediaeval monuments in each of the
French communes, which was drawn up and circulated by
the comité, and was the means of the collection of a good
deal of antiquarian information. A translation of the
'Questionnaire' is given from the *Gentleman's Magazine*
in Appendix A to Dr David Murray's *Archaeological Survey*

---

[1] Clemen, *Die Denkmalpflege*, p. 75. In more recent years the sums set apart
for 'Monuments Historiques' in the yearly budgets have not reached this figure,
but for any special work other sources of supply, diocesan, communal, etc., are
available.

of the United Kingdom. The comité is also responsible for the splendid Bibliography of the learned Societies of France mentioned pp. 36, 78. In the case of this 'comité' there have been several shiftings of names and functions, but it is still in operation. This was all the work of government acting through the Minister Guizot.

Meanwhile private agencies were busily engaged in the same cause. With all these is inseparably connected the name of Arcisse de Caumont, a man of restless energy whose power of organization was equal to his enthusiasm and his learning. De Caumont not only by his own lectures and writings roused the interest of the public in the ancient monuments of his own Normandy, but was the founder of societies and the organizer of Congresses, that have helped forward the work in all parts of France. The most important of these societies was the 'Société Francaise d'Archéologie pour la Conservation et Description des Monuments Historiques'. It was established in 1834 and its organ, the well-known *Bulletin Monumental,* has remained from that time to this one of the most valuable publications of the kind in existence. Among the Congresses which owe to him their initiative is the 'Congrès Archéologique de France', which still holds yearly meetings in different French towns, and has done much to rouse an interest in monuments among the cultured classes in each district visited. Especially valuable are these Congresses on account of the participation in them of the members of the older French families. These hold themselves apart from government organizations but show in connection with the private agencies their interest in the historical past of the land. 'At every Archaeological Congress of France' writes Dr Clemen[1] 'are to be found as habitués a whole number of members of the oldest families.' For it was de Caumont's idea to found the care of monuments upon the basis of a popular interest in the subject that he sought to awaken among all classes and in all regions. 'L'époque actuelle', he himself wrote, 'exige la réunion de tous les efforts individuels pour réagir contre

[1] Clemen, *Die Denkmalpflege,* p. 82.

le vandalisme; ce n'est pas seulement à quelques hommes
influents à prendre nos anciens édifices sous leur protection,
c'est à la population éclairée de toute la France à s'opposer
aux destructions qui désolent nos provinces[1].' In furtherance of this end de Caumont founded in 1839 the so-called
'Institut des Provinces' that was in a measure a protest
against the centralizing policy which in its monument
administration the government had adopted. De Caumont
covered France with correspondents, and appointed divi-
sional inspectors in various districts, who should report to
the 'Société Française d'Archéologie' on the condition of
monuments, and signalize every indication of danger from
time and decay or from ill-advised restoration.

As an outcome of the impulse he gave to the provinces
may be reckoned the numerous local antiquarian and historical
societies, whose combined energies produce a very substantial
body of work in each year on the national monuments. The
oldest is de Caumont's earliest creation, the 'Société des
Antiquaires de Normandie' (1824), and some of the most
important of the others are the 'Société Archéologique du
Midi de la France', the 'Société des Antiquaires de Picardie',
the 'Société Éduenne', etc. etc.

A full list and notice of these societies, with the titles of
the papers in their publications, is given in the work now in
course of publication by the Minister of Instruction, under the
editorship of R. de Lasteyrie and E. Lefèvre-Pontalis, entitled
*Bibliographie Générale des Travaux Historiques et Archéolo-
giques publiés par les Sociétés savantes de la France*[2].

It might have been expected that these various societies,
which cover the provinces like a network, would have been
taken up into the government organization, or at any rate
utilized by the central authority as adjuncts or affiliated
agencies. This however has not been the case. The government has on the contrary looked rather askance on the
societies, and officially ignored them. As Dr Clemen rightly
remarks[3] the President of the 'Société Française d'Archéologie'

---

[1] Clemen, *Die Denkmalpflege*, p. 78.
[2] Vol. I, Paris, 1888; Vol. II, Paris, 1893.   [3] p. 80.

should have had a seat ex officio on the 'Commission des Monuments Historiques', but no such recognition has been accorded to the private association. Not a little soreness of feeling has resulted from this ignoring of the provincial agencies by the central power, and this has found its expression in the criticisms freely lavished by provincial antiquaries and men of taste, on some of the restorations and other works carried out from Paris in the cities of the departments.

We must return now to the centralized organization, of which the 'Commission des Monuments Historiques' is the active agency, while the 'Comité des Travaux Historiques' is supposed to supply it with learned apparatus. It should be noted that the work of the commission can be dealt with quite independently of the Monument Act of 1887, for it had been going on for fifty years before that Act was passed. The Act indeed did not alter the work of the commission but only gave it a legal sanction.

The commission is attached to the Direction of the Fine Arts. Only for two brief intervals have the Fine Arts in France had a Minister all to themselves, and they are now in charge of the 'Minister of Public Instruction and of the Fine Arts' who however is often in the present connection called 'Minister of the Fine Arts'. This Minister is the official president of the commission, and is the executive officer for all proceedings relating to monuments. The commission has not and never has possessed in itself executive power and only acts through the Minister. The commission at first consisted of only eight members, but this number has since been increased till it has now reached thirty. Some of the members hold their seats ex officio. Among these are the Directors of the Fine Arts, of the National Museums, and of the Musée Cluny; the Director of Civil Buildings and the National Palaces, and the Director of Public Worship; the Prefect of the Seine and the Prefect of Police, etc. The other members are nominated by the Minister, a leet of three being presented to him by the commission when a vacancy has to be filled. Several of these elected members are men of affairs and deputies, the object here being to secure a proper repre-

sentation of the commission in the Chamber. Membership
of the commission is an honorary post, and is held to confer
high distinction. Some of the most distinguished names in
France are to be read upon its muster roll.

The appearance among the ex officio members of the
Director of Civil Buildings and National Palaces, and the
Director of Public Worship, calls attention to an anomaly in
the monument administration of the country. The Commission of Historical Monuments has not the direct oversight
over two important classes of public buildings, on the one
hand the Cathedrals and other diocesan buildings, and on
the other the Palaces and Châteaux and civil monuments
such as the Arc de Triomphe and the Panthéon. There is a
distinct service for each of these classes of buildings with a
distinct staff of administrators and a distinct column in the
national budget. The fact that the two directors of these
separate services have official seats on the commission shows
that an endeavour is made to secure harmonious working
among all the interests involved. Recently an important step
in this direction was made by bringing the administration of
the National Palaces into closer relation with the Commission
of Historical Monuments. The three General Inspectors of
Civil Buildings are now members of the commission, and this
body is thus able to exercise control over important works on
the great secular edifices, such as Versailles.

The duties of the commission have been defined in a
decree of January 3, 1889, in the following terms: 'La Commission des Monuments Historiques...a pour mission d'établir
la liste des monuments et objets ayant un intérêt historique
et artistique, de désigner ceux qu'il convient de restaurer,
d'examiner les projets présentés pour leur restauration, de
proposer au Ministre la répartition des crédits ouverts pour la
conservation des monuments classés[1].'

The first duty of making up the list of monuments results in
the so-called 'classement', which as a principle of monument
administration has been so much discussed. Something has

[1] Direction des Beaux-Arts: *Monuments Historiques*, Paris, Impr. Nat., 1889,
p. 13.

already been said in the Introduction on the principle in
general. Here in France it is a necessary consequence of a
centralizing policy. It is not the feelings and interests of
local districts that are consulted but only interests large
enough to touch the nation as a whole. Hence the first
clause of the Act of 1887 expressly states that it is only
meant to apply to monuments that 'may have, from the point
'of view of history or of art, a national interest' and this
evidently contemplates a limit to their number. In fact, the
councillor in charge of the Act, when it was being considered
by the Council of State, expressly stated that 'these monuments are intended to be few in number and their preservation
to be a matter of the highest interest[1]'. Inclusion in the list,
says a French writer on the subject, is 'a sort of official
consecration of the artistic and historical value of the monument in question[2]'. In this spirit the commission from the
first set about 'classing', that is marking with a note of
distinction, the monuments of a national importance, and by
the time that the Act of 1887 was passed it had made up a
list of over 2000 monuments. In 1889 there was published
an official list of the 'monuments classés[3]', amounting to some
2200 items, of which about 308 are pre-historic monuments,
such as dolmens and standing stones. The *eyes* of the commission are the General Inspectors of Historical Monuments.
These are now three in number, each receiving a yearly salary
of £250–300, and a fourth has been added since 1893 to take
in charge the movable works of art, which by the Act of 1887
have been included in the scope of the commission's labours.
It is the duty of these Inspectors to keep an eye over all the
monuments in the districts under their charge, to report if
any addition to the list of 'monuments classés' is advisable,
and if any work of reparation or restoration on the recognized
monuments seems called for. In carrying out such works the
commission needs *hands*, and these are provided by a staff of
forty artists, who have the title, an honourable and coveted

---

[1] Tétreau, *Législation*, etc., p. 24.
[2] Lucien Paté, quoted in Bredt, *Die Denkmalpflege*, Berlin, 1904, p. 22.
[3] *Monuments Historiques, Loi et Décrets*, etc., Paris, Impr. Nat., 1889.

one, of 'Architects attached to the Commission on Historical Monuments', and subordinate to these a body of Inspectors of Works who personally superintend any operations in progress. The Direction of Civil Buildings and National Palaces and the Direction of Public Worship are also served by their own staff of General Inspectors, Architects, and Inspectors of Works. Viollet-le-Duc was General Inspector of Diocesan buildings. The 'Diocesan Architects' as they are called numbered in 1896 fifty seven, but of these twenty seven also served as Architects attached to the commission. The Palaces, etc., have commonly each its own permanent architect. These Architects and Inspectors of Works receive a percentage on the work carried out.

It is part of the centralized system that all these operations, in whatever part of France they may be set on foot, must be under the direction of one or other of the official architects. Most of these live in Paris. When Dr Clemen wrote his book only twelve of the forty architects of the commission lived in the Provinces and only ten of the thirty diocesan architects who were not also architects of the commission. Paris men, imbued with the ideas and traditions of the central bureau, they are not naturally in touch with the local workers and local conditions to be found in distant parts of the country. The absence of really cordial cooperation between the central organization and the provincial antiquarian societies has also to be taken into account, so that it is not to be wondered at that many controversies have arisen between local experts and societies, and the representatives of the central commission, who have come down from Paris to restore some provincial Cathedral.

It is claimed by those who favour the French system that it is essential for the security of these historical monuments that no prentice hand should be allowed to touch them, and that only architects trained under a regular tradition should be entrusted with their restoration. There may be something in this view, though the traveller with artistic tastes must often sigh among these systematically restored French Cathedrals for anything rather than the cast-iron rigidity and sameness

of so much of the work.   In our own country we know something of official or semi-official restorers.   The English
Cathedrals are still distinguished above all others by their
variety and for the charming diversity of work even in a
single building.   Over all however is to be discerned what
has been called the 'trail of Sir Gilbert Scott', and even a
prentice hand, if guided by an artistic sense, would often have
left a more pleasing impress.   If one had to select in this
country an architect to restore a picturesque and weathered
pile, it would probably not be any of the architects who would
be chosen by a government department, and our system of
accidental choice probably leads on the whole to better artistic
results than the system of our more bureaucratic neighbours
across the Channel.   It should be stated on the other hand
that the International Congress of Architects at Madrid, in
1904, reasserted the orthodox principle, that ' the preservation
and restoration of monuments should be entrusted only to
architects " diplomés par le Gouvernement ", or specially
authorized and acting under the artistic, archaeological, and
technical control of the State'.

Besides advising the Minister on questions of ' classement '
and restoration, the commission has the care of the Cluny
Museum and of the fine collection of casts illustrating the
history of French Sculpture in the galleries of the Trocadéro.
It exercises moreover an oversight over the national treasure
in monuments in general.   ' The bureau of the commission is
the natural centre and place of business for all undertakings
connected with the care of monuments, it prepares reports,
collects material, keeps up constant connection with the
various government departments and ministries as well as
with the local officials in the Provinces...it is the natural
place of reception for the numerous inquiries, which come
from abroad as well as from home sources, and scholars as
well as artists find here the same kindly reception and help[1].'
The premises of the commission in the Palais Royal are
equipped with a library reported to be the best in existence
for the mediaeval art of France, and a noble collection of

[1] Clemen, p. 37.

6—2

reports, plans, and drawings, prepared in connection with the
restoration of important buildings, is preserved in its cases, and
some of these have been published under the title '*Archives
de la Commission des Monuments Historiques*'. Photographs
form a department by themselves, and by a judicious arrangement with private firms of photographers there has been
issued at a very small price an invaluable series of plates and
lantern slides which illustrate in the most effective manner
the untold riches of the mediaeval architecture and decoration
of the country.

All this activity had been in progress for half-a-century
before legislation came to set the seal on what had been
accomplished. Up to 1887 the commission, and the Minister
who acted as its mouthpiece, had possessed no legal power of
safeguarding in direct fashion the national monuments which
they had 'classed'. They could advise and warn, but had
no power to force their views upon recalcitrant public bodies
or private owners of monuments. In cases where a historical
monument was under the direct control of the Minister of
Public Instruction and the Fine Arts no difficulty could
arise, but when it was under that of some other government department the case was different. Thus, the Palace
of the Popes at Avignon is on the list, but has been used
as a barrack and as such was under the control of the
Minister for War. Military reasons might seem to demand
a treatment of the building quite opposed to the views of
the commission and the Minister of the Fine Arts. Hence
would arise a conflict for the settlement of which no machinery
was at hand. A monument in private ownership might be
'classé' without the proprietor having been informed of the
fact. Naturally he would resent the sudden interference of
a general inspector under the commission when he was going
to make some alteration on property he regarded as at his
own disposal. In such a case only one legal weapon was at
the command of the guardians of monuments, and this was
expropriation, or the compulsory purchase of the structure
in danger. A statute empowering the state to expropriate
on grounds of public utility had been in existence since 1810,

when it had been recognized by the Council of State that 'the acquisition of an edifice belonging to a private person might be declared to be of public utility, even when the administration was not going to claim it for the purpose of executing works, and when it had only the intention of preserving it, of preventing its destruction on grounds of the general interest[1]'. In 1841 an Expropriation Act was passed and here again public utility was officially recognized as covering historical and artistic considerations. On the strength of this legislation expropriation for artistic purposes had from time to time been carried through, as when in 1845 more than a hundred houses had been removed after compulsory purchase out of the interior of the Roman theatre at Orange, and the employment of this process was open to the Minister of Fine Arts and his commission. It was however an expensive and troublesome process not directly prescribed by statute, and in practice could not be much employed.

It was to remedy this condition of affairs that the Act of 1887 was framed. It is a short Act of 18 articles, but must be taken in connection with an administrative Order or Decree referred to in the Act itself and intended to explain its provisions and prescribe the machinery for carrying it out. This Decree, and a supplementary one, contain 29 articles. The Act and the Decrees, together with a list of Historical Monuments, were published officially in handy form in 1889[2].

The law is designed to give legal powers to the Minister, acting after consultation with the commission, in regard to monuments and to archaeological excavations, and the monuments contemplated are not only architectural structures, or dolmens, menhirs, and the like, but also movable objects, such as may form the apparatus of worship. It would have been natural to look in a French law of the kind for logic of arrangement and precision of language, but as a fact the document is faulty in form. For instance, there are four chapters in the Act of which the third is headed 'Excava-

---

[1] Tétreau, p. 93.

[2] Ministère de l'Instruction Publique et des Beaux-Arts. *Monuments Historiques, Loi et Décrets*, etc., Paris, Imprimerie Nationale, 1889.

tions'. This contains two articles, of which the first deals
with the subject of the chapter, while the second contains
a purely general provision without the slightest connection
with diggings! Another defect is a curious uncertainty in
wording. In its title the law claims to be one 'for the
'maintenance of monuments and objects of art having
'a historical *and* artistic interest', but Article one begins
as follows: 'The immovable objects...the maintenance of
'which may have a national interest from the point of view
'of history *or* of art....' It is clear that the latter is the
correct phrasing, and that the presence either of historical
or of artistic. interest, if sufficiently pronounced, makes
a monument suitable for enrolment. Thus the house of
Jeanne d'Arc at Domrémy is 'classée' though not for its
artistic value. The vacillation in the wording is curious,
and might have led to difficulties of interpretation. The
following is a brief account of the Act[1].

Art. 1 provides for the 'classement' of objects of the
above kind by the Minister of Public Instruction and of
the Fine Arts, while Art. 15 states that Ministerial decisions
under the Act will always be given after consultation with the
commission. If the immovable object (immeuble) or monument belong to the State (Art. 2) but be under the control
of another administrative department, then the Minister at the
head of this other department must have given his consent.
If this consent be refused the matter is referred for decision
to the Council of State (Decree, Art. 2). A similar procedure
obtains when the monument belongs to a Department, a Commune, a Religious body, or any other public institution. The
proprietory body and any Minister interested must consent,
and if the consent be refused the Council of State will decide.
A monument may be 'classé' either as a whole or in part,
that is to say the façade or doorway of a building may be
put on the list to the exclusion of the rest of the fabric.

Art. 3 introduces the case of a monument belonging to

[1] For the legal interpretation of the articles of the law the work of Louis
Tétreau has been followed. The author is a jurist, and at the same time a
member of the Commission des Monuments Historiques.

a private individual. This cannot be enrolled without the consent of the proprietor. Art. 5 *of the Decree* provides that this consent must be given in writing, unless the proprietor has himself applied for the 'classement'. It will be observed here that the old practice of placing a monument on the list without informing the proprietor is now forbidden. Art. 7 of the Act provides for the automatic 'declassement', or erasure from the list, in certain circumstances, of monuments enrolled before the law came into force. Art. 5 contains the important provision about the compulsory purchase of private property. It runs as follows: 'The Minister of Public Instruction and ' of the Fine Arts, can, in accordance with the prescriptions ' of the law of May 3, 1841 (the expropriation law), conduct ' the expropriation of enrolled monuments or of those that ' may be from his side the object of a proposition for enrol-' ment refused by the private proprietor.' Two cases are contemplated here, one in which a monument is already enrolled under the protection of the law and yet it seems desirable to expropriate it; another in which enrolment is refused by the proprietor so that the monument is left outside the protection of the law. The reason for purchase in the one case may be the inability of the owner to carry out the reparations necessary for the maintenance of the monument. It may be then more economical for the state to acquire the property than to spend money upon it and still leave it in its former ownership. The second case is the more important one of the recalcitrant proprietor who, possessed of a monument of national interest, refuses to allow it to be placed under the operation of the law. In these circumstances the Act (Art. 5) expressly authorizes the Minister to set in motion the machinery for a compulsory purchase of the property in question. This machinery however moves slowly. Some time would be needed for a decision whether after all the monument would be worth the cost of expropriation, and this would have to be discussed and reported on to the Minister by the commission. If he favoured the proposal, it would have to be considered by the Council of State before it could be sanctioned. All this would secure to

the recalcitrant proprietor time to alter, mutilate, or destroy
the monument in dispute, and in this way the provisions of
the Act could be made of no effect. The Act seems not
to have contemplated this possibility, but it is provided
against by Art. 12 of the Decree, which forbids all work
on a monument the object of a proposition of enrolment
till three months have elapsed from the receipt of the proposition by the proprietor. Jurists have complained that the
Decree in this respect establishes a new servitude not set up
in the Act, and have questioned its legality. There is no
doubt in any case that the Decree fills an awkward gap in
the actual law.

The effects of enrolment under the Act are explained in
Art. 4, which is thus conceived : The monument which has
'been enrolled (classé) cannot be destroyed even in part,
'nor be made the object of any work of restoration, repair
'or modification of any kind, unless the Minister of Public
'Instruction and of the Fine Arts has given his consent
'thereto.'

'The expropriation for reasons of public utility of an en-
'rolled monument cannot be carried out until the Minister, etc.,
'has been invited to present his observations on the matter.'
(This clause is to prevent a monument being expropriated
and destroyed for making a road or a railway or for some
other utilitarian operation.)

'Servitudes of frontage (alignement) and other building
'regulations, obedience to which would injure the structures,
'are not to apply to enrolled monuments.'

'The consequences of enrolment follow the monument
'enrolled into whosesoever hands it may pass.'

The provisions of these paragraphs need no comment
beyond what has been given, but the question will naturally
be asked what is the sanction of these prohibitory clauses, or
in other words what is the penalty for destroying or muti-
lating a monument contrary to the provisions of the first
clause of Article 4? The answer is given in Article 12 of
the Act which runs as follows :—'Works of whatever nature,
'executed in violation of the preceding articles, will give occa-

'sion for an action for damages in favour of the state against 'those who have ordered them or had them carried out.' It will be noticed that the penal law is not invoked and there is no question of imprisonment [1].

Arts. 6 and 7 deal with the removal of monuments from the list (déclassement).

Arts. 8, 9, 10, 11 are concerned with movable objects (objets mobiliers).

Such objects 'of which the preservation presents, from 'the point of view of history or of art, a national interest' are to be placed on a list, but only when they belong to the State, the Departments, the Communes, Religious bodies, and other public institutions. A copy of the list when made is to be on view at the Prefecture of each Department. Enrolled objects belonging to the state are inalienable and unassignable. Enrolled objects belonging to the other owners mentioned cannot be restored, repaired, nor alienated by sale, gift, or exchange, without the permission of the Minister.

No enrolment is attempted in the case of movable objects belonging to individuals or private corporations.

The third chapter of the Act (Art. 14) deals with excavations. In view of the fact that there are no regulations at all on this subject in our own country it may be worth while to give a translation of this Article as an illustration of how the matter may be dealt with.

'Whenever in consequence of excavations, of the carrying 'out of works, or of any accidental circumstance, discovery 'has been made of monuments, ruins, inscriptions, or objects 'of interest for archaeology, history, or art, on ground be-'longing to the State, to a Department, a Commune, 'a Religious body or other public establishment, the Mayor 'of the Commune must ensure provisional protection for the 'objects discovered, and must immediately advise the Prefect 'of the Department of the measures which have been taken.

'The Prefect will make a report with the briefest possible

---

[1] 'La seule sanction prévue par la loi est une sanction pécuniaire.' Tétreau, *Législation*, p. 76.

'delay to the Minister of Public Instruction and of the
'Fine Arts, who will decide on the definitive measures to
'be adopted.

'If the discovery have taken place on the land of a private
'person, the Mayor will give notice of it to the Prefect. On
'the report of the Prefect, and after taking the opinion of
'the Commission on Historical Monuments, the Minister of
'Public Instruction and of the Fine Arts may proceed to
'the expropriation of the said land in whole or in part on
'grounds of public utility, in accordance with the forms of
'the law of May 3, 1841.'

The fourth chapter of the Act provides for its application
to French possessions abroad, and will be noticed in the last
chapter of this volume.

The French Monument Act which has just been analysed
has had great influence on monument legislation since its
time. Its main provisions recur in Acts such as that of the
Canton de Vaud of 1902 and the Portuguese law or decree
on ancient monuments of 1901, and it is referred to in all
discussions on the subject in every land. It does not however represent the last thought of the French legislative mind
on the theme, for there is a project for an extension of the
law actually under consideration in the Chambers.

Apart from the care of the French for their ancient
monuments, we have to notice briefly their relation towards
the other objects of which this book takes account, towards
the preservation, that is, of the traditional aspect of their
cities, of civic amenity generally, and of scenes and objects
of natural beauty. If France be reckoned the classic land in
all that concerns the care of the artistic treasures of the
past, her reputation stands equally high as the country of
good taste in the outward apparatus of modern life. She
justifies this reputation, not only because in many respects
there is a fairly high standard of taste among the population
generally, but because the officials of the government are
more ready than similar personages elsewhere to give effect
to those aesthetic and historical considerations, which in most
countries are too often crowded out by utilitarian cares. A

highly-placed Indian official complained some years ago of the attitude of government servants in India towards the historical monuments of that country. 'It is surprising' he said 'to find how little support or encouragement archaeology meets with from the great majority of the officers of Government....I have seen how difficult it was at times to overcome the *vis inertiae* of those who, thinking the whole subject purely dilettantism and impractical...used all the powers of the Secretariat to delay and thwart the work[1].' In France, if anywhere in the world, the official mind is open on the side in question, and it will be sufficient here to quote in illustration a circular issued in September 1904 by the Minister of Public Works to the chief government engineers in charge of undertakings in the rural districts. The circular is indorsed 'Conservation des Sites et Monuments Pittoresques', and the text may be translated as follows.

'For a long time past public opinion has been occupied 'with the necessity of protecting the sites and scenes which 'form as it were the artistic domain with which nature has 'endowed our country. A society was founded three years 'ago with this aim under the presidency of a member of 'Parliament, M. Beauquier, Deputy, and quite recently the '"Touring Club" of France has formed a Committee for 'Picturesque Sites and Monuments, which has for its mission 'to discover practical means for assuring the protection of 'these.

'My administration, which has been often inspired with 'the thought that has prompted this double initiative, is in 'thorough agreement with these most praiseworthy efforts. 'The Service of "Ponts et Chaussées" has frequently and 'with success made demonstration that a public structure 'judiciously placed, or tastefully framed in picturesque sur-'roundings, will add in a true sense a beauty of art to the 'beauty created by nature; on the other hand it is only too 'well aware that it is possible for a jarring detail incon-'siderately introduced to mar the charm of some favourite 'site and to destroy for ever its harmony.

[1] *Journal of the Society of Arts*, vol. XXXIV, p. 562.

'However this may be, these truths, elementary as they
'are, lose nothing by being repeatedly enforced; an endeavour
'should also be made to bring them to some practical issue.

'I shall be obliged therefore if you will transmit to the
'agents under your orders the necessary instructions, according
'to which in all operations such as the opening of new routes
'of communication (roads, railways, tramways, etc.), alterations
'in thoroughfares and frontages, laying out of streets, planta-
'tions or clearances of timber, they shall have always in mind
'the obligation of respecting the existing beauties of nature,
'and as far as possible enhancing such beauties.

'All schemes submitted should contain all the indications
'necessary for calling the special attention of the superior
'authorities to the consequences which will follow from these
'schemes to the advantage or detriment of the interests in
'view.

'Kindly acknowledge the receipt of this circular, of which
'I send you a number of copies sufficient for the personnel
'placed under your orders.

'E. MARUÉJOULS.'

The society above referred to is called 'La Société pour
la Protection des Paysages'. It was founded in 1901 and
has as its main object 'to develope and bring into recognition
the principle that all the beauties of nature may be regarded
as of value to the community in general, and are part of the
national wealth and not mere ornaments'. Objectionable
advertisements, as well as all destructive operations carried
on in the name of utility, are as far as possible to be pre-
vented. Local laws and regulations are to be studied and
watched in their working, and legislative measures prepared
and forwarded.

One such measure is connected with the name of the
deputy mentioned in the circular, M. Charles Beauquier, who
is responsible for a draft Act which was introduced by him in
the French Chamber in 1903[1]. The protection contemplated
in this draft Act was not for ancient monuments, but was
to be extended to natural scenes. In introducing the bill

---

[1] *L'Ami des Monuments*, vol. XVII, p. 21.

the deputy declared that for years past a growing protest
had been rising up among all civilized peoples against the
recklessness with which engineers, artificers, and business
people were injuring and blotting out sites and scenes the
most beautiful and the most precious. Protection was
demanded for sites the preservation of which was of general
interest from the points of view of beauty, of history, of
natural science, or of legend. The provisions of the draft
Act favoured the principle of decentralization. In each
Department there was to be a Commission headed by the
Prefect for the purpose of scheduling sites of interest. The
proprietor was to be asked to accept a servitude according
to which no alteration could be made at the place except
by leave of the Prefect. In case of his refusal there might
follow either expropriation on grounds of public utility, or
the establishment of a servitude by decree of the Prefect, the
proprietor receiving an indemnity. It is good news that a
measure on these lines has now (1905) passed the French
Chamber of Deputies, but it is not yet law.

In the matters of the protection of the historical aspect
of cities, and of civic amenity in general, the following is in
brief the condition of affairs in France. As far as legal
regulations go, France is no better off than Great Britain
or Austria or Belgium, and as regards the former matter is
less favourably situated, as we shall see, than Germany.
The citizens of Paris and Vienna and Brussels, just like the
citizens of London and Edinburgh, have to form societies and
write to the papers and interview officials to save threatened
monuments and to secure a proper regard for aesthetic
interests in connection with new schemes. The French, and
to some extent too the Austrians, Belgians, and a few other
European peoples, have an advantage over ourselves that
officials are more sympathetic and approachable on questions
of amenity, and the general standard of taste among the
public is higher. What we are concerned with here however
is the question of definite regulations. Some of the historical
cities of Germany, as will presently be noticed, have protected
themselves by local enactments, through which they purpose

to hand down their characteristic buildings and coups d'œil as far as possible unimpaired to future generations. In French towns, any monument that is 'classé' is of course protected by the law, but structures and groups of structures not on the schedule are not legally defended. 'Hélas, nous n'avons point ici de ces bienfaisants règlements pour assurer l'aspect artistique des cités. On ne reussit à sauvegarder, ici ou là, quelque monument que par une volonté persistante, une tactique diplomatique, une offensive réfléchie dans la presse. So writes the representative of *L'Ami des Monuments*, while from the official side the writer is kindly informed from the Sous-Secrétariat des Beaux-Arts in the Ministry of Public Instruction that, while the 'Monuments Historiques' Act is sufficient to protect effectually all scheduled monuments, 'it is not believed that municipalities have had recourse in any large number of cases to special measures for the purpose of supplementing the law.'

The work of protection is therefore virtually in the hands of the public, and public opinion is educated and strengthened by the associations some of which have already been referred to. Some of these are of a semi-official character, such as the 'Commission Municipale du Vieux Paris' 'créée et présidée par M. le Préfet de la Seine, et qui a pour but de veiller à la conservation de tous les vestiges du passé, dans l'intérêt même de l'aspect artistique de la Capitale[1]', or 'La Commission Municipale du Vieux Lyon'. Others like 'L'Ami des Monuments Parisiens','L'Ami des Monuments Rouennais', etc., are private societies like the Cockburn Association of Edinburgh. It must be understood that all these agencies have at their back the established institution of the 'Monument Historique', and the legal procedure by which any building as yet unscheduled can be protected if made the object of a proposition for 'classement' (ante, p. 87). There is something definite therefore to appeal to as an effective means for resisting any proposed act of gross vandalism.

It should be explained that in Paris a certain amount

---

[1] Communication from the Prefecture of the Seine, see 'Bibliography and Sources of Information'.

of protection for the historical aspect of older parts of the city is secured by the existence of servitudes, referred to in the following extract from the communication mentioned in the note on last page. 'There exist in the City of Paris a 'considerable number of special servitudes imposed on struc- 'tures situated along certain public or private ways. This is 'notably the case with the buildings of the Place Vendôme 'and the Place des Vosges (letters patent of April 7, 1699, 'and July 1605). These servitudes, which generally fix a 'symmetrical architectural composition, and certain disposi- 'tions of frontage, such as for example a zone "non aedificandi" 'reserved for the gardens and in front of the facade, have 'been in most cases established at the time of the sale by 'the State or the City of Paris of large parcels of land, and 'are recited in the contracts of sale.

'If the proprietors of ground or buildings to which these 'regulations apply infringe such prescriptions, they are 'subject to penalties attached to contraventions of building 'laws (voirie) and administrative jurisdiction can prescribe, 'after judgement, the demolition and removal of structures 'or objects built or put in position in violation of these 'regulations.'

Some readers will remember references in the journals a few years ago to certain proposed alterations on some houses in the Place Vendôme that were opposed and vetoed. The prohibition was not, as was then supposed in Britain, due to the outraged public taste of the artistic Parisians, or to the intervention of a benevolent Minister of Fine Arts armed with despotic powers, but turned on the question of these building servitudes that the proposed alterations contravened[1].

In the case of new buildings, when these are of a public character there is no difficulty in securing the best available artistic advice and assistance. For government undertakings the administration of the 'Bâtiments Civils et Palais Nationaux' is available, and there is a 'Conseil Général des Bâtiments

---

[1] Similar servitudes exist, so M. de Lasteyrie informs the writer, in a certain number of provincial towns of France, but the protection afforded is of a partial and accidental kind.

Civils' presided over by the Minister of Public Instruction
and of the Fine Arts, that will consider and supervise projects
for new buildings for state purposes. In the Prefecture of the
Seine there is a similar 'Conseil d'Architecture' that takes
cognizance of the designs of all municipal structures. Semi-
public and private corporations are sometimes, as we have
seen in the case of historical monuments in such possession,
open to official pressure or even compulsion, and where this
is not the fact, they can generally be trusted, like similar
bodies in other lands, to take a pride in doing things well.
The new Orleans Railway Station in Paris has been repeatedly
referred to as an example of 'the way they do things abroad',
but we should not forget that long ago even in England
the North Western Railway Company tried to give a monumental aspect to their London terminus.

Private buildings, erected on a proprietor's own land, are
in France under no aesthetic control from the side of the
authorities. It was officially reported not long ago on this
subject that 'There is nothing to prevent the owner of any
'individual property in a street or square doing as he likes
'with regard to the building he intends erecting on his
'property, so long as his building conforms to the regulations
'concerning heights and projections, to the building frontage
'line already set out by the authorities, and to the Police
'regulations of safety and sanitation.' Not long ago the
Lord Dean of Guild of Edinburgh, speaking in his court
from his great interest in the city, complained that the law
gave him no aesthetic control over the plans for new
structures. It is a melancholy satisfaction to know that his
big brother, the Prefect of the Seine, is similarly powerless!

CHAPTER II.

GERMANY.

BIBLIOGRAPHY AND SOURCES OF INFORMATION.

The works of von Wussow and von Helfert. *Die Denkmalpflege* (Zeitschrift). Reports of Monument Congresses, see ante, p. xiii.
Kunsthandbuch für Deutschland (Konigliche Museen zu Berlin), Berlin, Reimer, 1904.
Handbuch der Gesetzgebung in Preussen und dem Deutschen Reiche, Theil IX, das Bauwesen, Berlin, Springer, 1904.
Die Denkmalpflege in der Rheinprovinz, von Dr Paul Clemen, Provinzialconservator der Rheinprovinz. Düsseldorf, 1896.
Die Denkmalpflege und Ihre Gestaltung in Preussen, von Dr Jur. F. W. Bredt, Berlin, 1904.
Denkmalschutz und Denkmalpflege im Neunzehnten Jahrhundert, von Dr Georg Gottfried Dehio, Strassburg, 1905.
Baupolitzei-Verordnungen (Local Building Regulations) of Hildesheim, Frankfurt, Augsburg, and other German cities, kindly forwarded to the writer by Dr Robert Mielke, of Charlottenburg, Honorary Secretary to the 'Bund Heimatschutz' (League for the Defence of Home).

For these documents, as well as for other valuable information, the writer's grateful acknowledgements are due to Dr Mielke. Thanks for help and information are also tendered to Professor Dr J. Lessing, Director of the Kunstgewerbe-Museum, Berlin; to Dr K. Büttner, Provinzialconservator for Brandenburg; and to the writer's colleague Dr Otto Schlapp of the Department of Teutonic Philology in the University of Edinburgh. The writer also thanks the Ministry of Justice, etc., of the Grand-Duchy of Baden, for the communication of the draft Monument Act for that State of 1883-4.

WRITING in 1897, the Chairman of the executive committee of the National Trust, in his report on the condition of legislation in foreign countries on the subject of monuments, stated about Germany that she appeared to have no machinery for preserving historic monuments, and that there was 'cer-

tainly no compulsory power in relation to buildings in private
hands in force in any German State'. The statements may
have been partly due to the fact that for some unaccountable
reason Germany, meaning in this sense Prussia, is almost
completely ignored in the Reports presented to the British
Foreign Office in 1896, though, as was mentioned before,
it is the fact that successive Prussian governments had been
active in the care of monuments for the best part of a century,
and von Wussow had filled nearly 300 pages with their
rescripts and circulars. It is true however that this activity
had been bureaucratic; and had not represented the popular
feeling, which had remained on the whole indifferent. This
is acknowledged by a German writer who is one of the leading
authorities on monuments and their treatment, Dr Paul
Clemen, Provincial Conservator of Monuments in the Rhine-
land. Writing in 1898 he recognized that his own country
was in this matter still in the background, and he noted
especially the absence of any organ in the German press to
represent the subject[1]. At that time also it was no doubt
true that there was no compulsion upon private owners.
Within the last few years however there has been a remarkable change, as a result of which Germany has become just
the very country to which one must first turn for materials
bearing on the study of all monument questions, and for
examples of legislative measures, which, though many of them
remain as yet mere proposals, are none the less instructive to
the inquirer. The public in general has had its attention
drawn to the matter, and has acquiesced in restrictions upon
private rights that cannot elsewhere be paralleled. In their
own systematic fashion the Germans have taken up the task
of collecting evidence and initiating experiments, by means
of which light is being thrown on every side of this somewhat
complex subject.

The present popular movement began about five years ago,
and may be said to have had its birth in 1899 at the General
Congress at Strassburg of the German Historical and Artistic
Societies. This General Congress passed certain resolutions

[1] *Die Denkmalpflege in Frankreich*, Berlin, 1898, p. 82.

which were signed by representatives of 124 German historical and artistic societies, and were afterwards submitted to the governments of all the German states. While acknowledging the interest already shown by the governments in these memorials of the past greatness of the states, the Congress strongly urged increased attention to what was ' a question of 'life and death for the historical sciences and for the main-'tenance of the national consciousness', and asked for further legislation with a development of organizations for carrying out the protective rescripts, and above all an increased liberality in the financial provision for the care of monuments. Four resolutions were drawn up to the following effect, and these may be quoted to show the trend of public opinion in the Germany of to-day.

I An immovable monument of artistic or historical importance in the possession of the state or a public corporation should not without permission of the authorities be destroyed, suffered knowingly to go to ruin, restored, essentially repaired, or altered.

II Movable objects similar in character and situation should not be dealt with as above *nor alienated* without the same permission.

III Archaeological excavations on public land should be under the control of state authorities.

IV Immovable monuments of artistic or historical importance in the possession of private individuals that are in danger, and ground in private ownership that conceals archaeological treasures of a movable or immovable kind, should be subject to expropriation.

As regards legal provisions touching this question of expropriation, the General Congress declared itself in accord with all lovers of art and history in the Fatherland in laying stress on the necessity for these, on the ground that they were the only means by which innumerable monuments and artistic objects, hitherto without any protection, could be rescued from injury and destruction.

Finally, the principle of 'classement', as it obtains in France, was recommended, though in guarded fashion, as a

valuable aid to the care of monuments. These resolutions
were also adopted by the sixth International Congress for the
History of Art held in Lübeck in 1900, though misgivings on
the subject of 'classement' were somewhat strongly expressed.

An outcome of the Strassburg Congress was the determi-
nation to hold yearly in different German towns meetings
devoted to the discussion of monument questions. Five of
these meetings, each called a 'Tag für Denkmalpflege', have
been held at Dresden, Freiburg-i.-Br., Düsseldorf, Erfurt, and
Mainz, and in each case the proceedings are fully reported in
a volume, part of the cost of which has been borne by the
state in which the particular meeting was held. The meetings
were attended from the first by official representatives of
monument-lore, such as the various Conservators in the
service of the different German states, and by representatives
of numerous Ministries of the Interior, of Religion, and of
Education, to whose departments the care of monuments
belongs. Many of the most distinguished German architects
have taken part in the deliberations, but the burgomasters
and councillors of the towns were at first, as a rule, conspicuous
by their absence. This only meant that in Germany, as in
our own country, the extreme shyness of the average town-
councillor in face of devotees of the old monuments he so
often finds a nuisance, had not yet been overcome. At the
last congress, held at Mainz in September 1904, it was
reported that the number of these adherents had doubled.

The movement of which these meetings are the symptom
did not have to wait long for its journalistic organ, for from
1899 onwards the *Centralblatt der Bauverwaltung* of Berlin
has published a monthly illustrated supplement entitled '*Die
Denkmalpflege*' or '*The Care of Monuments*', and the parts
bound in yearly volumes, admirably indexed, contain a most
interesting and valuable record of all that is done or is
attempted or fails in different countries for the care of ancient
monuments.

On the basis of the information thus supplied, and of
private communications kindly sent by correspondents, there
has been drawn up the following account.

Legislation on the subject of monuments is not imperial business, but is a matter left to the separate states that are grouped together under the Germanic Empire. Of these states as yet only one, the Grand-Duchy of Hesse, has passed a formal Monument Act, yet each state has given official attention to the subject. Some of the German Grand-Dukes and Margraves issued protective edicts in the eighteenth century, and as soon as the War of Liberation against Napoleon was over, we find evidence of activity in more than one quarter. The chief measures were the establishment of custodians or inspectors of monuments and the planning of state-aided publications, giving a catalogue raisonné, often on an elaborate scale, of the monuments of a kingdom or principality.

PRUSSIA.

Here the credit of the initiative belongs to the famous architect Schinkel, who in 1815 sent in a report to the Minister of the Interior which is regarded as the foundation stone of all subsequent operations towards the end in view. He asks for the appointment of officers specially charged with the care of monuments, and for the preparation of a complete inventory of movable and immovable objects of artistic value, and of earlier date than the middle of the seventeenth century. He also protests against the centralizing policy pursued in France, and favours local museums, which should serve as shrines in each district sacred to the memory of its past. Schinkel's memorial produced at once a royal rescript of protective intent, and this has been followed by a number of royal orders and ministerial circulars issued between 1815 and 1881. Von Wussow prints no fewer than forty nine of these, and among the most important are the following. An order and circular of 1830, intended to protect the ancient walls and fortifications of cities from destruction, was repeated in 1854, 1857 and 1881, when it was laid down in the ministerial circular that in the case of any proposal for the demolition or alteration of city walls, gates, towers, etc., the value of the structures as artistic and historical monuments should be taken into full account. In 1843 von Quast was appointed Conservator of Artistic Monuments; in 1844 arrangements were made for an inventory; in 1853 a Commission was appointed for the investigation and safeguarding of monuments, and in 1854 local correspondents for the Commission were called into being. The Commission, however, soon came to an end because no funds were placed at its disposal.

In 1891 the important step was taken of appointing Provincial Commissions and Provincial Conservators to assist in the work which no single central custodian could overtake. At present, 1905, there are fourteen provincial and district Conservators in the different parts of the Prussian dominions, and they dispose of funds which in the five and twenty years previous to 1902 had amounted altogether to about £200,000. The office itself is an honorary one, but expenses are allowed. The office of General Conservator for Prussia still remains. Von Quast, who held the post till 1877, was succeeded by von Dehn-Rotfelser, and he in 1886 by Reinhold Persius who resigned in 1901. To the last named the cause of ancient monuments owes much, as he endeavoured to provide a sound basis for future legislation in the education of public opinion, and the organization of voluntary agencies in the form of associations and congresses.

It is to be noted that a Prussian law of June 2, 1902, gives power to local police authorities to forbid the display in rural districts of posters and other advertisements that disfigure the landscape[1].

The fact that a state Monument Act has been for some time under consideration in Prussia has already been mentioned. There is some prospect that this project of law will come before the Prussian parliament in 1906, and its provisions will be scanned with great interest.

In measures of these kinds the other German states have worked on the same lines as those followed in Prussia, and without possessing (save in one case) formal Monument Acts they have established conservators and initiated sumptuous

---

[1] *Handbuch der Gesetzgebung*, das Bauwesen, p. 271.

works of inventory.   A brief notice of the work carried on in
the more important of these states may be of interest.

BAVARIA.

Here was instituted as early as 1835 a General Inspector
of Monuments of the Plastic Art, and in 1868 there was
appointed a General Conservator of Monuments of Art and
Antiquity attached to the Ministry of the Interior.   With
this post is united the direction of the National Museum at
Munich, and there is a well-equipped staff of subordinates
with a literary and technical apparatus, so that the care of
monuments that belong to the state can be conducted with
thorough efficiency.   The drawing up of an inventory of
artistic treasures was also in 1868 decided on.   On the other
hand there are no means except persuasion available for the
protection of monuments in private hands, and for that and
other reasons legislation is demanded in Bavaria as well as in
the other Germanic states.   This demand has been for some
time under consideration in Bavarian government circles but
no draft of a general Act has yet seen the light[1].

A step of some importance on the part of the Bavarian
state was taken on the first of January 1904, when the
Ministers of the Interior and of Religion issued a joint minute
addressed to the representatives of the towns and of the rural
communes[2], encouraging them to promulgate local by-laws to
control building in the interest of the amenity of their districts;
urging the maintenance of the traditional fashions of construction in the country, and especially the mountain,
regions; and laying stress on the importance of preserving
not only the few outstanding monuments but more especially
the general aspect of entire ancient streets and groups of
houses.   The necessity for considering the relation of new
structures to their natural surroundings and of safeguarding
landscape beauty, is also dwelt upon in this minute, at which

---

[1] *Zweiter Tag für Denkmalpflege*, p. 48.

[2] *Die Denkmalpflege*, 1904, pp. 7, 15. The text of this minute is given,
postea, p. 116.

some may smile as an example of the paternal legislation we
are prone to associate with Germany. The question of local
building regulations is one of great importance and interest
and to this we shall have to return.

In an important department of 'Denkmalpflege' Bavaria
has recently pursued an advanced policy. This is the protection of natural scenes and objects, referred to in the
minute just quoted. In 1901 a ministerial edict urged the
maintenance of the natural beauty of interesting and conspicuous spots, and declared for the protection of trees of a
special beauty or character from the axe and of fine rocks
from the quarryman—always provided that these provisions
did not involve any excessive sacrifice of material interests[1].

WÜRTEMBERG.

This state enjoys the reputation of having been beforehand in the intelligent attention to monuments. What is
said of it by von Wussow applies to most of the German
principalities. 'The statute book of the Kingdom provides
no protection for monuments, nevertheless in the way of
Administration a very great deal is done in their interest[2].'
In 1824 the government was already paying attention to
them; in 1841 the issue of a short inventory was begun.
In 1858 a General Conservator of Monuments was appointed
as the head of a standing commission on the subject. These
officers manage all monuments in state possession but in
respect of those in other ownership they can only act by
way of recommendation and advice. In 1902 official directions were given to all local authorities to send in information
of all proposed alterations on or alienation of artistic monuments within their districts, whether these belonged to public
corporations, religious bodies, or private individuals. The
last provision is one of some importance. At the close of
1904 a ministerial rescript was issued embodying provisions
for the protection of ancient monuments of the same kind

[1] *Zweiter Tag,* p. 48.
[2] *Erhaltung der Denkmäler,* I, 83.

as are contained in state Monument Acts like that of Hesse, presently to be noticed. Würtemberg is not herself contemplating a formal Act of the kind [1].

In the official publication of a detailed inventory Würtemberg has been exemplary. The *Kunst- und Alterthums-Denkmale im Königreich Würtemberg*, edited by Dr Paulus for the Ministry of Religion and Education, was resolved on in 1889 and is not yet completed. The text is in octavo with illustrative cuts, while the plans and measured drawings are issued in atlas form. It occupies a high place among the numerous German publications of the kind.

SAXONY.

The Kingdom of Saxony on the other hand has been one of the last of the states to give official attention to the subject. Not until 1894 was the Saxon Commission for the Maintenance of Artistic Memorials called into being, and as yet there is no General Conservator such as exists in other German states. The operations of the commission have been much furthered by the intelligent cooperation of the authorities both of the Roman Catholic and the Lutheran communions. The latter issued in 1899 a series of recommendations for the restoration and general treatment of ecclesiastical buildings which are said to be models of their kind.

A fully illustrated inventory was started here in 1881 under the Ministry of the Interior, and is now being carried on by Professor Gurlitt as editor. It is worthy of notice that the fund provided by Government for this work and for restoration purposes amounted in the period up to 1897 to £650 yearly, but since 1900 it has reached the yearly total of £2150. A draft of a general Monument Act has been for some time under consideration.

---

[1] *Die Denkmalpflege*, 1905, p. 7.

BADEN, HESSE-DARMSTADT, AND THE OTHER GRAND-
DUCHIES.

The Grand-Duchies of Baden and of Hesse-Darmstadt
are of special importance in connection with monument
legislation, but before going on to them it may be noticed
that the smaller principalities, numbering a dozen or more,
have all done their part in the care of monuments. Anhalt
may suffice as an example. In 1902 a Conservator for
Artistic Monuments was appointed and a revision of the
general inventory of these set on foot, while the full publication of important examples was also begun. It is a feature
of the work at Anhalt that the same department is concerned
with the encouragement of the art of to-day that busies itself
with the artistic monuments of the past.

In the matter of inventorization, Mecklenburg-Schwerin
furnishes a model. The state-publication *Die Kunst-
und Geschichtsdenkmäler des Grossherzogtums Mecklenburg-
Schwerin*[1], is one of the best of its kind, and embraces
a notice of buildings and other monuments of interest in
the villages as well as the towns of the Duchy.

Baden began very early its 'Denkmalpflege' with an
edict of 1749 regarding Roman antiquities. A Conservator
was appointed in 1853 and after 1875 there were for a time
two, one for antiquities the other for public architectural
monuments. The duties of the latter were thus defined.
He had to collect accurate information about all the monuments of the Grand-Dukedom, and to draw up a complete
inventory, with a full publication of the most important
examples. Further, he had to take measures for the safeguarding of the monuments. Later on the two offices were
again united in one person, but since 1884 there has been
a distinct Conservator for ecclesiastical monuments. On
this official interest in the subject the seal was set by the
preparation in 1883-4 of a formal Monument Act. It was
reported on this however, by a representative of the Minister

---

[1] 5 volumes, Schwerin, 1896, etc., edited by Fr. Schlie.

of Religion, at the monument congress at Freiburg-i.-Br. in 1901, that this draft, already in the preliminary stages met with so many difficulties, that at that time it could not be carried further[1].' Dr Clemen pronounces the draft Act to have been in many respects exemplary, and the preamble is especially full and instructive[2].

It may be of interest to give here the headings of the sections of this draft Act which furnish an indication of its scope and arrangement. § 1 is headed 'Meaning of the term 'Monument; care of the State for Monuments and arrange-'ments for its exercise'; § 2, 'Extent of the State care of 'Monuments'; § 3, 'Declaration in the case of certain objects 'of their character as Monuments'; § 4, 'Prohibition of the 'destruction of immovable Monuments of every kind'; § 5, 'Necessity for notice when any part of an immovable 'Monument is to be removed: right of pre-emption of such 'part reserved to the State'; § 6, 'Protection and maintenance 'of Monuments in public ownership'; § 7, 'Operations needful 'for protection and maintenance, and their cost'; § 8, 'Places for the display of Monuments, their reception in a collection'; § 9, 'Alienation or mortgage of a movable or immovable 'Monument, and the removal of such from the country'; § 10, 'Alterations on, or restorations of, immovable Monu-'ments'; § 11, 'Official care for the Monuments in State 'ownership'; § 12, 'The Discovery of Monuments'; § 13, 'Ex-'cavations'; § 14, 'Arrangements for excavations under State 'control'; § 15, 'Indication of Monuments and their surround-'ings by distinctive marks'; § 16, 'Penalties' (these are fines, up to £250); § 17, 'Franking of communications about 'Monuments'; § 18, 'Department for the administration of 'the law.' It has been pointed out already that in draft Acts we find a completeness and a logic which measures actually passed after parliamentary struggles have seldom retained.

What Baden attempted but failed to effect was accomplished in the territory of Hesse-Darmstadt, where in 1902 an elaborate Monument Act was after much consideration unanimously adopted by the legislature—the first example

---

[1] *Zweiter Tag*, p. 1.　　　　　　　[2] *Erster Tag*, p. 17.

in Germany of the ratification of a formal measure of the
kind. The previous history of 'Denkmalpflege' in Hesse
had been much the same as in the other states, and the
only point of real interest is the law of 1902. This is
printed in the report of the monument congress for 1902[1]
and in other publications, and has naturally been the subject
of considerable discussion. It is a fortunate circumstance
that the author of the law, Freiherr von Biegeleben, gave
full accounts of it to the congresses of 1901[2], 1902[3], and
1903[4] and explained the difficulties which had to be en-
countered and the changes that the draft underwent in its
passage through the legislature.

The Hessian Law, which came into force on October 1,
1902, falls into seven sections and contains thirty nine
articles; each of the main and subsidiary divisions has a
useful heading. The first section, articles 1 to 8, is concerned with monuments in the possession of corporations
and public bodies, and the expression 'monuments' includes
movable objects as well as architectural structures, and takes
in documents as well as works of art. These bodies are
forbidden not only to destroy or alienate any monument
in their possession, but to effect on it any alterations or
restorations, without previously obtaining the permission of
the authorities, such permission being given or withheld upon
considerations of an artistic or historical kind. Alterations
in the adjuncts or surroundings of a monument are included in this prohibition. The authorities in question are
the 'Kreisamt' corresponding roughly to our County Councils,
and there are appeals to higher bodies up to the Minister
of the Interior. On the Kreisamt is enjoined the duty of
drawing up an inventory of all monuments belonging to
public bodies within its district.

The second section, articles 9 to 17, is concerned with
monuments in the possession of private persons. Movable
objects in such ownership are excluded from the operation
of the law, and with regard to other (architectural) monu-

---

[1] *Dritter Tag*, p. 145 f.   [2] *Zweiter Tag*, p. 22 f.
[3] *Dritter Tag*, p. 15 f.   [4] *Vierter Tag*, p. 125.

ments, only those are protected which are included in an official list, or as the French would say are 'classés'. The task of drawing up this list (which is quite distinct from the mere inventory kept by the Kreisamt) is in the hands of a Council on Monuments (Denkmalrat) the constitution of which is defined in article 32 of the Act. It is called together by the Minister of the Interior and consists of representatives of the Catholic and Protestant churches, at least two members of the Hessian antiquarian, historical or artistic societies, and two resident Hessian owners of architectural monuments. A private proprietor of a monument must be informed when it is in this manner classé', and is allowed to appeal against the inclusion to the Minister of the Interior within a period of four weeks (art. 10).

The law is not very explicit on the important matter of this appeal[1]. Till the appeal is decided the monument appears to be provisionally protected by the 'classement' (art. 10, cl. 4). If the appeal be upheld, the monument will be excluded from the schedule, but by article 19 it will still be possible to save it, if needful, by compulsory purchase. The Minister may, on the other hand, disallow the appeal and confirm the scheduling, but the law does not say on what grounds or within what time he must give his decision. The words used are 'ist sie' (the act of 'classement' 'Eintragung') 'durch ministerielle Entscheidung bestätigt worden, so wird', etc. The articles that follow assume the 'classement' to hold good.

Any proposed alienation, alteration, or restoration of a monument thus scheduled in private hands must be reported to the 'Denkmalpfleger', that is the General Conservator of monuments for the state at large, and unless the proprietor receive official sanction he is bound to take no steps involving a carrying out of the proposal till six weeks have elapsed. During that interval, if the proposal seem to involve danger to the monument, the Conservator has to exercise what moral

---

[1] The account given of these sections by the author of the Act, (*Dritter Tag*, p. 17,) and the Ministerial Rescript on the working of this part of the Act issued in 1905 (*Die Denkmalpflege*, 1905, p. 28) do not make the matter any clearer.

pressure he can on the proprietor to induce him to modify his intentions, and to give time for this the Minister of the Interior may prolong the period of six weeks to one of three months. In case of a proposal on the part of the proprietor to *destroy* the monument or to alter injuriously its surroundings permission must be asked either from the 'Kreisamt' or from the 'Denkmalpfleger'. If permission be refused, the proprietor may appeal to the Minister of the Interior within a period of four weeks to which no extension can be allowed. If the answer to the demand for permission be not sent within a space of six weeks (which the Minister can extend to three months) then the proprietor is allowed to carry out his original proposal. In case the permission be refused or only granted partially, and the appeal to the Minister of the Interior be rejected, then the proprietor can within six weeks claim compensation from the Minister for the curtailment of his right of disposal over his property, or can call upon the state to acquire the monument or its surroundings at a valuation.

Section three, articles 18 to 24, deals with special cases. Article 19 entitled 'Right of Expropriation in the Interest of Monuments' is of enough importance to be quoted in full.

'The state is authorized to limit the rights of private 'property on land to such an extent as is needful

'1, to secure the preservation of an architectural monu-'ment, the maintenance or security of which is being 'neglected in such a manner as to endanger its existence 'or the upkeep of essential parts of it or

'2, to effect such an opening out of a monument as is 'demanded by artistic or historical considerations, provided 'that no overpowering public or private interests come in 'the way.

'The proprietor, in so far as circumstances make this rea-'sonable, may demand in place of the limitation of his rights 'their entire acquisition by the state.

'The state is empowered, by a rescript of the Minister of 'the Interior, to transfer the right of expropriation given to 'it in the first paragraph of this article to the commune, the

'district, or the province in which the architectural monument
'is situated.' (This last provision is an important one as will
be explained later on.)

Other articles of this section secure to the state the right
of visitation, and of making plans and drawings, of monuments; and the right of ordering a proper expenditure on
monuments on the part of public bodies that own them.
Article 23 provides that any projected road or railway line
that threatens the existence or amenity of a monument shall
not be made without leave of the Minister of the Interior.
Also that in the interest of the amenity of an architectural
monument local regulations may be made to prevent new
buildings being erected within a certain distance of it, or
the buildings in its vicinity being raised above a certain
height.

The fourth section, articles 25 to 30, is concerned with
the question of excavations and 'finds'. The former cannot
be undertaken without previous notice to the authorities; the
latter must immediately be announced to the burgomaster or
Kreisamt of the place.

Land may be expropriated for the sake of carrying on
excavations.

The fifth section, articles 31 and 32, deals with the organization of the bureau for the care of monuments, etc.

Section six, articles 33 to 36, introduces us to a new and
interesting feature in Monument Acts, the care of 'Naturdenkmäler' or natural scenes and objects. Article 33 begins
as follows :—

'Natural phenomena of the earth's surface, such as water-
'courses, rocks, trees, and the like, the maintenance of which
'is a matter of public interest on grounds of history or of
'natural history or from considerations of the beauty or
'special character of a landscape (Natural monuments), can
'be placed under a special protection to be exercised by the
'Kreisamt on the demand of the department of Forests in
'the Ministry of Finance.

'This protection can be extended to the surroundings of
'a natural monument.'

The owner, be it a public body or a private person, is to be informed that the natural monument is scheduled, and can appeal as in the case of the monuments referred to in previous sections.

Article 34 continues :—

'Operations which threaten the continued existence of 'a natural monument that is officially protected, or promise 'to injure either this or its officially protected environment, 'can only be carried out after the permission of the Kreisamt 'has previously been obtained.'

Such permission is to be refused when the proposed operations give rise to apprehensions in respect to the maintenance of the monument or to considerations of the kind referred to in article 33, 'and when such apprehensions outweigh the 'public or private interests that may be injuriously affected by the refusal '.

In furtherance of the aim of this section of the Act it should be noted that in 1904 the Hessian Ministry of Finance published an illustrated book entitled *Noteworthy Trees in the Grand-Duchy of Hesse,* the aim of which was to secure the protection of these precious natural monuments. It has been rightly remarked that ' It is now beyond doubt that for the future Hesse has secured the protection and care of her natural monuments, and that the forests will be managed with a view to the beauty of her landscapes[1].'

Article 35 will appeal to the sorely tried British lover of amenity and quiet.

' 35.

'PROHIBITION OF ADVERTISEMENTS, POSTERS ETC.

'On a natural monument officially protected, or in its 'officially protected environment, no advertisements nor the 'like, nor objects such as posters, shall be placed or set up, 'of such a kind as to injure the effect of the monument.

'At the bidding of the Kreisamt, advertisements or objects 'of the kind referred to, which at the time of the promulga-

[1] *Die Denkmalpflege,* 1905, p. 6.

'tion of this Act are already in existence, must be removed.
'The proprietor can demand from the state an indemnifica-
'tion for the loss sustained by him through the removal of
'what he had put up.

'It shall be competent for district authorities through
'local police regulations to forbid the importation or display
'of advertisements, etc., or of objects which in localities of
'great natural beauty are injurious to the landscape; and
'further, to direct the removal of those already in existence
'at the localities in question.'

In the seventh and last section, articles 37 to 39, there
are provisions for penalties for breach of the Act. These are
fines up to fifty pounds or imprisonment.

At the fifth monument-congress held at Mainz in Hesse,
Freiherr von Biegeleben, the author of the Act, gave an
interesting account of its working up to that date. The
Denkmalrat had already placed a large number of buildings
in private possession under the protection of the law. A few
proprietors had appealed against the act of 'classement',
but others had expressed a wish to have their monuments
scheduled. A limit of about thirty years had been agreed on
for the age of a monument to bring it under the law.

In its more general aspects it was claimed that the law
promised to work well, and the principles under which it was
being administered are worth a word of notice. 'What have
we gained,' asked the speaker, 'in Hesse since October 1,
1902, through the law and its administration? The study
of antiquity has been forwarded by the regulations concerning excavations and "finds"; proprietors both corporate
and private have been influenced in the proper management
of their monuments; needless destruction has been avoided;
but, above all things, in the mind of the people there has
been aroused a new and living interest in the memorials of
the land....The care of monuments has this special character,
that it touches the whole soul of a people. It cannot be
dealt with in the cut-and-dried fashion of a cold-blooded
official, nor yet with the passionate fervour of a fanatic for
antiquity. A warm enthusiasm for the memorials of the

past must go hand in hand with a reasonable estimate of
the needs and demands of the new age, and a fair recognition of the ways of thinking and feeling of the individual
monument-proprietor, as well as of his practical powers of
action. On this account, in every case as it presents itself,
we must form a rational judgement as to what can fairly be
demanded. But, some may ask, are not the care of monuments and an interest in modern works necessarily at opposite
poles? By no means. The same man can well be a patron
of the newest artistic developments and a warm-hearted friend
of the old historical art....Laws and administrations are not
intended to make the encouragement of art a mere matter
of state, nor to erect into power an artistic bureaucracy; but
rather through stimulus, advice, and warning, and by the avoid-
ance of official pressure, to exercise an inspiring influence alike
upon public bodies and upon individuals[1].'

Some notice has now been given of the action in Germany
of official commissions and conservators in the interest of
artistic and historical monuments, and of attempts at state
legislation, which so far however have only in the case of a
single principality produced any definite result. Another
side of Denkmalpflege' in Germany must now be discussed.
The reference is to the action not of the state but of smaller
communities, especially the older historic towns for which
Germany is so famous.

As compared with France Germany is a decentralized
country. The numerous states included under the Germanic
Empire have their bodies of domestic legislation, and as we
have seen, Monument Acts are matters for each of the states
to consider for itself. Furthermore, within the several states
the towns have a considerable amount of independent life of
their own, fed by memories from the days when each was for
practical purposes a self-governing community. There was
an epoch not long ago when the State seemed disposed to
take everything into its own hands, and the independence
of the towns was seriously curtailed, but as a reaction from
this the towns are now managing their own affairs with

[1] *Fünfter Tag*, p. 13.

considerable freedom and spirit[1]. Hence there is a town 'Denkmalpflege' as well as a state 'Denkmalpflege', and in connection with this there emerge matters of much practical interest to ourselves in Britain.

All states possess Local-Government Acts under which the different civic communities are empowered to make their own by-laws, of course within limits fixed by the Acts. Some of these general Acts in the German states appear to allow and even to encourage local authorities to make by-laws in the interests of amenity, while others do not directly authorize such a proceeding. The legal competence of such by-laws varies accordingly in different parts of Germany, and under the impulse of the new enthusiasm for monuments the temptation is strong for a city living under a discouraging Local-Government Act to push its aesthetic by-laws out as far as those of some rival town that is under a different administration. An illustration of how these differences work was given by the Burgomaster of Hildesheim in his address to the Congress at Düsseldorf, already referred to as the fullest expression of advanced German views on this subject. The higher Court of Justice in Prussia decided a case in which an aesthetic restriction in Nassau had been called in question. It was decided that the restriction would not stand in Old-Prussia, but 'in Nassau there was an old Local-Government Act which provided that the building authorities (Baupolizei) were entitled to take account of considerations of beauty. On the ground therefore of this ancient regulation, which happily survived in Nassau, the Court upheld a restriction that had been launched to protect a city from disfigurement[2]' In Prussia proper the general Local-Government Act (Allgemeines Landrecht) is unfavourable, and only allows the local authorities to forbid any absolute open disfigurement of a town (grobe Verunstaltung), more refined aesthetic requirements not being covered by it[3]. In Hanover, on the other hand, in which

[1] The subject was discussed in the interesting speech by the Burgomaster of Hildesheim at the Congress for the care of monuments at Düsseldorf in 1902. See *Dritter Tag*, p. 97.

[2] *Dritter Tag*, p. 113.   [3] *Das Bauwesen*, p. 260 f.

province lies Hildesheim, the Prussian law is not in force, and the regulations which there obtain allow of building prescriptions that take full account of aesthetic demands[1]. Building Acts in Würtemberg and Hesse are also said to be favourable to those who desire to restrict the freedom of constructors in the interests of good taste. In the Kingdom of Saxony a general Building Act was a year or two ago under consideration and the draft of this Act contained a provision perhaps in advance of any other in Acts of the kind: 'Building operations which threaten to involve an open disfigurement to a place can be forbidden. By local regulations there can be fixed a higher architectural standard for new buildings to be erected in certain streets or parts of streets[2].' Bavaria however seems to be the classic ground for these local prescriptions, for the state authorities there not only allow or encourage but even urge the towns to take up this as part of their business.

Attention has already been called to a Bavarian Ministerial Minute issued on January 1, 1904. The following are some of the directions contained in this minute for the guidance of civic or communal authorities in framing their local regulations.

'(1) The ancient works of fortification with their fosses, 'city walls, gates, towers, and all thereto appertaining, are to 'be preserved as carefully as possible; for every constructive 'alteration on them permission must be obtained.

'(2) Constructive alterations, interior or exterior, on other 'buildings of historical or artistic importance must depend on 'official permission. It should be a condition that in rebuild-'ing or alteration the style and character of the original must 'be conformed to.

'(3) In the case of all new buildings or alterations in the 'vicinity of the fortifications or of structures mentioned in the 'last paragraph, the character of the latter must be taken into 'account. Especial attention should be paid here that the 'new structure should as regards its proportions take its 'proper place in the general picture, and in its details and

---

[1] *Zweiter Tag*, p. 40.   [2] *Die Denkmalpflege*, 1900, p. 8.

'ornament should be in harmony with the older surroundings.
'In order to avoid anything that offends the eye in the
'general view of the town, the form and material of the roofs
'ought to be carefully considered.

'(4) When new lines of houses are in contemplation, care
'should be taken to safeguard the picturesque views of streets
'and open spaces, and the tyranny of the engineer's rule and
'level must naturally be resisted. In general, in the case of
'all new buildings, especially in the older parts of cities, it
'should be made a matter of duty to adhere as closely as
'possible to the traditional building-style of the place, and in
'this connection again the form and covering of the roofs
'become of importance.

'(5) In the case of new buildings in other situations,
'especially when fresh quarters have to be laid out, it would
'be enough to keep general aesthetic requirements in view.
'Directions however on such matters as the proper plastering
'of rubble walls and the correct slope of mansard roofs would
'always be welcome.'

The minute from which these are extracts is not the work
of an irresponsible artist, of some William Morris generally
at war with constituted authorities, nor even of a single state
official with a personal crotchet on the subject of 'Denkmalpflege', but is the combined production of two responsible
Ministers, of the Interior and of Religion; and these go out
of their way, as we should think, to excite in the minds of
town councillors unholy aspirations towards civic beauty,
which it would be the instinct of the English official rather to
repress. That the Bavarian government is prepared to back
its own opinions is shown by the following incident which
recently occurred.

In Bamberg in 1899, a very fine Renaissance house of
about the year 1700, called Prell's House, was sold by its
proprietor to a Munich sculptor who proposed to remove it
and set it up again in the Bavarian capital. On the ground
of their local regulations the Bamberg magistrates forbade
the demolition of the monument, but when recourse was had
to law the court gave judgement against the magistrates. The

magistrates then appealed to the Bavarian Minister of the Interior, and with complete success, for on the report of the General Conservator of Monuments, the Minister upheld the appeal and added that ' no further opposition was to be made to the efforts of the urban authorities to preserve the ancient appearance of the city[1].'   This may seem to us in this country a lordly way of doing things and one that savours a little of the Arabian Nights, but the outcome of the affair is the prevention of a foolish act of vandalism.

In Nürnberg in 1899, on the occasion of a peril which threatened the so-called Nassauer Haus (opposite the western end of the Lorenz-Kirche), the magistrate issued an order which forbade any alterations either in the interior or on the exterior of a historical and monumental building, without leave of the local authorities.   This order was appealed against to the law courts, but the decision of the magistrate was upheld.   It was stated that the Minister of the Interior approved of the magisterial order.

Nor is it only in Bavaria that this local care for monuments is encouraged by state authorities.   The Burgomaster of Hildesheim reported that he and his colleagues had consulted the Prussian Minister of the Interior on their own proceedings in this kind, and that he had replied in encouraging terms, though he advised them to be cautious and moderate in the use they made of their regulations[2].

The uncertainty, which hangs over these well-meant efforts at local monument legislation, makes it natural that those who believe in this potent weapon of ' Denkmalpflege' should demand some distinct regulation of the whole matter by state legislation.   It will be noticed that the Hessian Monument Act, the only German achievement in this line, does not contain any definite pronouncement on the matter, but it does on the other hand recognize the importance of independent local efforts in this direction, as distinct from state action, in an important provision authorizing the State to delegate to communes or town-councils its right of expro-

---

[1] *Die Denkmalpflege*, 1900, pp. 4, 15.
[2] *Zweiter Tag*, p. 40.

priating private property in the interests of monuments. This puts into the hands of local authorities a weapon as effective in its way as the building regulations.

The question of the general policy of such regulations in the best interests of monument preservation is one on which a good deal might be written. It needs only to be said here that it is fully recognized in Germany how much care must be taken in the framing and enforcement of restrictive ordinances of the kind. They may easily go too much into detail and may lay down the law on matters on which people of good taste can take different views; or they may be applied too widely, without observance of the distinction noted in the Bavarian minute between the old parts of towns, where a jarring note may too easily be struck, and new quarters where more freedom should be allowed. They may be enforced too often and too rigidly and by producing a feeling of irritation in the minds of the citizens do more harm than good. When administered however in a spirit of moderation and common-sense they may do much good, and their existence in the background will always render moral methods of suasion more effective. Recent experience in Lübeck has shown this to be the case[1].

Local building regulations of the kind contemplated are in operation in the Bavarian towns Augsburg, Würzburg, Nürnberg, Rothenburg, Amberg, Lindau; in Frankfurt, Hildesheim, Wimpfen-am-Berg, Danzig, Lübeck, and other places. A few go too much into detail and lay themselves open to the charge of pedantry, most of them wisely limit the restrictions to the central and oldest parts of the cities. There may be quoted as a specimen the regulations at

HILDESHEIM.

After a reference to the general Acts which sanction the by-laws these proceed: '(Art. I.) In the streets and 'open places referred to below, those parts of any new 'building which can be seen from any street or public place

---

[1] *Die Denkmalpflege*, 1905, p. 7.

'must be carried out in architectural forms which agree with
'those in use in Germany up to the middle of the 17th century.
'Further, the new work must as far as possible be in harmony
'with its nearer surroundings, and especially with any con-
'spicuous building which gives a character to the whole
'neighbourhood.' Under certain conditions the magistrate
may relax the stringency of this restriction.

'As a rule the parts of new buildings referred to
'above must be so carried out that the general appearance
'of the surroundings be not interfered with. This applies
'especially to the materials, including those used in the
'roofing and the ornamentation, and to colouring.

'The above regulations apply also to any alterations made
'on structures which already conform to them, as well as to
'restorations and important additions and reparations on
'buildings that do not yet so conform.' Here again the
magistrate may relax the prescriptions, especially when the
difficulty or cost of carrying out the new work in this style
would be disproportionate, in view of the character of the
existing parts of the structure.

'The following are the streets and open spaces to which
'these regulations apply......(47 names follow).

'Art. II.......Offences against the provisions of these
'regulations may be punished with a fine up to 30 marks
'or in case of inability to pay with a corresponding term of
'imprisonment.

'Art. III.   These regulations come into force on July 1,
'1899.'

AUGSBURG.

In 1902 the magistrate issued local regulations concerning
new buildings, and additions to or alterations of old, within
the former circuit of the-walls. Alterations even in the
interiors of buildings of historical, artistic or architectonic
importance must be reported to the authorities before operations are begun. In the case of new additions to or alterations
on such buildings, their style and character must be conformed
to; this applies also to work in their immediate neighbourhood.

Prohibition may be issued against construction in rough brick work or mixed walling of harsh tones of colour, as well as against flat or mansard roofs in the neighbourhood of buildings of the above character.

In parts of the city where building is not restricted the new regulations prescribe attention to the artistic design of new edifices. Further, in the case of structures in bad condition that are a disfigurement to the streets, the local authorities may require them to be repaired in accordance with the above. Unsightly advertisement-posters and bills, offensive colours, and by-structures (Anlagen) which injure the look of the streets must be removed at the demand of the magistrate within a time fixed by him.

ROTHENBURG-ON-THE-TAUBER.

Pilgrims to Germany in search of the picturesque will naturally expect to find the Rothenburgers in the fore-front of any battle waged in defence of ancient monuments. Here are some of their building ordinances, to our views minute and even pedantic but natural enough in a town which is run frankly on antiquarian lines.

' *A.   Ordinances applying within the walls.*

'§ 1.   All buildings to be erected within the circuit of or ' upon the city walls must be so carried out as to agree with ' the general architectural traditions of Rothenburg, and ' especially with the ancient structures in the vicinity, and ' must be in harmony with the whole aspect of the streets and ' of the town.

'§ 2.   The same applies to any important reparations or ' alterations on buildings which in whole or in part are visible ' from a street, an open place, or a road.

'§ 3.   Every other constructive alteration in the outer ' walls and roofing of buildings thus visible must be carried ' out in the way prescribed in § 1, and needs the permission ' of the local authorities.

' This applies specially to any alterations in gateways,

'doors, and windows, which as far as possible must be kept
'to the beautiful ancient forms.

'§ 4. In the case of any reconstruction or alteration on
'monumental buildings of historical or architectonic import-
'ance, attention must be paid to the style, character and
'appearance of the main structure. Constructive alterations
'inside or outside such buildings require the consent of the
'local authorities.

'§ 5. Rough brick buildings, buildings in mixed masonry
'with harsh colouring, and flat roofs are to be avoided. For
'structures visible as in § 2 roof coverings in slates or zinc are
'inadmissible.

'§ 6. In the painting of buildings referred to in §§ 1–4
'harsh colours are to be avoided. Suitable colours are to be
'selected for painting the windows, doors and other wooden
'portions of the facades.

'When painting is contemplated, before the work is com-
'menced the authorities must be informed exactly what is
'intended, and their directions with regard to the work must
'be followed.

'§ 7. Any woodwork which is brought to view in con-
'nection with alterations shall as a rule remain visible when
'it adds to the artistic effect of the building, but the authorities
'can from time to time decide about this.

'B. *Ordinances applying outside the walls.*

'§ 8. Buildings without the town walls on the old outer
'fortifications or in their vicinity, must correspond as closely
'as possible to the architectural forms of the inner city, and
'must be in harmony with these old fortifications; they must
'not injure the view of the city. For all such buildings, and
'for all alterations on their exterior, leave of the authorities
'must be obtained. The provisions of § 6 apply to the
'painting of them.

'§ 9. In the case of all other new buildings and important
'alterations on street frontages aesthetic requirements must
'be satisfied. All constructive alterations of facades of build-

'ings on streets, roads, and public places require the approval
'of the authorities.

'In regard to painting the provisions of § 6 must be
'observed.

'§ 10. The provisions of § 4 apply to buildings of the
'kind contemplated when they are outside the city walls.

C. Ordinances applying to the old fortifications.

'§ 11. The town walls, barbicans, fosses and ramparts
'with their appurtenances (wall-towers, postern doors etc.)
'are as far as possible to be preserved intact. All alterations
'on the exterior of these works of fortification require the
'approval of the authorities.

'D.   Final Provisions.

'§ 12. The magistrate, as Local Building Authority,
'reserves the power of taking the opinions of experts on
'doubtful questions, especially whether a given building-project
'agrees with the architectural style of the place, or whether
'a given building belongs to the class of monumental structures,
'etc.

'§ 13. Infringements of these ordinances involve fines up
'to 150 marks, or imprisonment up to six weeks; furthermore
'any work done in contravention of the regulations may be
'removed.'

AMBERG-I.-D.-OBERPFALZ.

This smaller Bavarian city issued a set of ordinances in
January 1904 which follow in most of their provisions those
of Rothenburg. The roofs in the important parts of the
town are not to be covered with slates or zinc or black
glazed tiles, and red tile roofing is recommended. Mansard
roofs are not to rise at a steeper slope than 60 degrees with
the horizontal. The advice of experts is to be taken on
doubtful questions.

LÜNEBURG.

This is another of the smaller towns that, inspired by the
example of Hildesheim, has set itself seriously to consider

the question of preserving its characteristic ancient features. Over and above its picturesque Rathhaus in the old market place with the buildings behind it, Lüneburg still possesses a very large number of private houses of the 16th century, with lofty arcaded gables, that give the streets a very distinct character of their own. A report of the middle of 1903 states that an association for the protection of these features has been formed, and that the civic authorities are prepared to subsidize it in its efforts to keep alive the old building traditions.

To show that these efforts are not only made in small towns, or in such as depend largely on their reputation for picturesqueness, this series of extracts may close with the ordinances of Lübeck and of Frankfurt, issued the one in 1903 the other in 1900.

LÜBECK.

The following is an extract from the recent building ordinance of Lübeck. It will be noticed that care is taken for the natural scenery around the city.

'All new buildings and additions to existing structures
'must on every side that is visible from thoroughfares
'or public places be so carried out that they do not injure
'either the aspect of the streets or the natural surroundings
'of the city, nor injuriously affect the appearance of existing
'buildings, especially those of historical value.

'Placards, posters, bills, and other such arrangements for
'advertising, or coloured surfaces that disfigure the streets or
'the landscape, or injuriously affect historical buildings, are
'prohibited.'

FRANKFURT-AM-MAIN.

The following is a local ordinance issued in the year 1900.

'§ 1. For the preservation of the artistic and antique
'character of the following historically interesting streets and
'public places (here follows a list of seven such localities) all
'buildings which are to be erected thereon, in so far as they
'are visible from the street, must be so treated externally

'that the existing aspect of the streets is not disfigured or
'essentially altered. For the attainment of this end the
'authorities may limit the otherwise legal height of the
'building or of its several stories. As a set-off against this,
'the authorities may allow exemptions from the usual legal
'provisions in regard to height of roofs, height and breadth
'of gables and dormers, balconies and oriels, and overhanging
'parts.

'§ 2. These provisions apply also to the case of altera-
'tions on older structures which already agree with these
'prescriptions, as well as to the case of important alterations,
'enlargements, etc., on buildings which do not yet agree
'thereto.' In the last case the authorities may relax these
prescriptions (on the same grounds as explained in the case
of Hildesheim).

'§ 3. The local authorities shall decide whether the
'above prescriptions have been fulfilled, and before their
'decision they must consider a report from a special civic
'commission, consisting of the custodian of the city antiquities,
'a member of the civic commission for art and antiquities,
'two members of the association of architects and engineers,
'and one member from the magistracy, who acts as president.

'§ 4. This ordinance comes into force on the day of its
'publication.'

CHAPTER III.

ITALY.

Bibliography and Sources of Information.

Mariotti, *La Legislazione delle Belle Arti*, Roma, 1892. Contains a large collection of the older laws and edicts, with reports of Parliamentary discussions on draft Monument Acts, etc.

Regolamento per l' Esecuzione della Legge 12 *Giugno* 1902 *sulla Conservazione dei Monumenti, etc.*, Roma, Cecchini, 1904. An official publication containing the text of the Monument Acts of 1902 and 1903 and the Regulations for the carrying out of these Acts.

L' Amministrazione delle Antichità e Belle Arti in Italia, Roma, Cecchini. An official yearly report on Monument Administration to the Minister of Public Instruction.

Elenco degli Edifizi Monumentali in Italia, Roma, Cecchini, 1902. An instalment of the official inventory of the artistic treasures of the kingdom.

Catalogo degli Oggetti di sommo pregio per la Storia e per l' Arte, appartenenti a privati, Roma, Cecchini, 1903. A special section of the forthcoming inventory.

Regolamento Edilizio del Comune di Roma, Roma, Cecchini, 1887. The Municipal Building Laws of the City Rome, with

Elenco delle fabbriche aventi carattere artistico e storico, Consiglio Comunale di Roma, 1897. These documents have been kindly furnished for the purpose of this book by Cavaliere Vittorio Caroselli, Capo-Sezione in the Commune of Rome.

The thanks of the writer are due to his Excellency the Director for Antiquities and the Fine Arts in the Ministry of Public Instruction, Signor Carlo Fiorilli, for his kindness in giving information about the Italian Catalogue or Inventory of works of art, referred to in the Italian Monument Act. The writer also desires to thank Signor Cannizzaro, president of the Associazione Artistica fra i Cultori di Architettura, of Rome; and Count Gallenga Stuart of Perugia, for kind assistance through correspondence, and for documents furnished.

MANY causes combine to vindicate for Italy a position of special importance in all that concerns the ancient monument or the site of historic interest and beauty. The wealth of the country in historic monuments and towns and sites, and in scenes of entrancing beauty, is unrivalled. The care of monuments has there a very long history, and is associated with men of world-wide fame. These monuments have at times in the past been so dealt with as to furnish the most terrible examples for warning, for the barbarism of the men of the Renaissance towards the remains of ancient Rome was a disgrace to civilization[1]. Though at the present day they are conserved with the most jealous care, the question of their proper treatment in the matter of restoration furnishes much matter for thought; while the important and ever-present problems, connected with the modern treatment of ancient cities, have been brought into the sharpest relief in the conspicuous instances of Rome, and of other world-famous towns of the peninsula. If the aedilic policy of the Italian administrators of to-day be made sometimes the object of foreign criticism, this is only a proof of the intense interest taken all the world over in cities and monuments that are the common glory of mankind. The cordial sympathy which the lovers of Italy feel with the great national revival of the last half-century cannot blind them to the danger that these ancient monuments may be summoned to an artistic 'risorgimento' which will 'restore away half their charm, and that the straight broad monotonous streets borrowed from a Housmannized Paris may drive away the *genius loci* of the seven hills[2].

The subject of Italian monuments in general, and of their

---

[1] 'Why do we complain of the Goths, the Vandals and other foes of the Latin name, if those very men who as fathers and governors should defend these poor relics of the Roman city, have themselves bent their energies with all zeal and through a long space of time to destroy them and blot them out?' Letter of Raphael (?) to Leo X. See ante, p. 11.

[2] An excellent address, delivered in 1902 in the Capitol at Rome on the invitation of the Syndic, by M. Charles Buls of Brussels, on 'the Aesthetic of Rome' contains some timely counsels and warnings, of which the Roman Aediles have taken count. It was actually determined at one time to run a new broad street into the Piazza Navona practically destroying its curved end!

treatment at various epochs, and in the different states into
which the country has till recently been divided, is too vast a
one to be entered on here with any fulness.   The selfish and
inconsiderate policy of some of the Popes of the Renaissance
period must not be regarded as the rule for all times and
places.   In the fifteenth century, before the *ombra funesta* of
the new St Peter's began to darken the Leonine city, wise
measures for the preservation of Roman antiquities were set
on foot by men like Aeneas Sylvius Piccolomini Pope Pius II,
and Sixtus IV   Later edicts applying to the States of the
Church lay special stress on the prevention of the export of
works of art and on the supervision of excavations and
disposal of finds, which from the seventeenth century downwards have formed the chief objects of Italian monument
legislation.   Mariotti prints edicts issued by Cardinal-
Camerlenghi in 1624 and successive periods of the seventeenth
and eighteenth centuries[1], which not only bind proprietors of
works of art not to sell them beyond the borders, but threaten
with dire penalties any makers of wooden cases, packers,
porters, waggoners, muleteers, boatmen, frontier officials,
guards, and the like, who may by act or omission further the
forbidden traffic.   No excavations could be undertaken without the supervision of the Papal Commissioner, and any work
of art accidentally found had to be at once declared.   In
1802 Pope Pius VII appointed the sculptor Canova General
Inspector of Antiquities and the Fine Arts for the Papal States,
and in the same year was issued the famous Doria Pamphilj
edict, so called from the Cardinal-Camerlengo with whose
name it was subscribed.   This edict, with that bearing the
name of Cardinal Pacca and dated 1820, embodies Italian, or
at any rate Papal, monument policy, as it existed prior to the
more recent attempts at legislation which found final outcome
in the national Monument Act of 1902.

      The Doria Pamphilj edict of Oct. 1, 1802, contained seven-
teen articles, of which the first began ' We (that is the reigning
Pope) desire in the first place that it be prohibited to export
from Rome or from the State any statue, basrelief, or other

----

[1] *La Legislazione*, p. 208 f.

similar work, representing human figures or animals, in marble, bronze, ivory, or any other material ; or any ancient pictures Greek or Roman, or mosaics, or vases called Etruscan ' and so on for a long list of ancient works of art (*antichità*) including architectural fragments. Pictures and other works of art of the Renaissance were included under Article 2, while in Article 3 the prohibition was made to apply absolutely to those in high places as well as low, to foreigners as well as native Romans. Article 4 laid down the penalties for infringement, which could involve five years at the galleys. By Articles 5 and 6 antique objects could change hands through sale or be moved within the limits of Rome, or, on leave given, within the limits of the Papal dominions, while the works of living artists were to be subject to no restrictions. Articles 7, 8 and 9, recalling similar rescripts of the Popes of the fifteenth century, prohibited injury to any ancient monument or work of art either within or without the city, or the filching of any object of the kind from the churches ; while by Article 10 the churches were protected in that no picture was to be moved out of or in them nor alienated, nor even repaired or copied without the express leave of the authorities, that is the Inspector General of the Fine Arts, the Commissary of Antiquities, or their representative. Article 11 concerned private proprietors of collections or single works of art. These were directed within a fixed time to give in an exact and detailed list of their possessions, under penalty of the forfeiture of any object not so declared, and every year an official inspection was to be made of the collections or objects for purposes of verification. Article 12 dealt with the offence of taking materials from ruined structures and 13 and 14 with excavations and ' finds '. Any object of value accidentally discovered must be declared, under pain of the forfeiture of the object and other penalty, and the same obligation followed the discovery of any fragment of antique masonry. No excavations were to be undertaken without the licence of the authorities, who had the right to levy a tax on the objects found. Notice was to be given of the commencement of the actual excavations and these were subject to official

inspection. A full list of all objects found was to be given in
to the Papal authorities. Any failure under these sections
was punishable by forfeiture of discoveries and a fine of five
hundred golden ducats. Objects found accidentally or after
search remained the property of the owner, but if he wished
to part with them the state had the right of pre-emption at a
reasonable price. The last three articles contained administrative regulations.

In the year 1820 was issued under the same Pope, Pius VII,
the well-known Pacca edict, the intention of which was 'to
renew, enlarge, and make public all existing regulations on
this subject'. In sixty one articles the edict goes over the
same ground as the previous one. A special Commission of
the Fine Arts is charged with the work of administration and
inspection.

These provisions for monument administration in the
States of the Church can be paralleled by a series of similar
edicts, promulgated during the seventeenth, eighteenth, and
nineteenth centuries, in all the political divisions into which
the peninsula was then broken up. Mariotti has printed a
long series of these, and the general objects of them are the
same as those of the Doria Pamphilj and Pacca edicts.
Prohibition of the export of works of art of old date, inventorization of private collections, the preservation of ancient
monuments, the regulation of excavations, and restraint on
the free disposal of finds ', are contemplated in most of them.
There is one regulation however of early date that is of
special interest. This was issued in 1571 by the Grand-Duke
of Tuscany, and concerns the preservation on the palaces of
Florence and other Tuscan towns of the arms, insignia and
inscriptions of their founders. In terms which remind us of
those in which an enlightened County Council of to-day
might instruct the heedless citizens, the edict points out the
value of these historical records, and forbids their mutilation
or effacement, even in cases where the original family is
extinct, or the house has passed into other hands. No
new proprietor is to presume to put his own arms by the side
of the old. Only in cases where nothing has survived from

the older time may a new lord place his own insignia on the facade.

The existence of multitudinous rescripts relating to monuments in all parts of Italy shows that, at the time of the national consolidation, a body of legislation already existed in the peninsula, that might have seemed easy to codify into a single general law. In 1872 such a proposal was introduced into the Italian parliament, and the Minister of Public Instruction, Correnti, took occasion in bringing forward the bill to give a summary of these local enactments which had been in force in the different principalities. In the older provinces of the kingdom there existed by a law of 1865 a right of compulsory purchase, on the part of the state or a province or a commune, of any national monument in corporate or private hands that might be in danger of injury. In Lombardy and Venetia the state had the right of pre-emption of any object its proprietor wished to alienate, and powers to prevent damage to monuments of a public character when in private or municipal control. In the Duchy of Modena there was a strict prohibition of exportation, under pain of the forfeiture of the object and a fine of ten thousand Lire. In the Emilia, powers had been given in 1860 to the Commission of Preservation for monuments to protect these from injury, while the Academy of Fine Arts in the province of Parma could control the exportation of works of art without the confines. The Tuscan laws were particularly strict. A list of eighteen of the best painters of the Italian schools was drawn up, and it was forbidden to take any substantial work by any one of them outside the limits of the territory. Works of art belonging to government institutions, communes, religious foundations, churches, confraternities, were inalienable without the consent of the authorities. Monuments in open view of the public, even when in private hands, could not be dealt with at the will of their proprietors. Excavations might be freely carried on, but the objects found had to be disclosed and the royal gallery might purchase them if it so desired. In the province of Lucca there was a lien on alienation, and a power of veto on any proposed restoration of an

ancient monument. In the States of the Church the Pacca
edict was in force, and similar restrictions existed in the
provinces of Naples and Sicily.

These local regulations remained in force after the unifica-
tion of the kingdom, but ministers naturally felt desirous of
obtaining a single Act which would consolidate the whole
monument legislation of the country. Such a measure was
accordingly introduced in 1872, but it was not carried into
law. The fact is one of great significance for the whole
subject. The local measures had applied to comparatively
small districts, and been framed by comparatively despotic
governments which issued them as edicts. As will have been
observed in the case of some already noticed, their provisions
were often of the most drastic kind, and the rights of private
proprietors were treated with very scanty consideration.

When an attempt was made to carry through an Act
embodying similar provisions in a deliberative assembly
representing the whole kingdom, the matter proved to be by
no means simple. Many interests were up in arms, and the
defenders of the rights of private property made themselves
conspicuous in opposition. Not only did the draft of 1872
fail to pass the legislature, but several successive projects of
the same kind were rejected in one or other of the Italian
Chambers, and it was not until the year 1902 after thirty
years of discussion that the long-expected general monument
law of Italy finally received the royal assent. The history of
the measure is another proof how much easier is monument
legislation in small or despotically governed communities
than in more advanced countries, where democratic sentiment
is keen, and where the individual is accustomed to contend
boldly for what he conceives to be his personal interest.

The draft law of 1872 boldly asserted the control of the
state over monuments of national interest in private hands.
Such were not to be destroyed, injured or altered, under a
penalty of 500 to 3000 Lire. If the legitimate interests of a
proprietor demanded any measures inimical to the monument,
the state might acquire it by compulsory purchase. No
objects of artistic or historical value could be exported with-

out permission, and to secure their retention compulsory purchase might be resorted to. Even to remove such objects from one part of the kingdom to another required authorization. Excavations could only be carried out on private lands under official permission, and a notice of all objects found had to be periodically sent in. The proprietor could retain what he found, but could not sell anything until the government had had the opportunity of purchasing. Land on which there were ancient remains of value could be expropriated. Commissions of Preservation were to be constituted in each province under the Act, and one function of these was to be 'to compile and to transmit to the Minister a complete 'artistic and archaeological inventory of the monuments, the 'collections, and the objects of art and archaeology, existing 'in each province, and belonging to the state, to corporate 'bodies, or to private individuals'.

For one reason or another[1], neither this draft nor any of the half-dozen successive ones which were introduced at intervals from this date to the end of the century, actually passed the legislature, and it was not till June 12, 1902, that Italy obtained, as we have just seen, a general Act, which abrogates, with certain exceptions given in its thirty fifth article, all the earlier local regulations so abundant in the different parts of the peninsula. It must be confessed that the Act as it stands compares very unfavourably, as regards its form, with the earlier drafts which Mariotti has printed in his useful work. The fact is that a measure of the kind when first introduced is generally both logically arranged and clearly expressed, but it finally emerges from the Parliamentary battle-field in a somewhat ragged and disjointed condition. The Italian Act is no exception to the rule, and to go through it clause by clause would be wearisome. It has not even the useful grouping of the articles under chapters of the draft of 1872, where chapter I was headed 'Preservation of Monuments and of Objects of Art and Archaeology'; chapter II, 'Exportation and Sale of Monu-

---

[1] Freiherr von Helfert, *Denkmalpflege*, Wien, 1897, p. 27, says that the reason for rejection was the threatened invasion of the rights of private ownership.

ments and of Objects of Art and Archaeology', chapter III, 'Archaeological excavations'; and chapter IV, 'Commissions of Preservation'. The thirty seven articles of the law of 1902 have no such grouping and are anything but clear in their wording. The main intention of the measure appears to be to check the sale to foreign purchasers of works of art which are part of the national wealth, but the difficulty of interference with the rights of private proprietorship has been the cause of considerable obscurity and confusion in the various articles. As a fact, in the next year after the passing of the main Act, that is to say on June 27, 1903, there was issued a short supplementary Act of a temporary character which contains provisions prohibiting the export of works of art more drastic than those of the main Act. On July 17, 1904, there was promulgated the official 'Regolamento' or code of regulations for the practical carrying out of the two Acts, and this is of course of great help in their interpretation. The essential element in the legislation however, a Catalogue or schedule of works of art, constantly referred to in the texts and the regulations, has not yet seen the light[1].

Taking the Regolamento together with the texts of the two Acts, we may hazard the following summary of their main provisions. In the Act of 1902 the first thirteen articles deal with the relation of the authorities to movable and immovable monuments in the hands of corporations or private individuals. Articles fourteen to seventeen are concerned with excavations, eighteen to twenty two with the care for and acquisition of specimens for museums, twenty three and twenty four with the catalogue just referred to, twenty five to thirty four mainly with penalties, while article thirty five abrogates former provisions, thirty six refers to the contemplated Regolamento and thirty seven substitutes new rates on exported works of art for those previously in force. The Act of June 27, 1903, has only four clauses all dealing with the prohibition of exportation of works of art, but it was only to remain in force for two years. The Regolamento runs to four hundred and eighteen articles, and is conveniently divided

---

[1] About this catalogue, see postea, p. 138 f.

into three Parts, each with a subdivision into 'Titoli', Chapters, and Articles.

The Regolamento devotes Part I to a subject not dealt with in the Acts, 'The Ordinance of the Bureaux and Commissions for the Preservation of Monuments and Objects of Antiquity and Art'. Before the Act of 1902 there had been an extensive service of Commissions, Inspectors, and the like, in different parts of the kingdom, and for these there is now substituted a coordinated system applying to the whole country. The system is not however centralized to the same extent as that of France. The ancient provincial divisions of the country are still recognized and the administration is carried on at centres corresponding to these divisions. There are four branches of the administration, one for monuments; another for excavations, museums, and objects of antiquity; a third for galleries and objects of art; and a fourth for the superintendence of exportation. There are about a dozen centres. For monument administration the kingdom is divided into ten provinces, I, Piedmont and Liguria; II, Lombardy; III, Venetia; IV, Emilia and Romagna; V, Tuscany; VI, The March and Umbria; VII, The Province of Rome; VIII, The Southern Provinces; IX, Sicily; X, Sardinia. (For the other branches the division is slightly different.) These provincial establishments are commonly called 'Uffizi Regionali per la Conservazione dei Monumenti' and they act as advisory and as executive boards under the Minister of Public Instruction. Each has a staff of Superintendents, Inspectors, Architects, Draughtsmen, Overseers, and minor officials. Besides these state-appointed officials, there are called in to give honorary aid persons of artistic culture and experience, who form with the higher officials Provincial Commissions for the Preservation of Monuments and Objects of Antiquity and Art. There is also at Rome a Central Commission composed of 'eighteen 'members selected from among persons of most authority for 'their learning in archaeological, historical, or artistic subjects, 'and nominated by Royal Decree[1]'. There are two sections, one for ancient the other for mediaeval and later art, and they

---

[1] Regolamento, Art. 51.

form a privy council for the Minister on all that concerns the
care and the preservation of the archaeological and artistic
patrimony of the nation[1]. In most respects the Central
Commission will supersede the earlier Giunta Superiore di
Belle Arti which was instituted in 1844, but the Giunta is still
to exercise such of its functions as are connected with the
artistic instruction and output of the day[2].

The above machinery is to carry out the provisions of the
laws of 1902 and 1903, and Art. 1 of the former states that
the subject matter of the Act comprises 'monuments and
'immovable and movable objects which have antiquarian or
'artistic value'. Buildings and objects of art by living authors
or not more than fifty years old are excluded from its
operations (Act, 1). The next dozen articles (Act, 2–13)
contain the chief provisions of the Act and must be read in
connection with Part III, Titoli 1 and 2 (Reg., 101–315), of
the Regolamento, headed 'On the Preservation of Monuments
and Objects of Antiquity and Art'.

The crux of the matter is the sale or exportation of
monuments or movable objects of art. These may belong
(1) to ecclesiastical corporations, (2) to civil corporations,
(3) to private individuals. Ecclesiastical property and property
of special value belonging to civil bodies cannot be sold to
individual purchasers, though the Minister may authorize a
sale from one corporation to another (Act, 2, 3). Property
not of special value[3] belonging to such bodies can be sold
without such restriction but only by leave of the Minister
(Act, 4). In the case of property belonging to these bodies,
no repairs nor alterations can be carried out without the
authorization of the Minister (Act, 10). When the property
is in the form of a monument and belongs to communes, care
has to be taken that new constructions do not interfere with
the view of, or the lighting of, the monument (Act, 13). The
right of initiating the process of expropriation (according to

---

[1] Regolamento, Art. 53.

[2] ibid., Art. 409 f.

[3] These degrees of value are to be fixed on the authority of the catalogue
already mentioned as in preparation.

the older law of 1865) is given to monument administrators (Act, 7)[1].

In the case of monuments or works of art in private possession the following are the provisions of the Act.

No proprietor may demolish or alter monumental remains existing on his estate unless he can convince the authorities that they are not worth preservation (Act, 11), nor without express leave do any work upon any part of them that is exposed to public view (Act, 10). If the officials responsible for the care of monuments become aware that works of repair or protection are necessary on a monument in private hands, they can call on the proprietor to carry these out within a certain time, and if he fail to do this they can step in and execute the work required, charging the proprietor with the economic value of the improvement (Act, 12; Reg., 127–8). If the private proprietor desire to sell a monument or object of art of special value, or have entered into a contract for such a sale with another party, he must give timely notice to the proper authorities, and must also make the proposed purchaser aware that the object is one on which the authorities have a lien (Act, 5; Reg., 115–118). In such cases of desired or proposed sale the government has a right of pre-emption, that must be exercised or waived within a space of three months, which can however be extended to six (Act, 6; Reg., 123–4). If the proprietor desire to sell his property to a foreign purchaser, and the government have waived its right of pre-emption, article 8 of the Act allows the exportation, subject to special progressive rates of export duty according to value. These rates are given in the last article, no. 37, of the Act, and amount to 5 °/₀ on the first L. 5000 (£200), 7 °/₀ on the second, 9 °/₀ on the third, and 11 °/₀ on the fourth L. 5000, with a final limit of 20 °/₀. In the Regolamento a long chapter of sixty three articles (252 to 315) goes minutely into the whole matter of exportation, but all this appears in

---

[1] Article 83 of the Law on Expropriation of 1865, no. 2359, runs as follows :— 'Every historical monument or national antiquity of an immovable kind, the 'preservation of which is in danger so long as it continues in the possession of any 'corporation or private citizen, can be acquired by the State, by Provinces or by 'Communes by the process of expropriation for reasons of public utility.'

the meantime to be superseded by the short supplementary Act of June 27, 1903, which prohibits for a space of two years all exportation of works of art of recognized value, or such as seem to the officials in charge of the matter to have a notable archaeological or artistic importance.

Article 23 of the Act, and Part II of the Regolamento, articles 62 to 100, are concerned with the important matter of the Catalogue or schedule of monuments and works of art, according to which the value of the objects in question is to be fixed. According to Reg., 62, there are to be two catalogues, one of immovable objects or buildings and the remains of these, and the other of movable objects of antiquarian or artistic value. Each catalogue is to be in two parts, one for entries belonging to private persons, the other for entries belonging to corporate bodies. Objects belonging to private persons can be inserted either on the initiative of their owners or officially. Official insertions however are to be confined to objects of which the value is so great that their exportation from the kingdom 'would ' constitute a serious loss to the artistic patrimony of the nation 'and to history' (Reg., 66; Act, 23). Notification is to be given to private proprietors and to corporations of the insertion of property belonging to them. Such insertion carries with it important legal consequences. The mere insertion is to be a recognition of archaeological or artistic value, but in the case of certain objects there is to be an indication of special value, and objects thus distinguished are to occupy a special position under the law. Thus corporations may not sell such objects to individuals (Act, 2). Private persons must give the government in regard to them the right of pre-emption (Act, 6) and in the meantime no such objects may be sent out of the kingdom (Act of 1903). A necessary provision is contained in Act, 5, according to which, before the promulgation of the catalogue, an intimation from the Minister to the proprietor that such and such an object is officially regarded as of special value, is to carry with it the same legal consequences as the official insertion in the catalogue.

The directions given for the catalogue in the Regolamento

show that it is intended to be most searching and elaborate, and in view of the vast treasure in works of art of almost all kinds of which Italy is the repository, it will be, if it is ever completed, the most comprehensive work of the kind in existence. According to articles 75 and 76 of the Regolamento every edifice or ruin is to be entered with its situation, the name of its proprietor, its description, the century of its origin and if possible the builder's name; with a note of all inscriptions on it and of all the works of art permanently attached thereto, and any other particulars that may usefully be added. In the case of a movable work of art we are to have its description, dimensions and material; the subject, if any, represented; the name of its author or the school and century to which it belongs; with all indications, such as inscriptions, restorations, parts wanting, etc., that may serve for its better identification. According to article 35 of the Act of 1902 this stupendous catalogue was to be completed within a year! As a fact only a small portion of it has seen the light. This small portion consists in a list of 'objects of special value for history and for art belonging to private persons', and was issued in December 1903, in accordance with the subsidiary Act of June 27, 1903, which deals, it will be remembered, with the prohibition of the export of artistic treasures. The catalogue in question contains a list of works of unique value that are on no conditions to be allowed permanently to leave the country, and we find in it masterpieces like the Greek marbles in the Villa Albani and Prince Giovanelli's 'Family of Giorgione' at Venice. There are only about 150 entries. The full catalogue, as will easily be understood, represents a vast labour and it will probably be a long time before it is completed, though the work is being pushed forward with all diligence[1]. Shortly before the passing of the Act of 1902 there was published a sort of preliminary sketch of a catalogue of architectural monuments, that is to be regarded not as part of the final catalogue but as a preparation for it[2].

---

[1] Information kindly furnished by the General Direction of Antiquities and the Fine Arts in the Ministry of Public Instruction.

[2] *Elenco degli Edifizi Monumentali*, Roma, 1901.

The sections of the Act relating to excavations, articles
14–17, are clearly expressed, and as this is a matter which
partly concerns foreigners, they are of sufficient importance to
be translated verbatim.

'Art. 14.

'Whosoever desires to undertake excavations for the
'discovery of antiquities must make application to the
'Minister of Public Instruction, who is empowered to
'supervise them and to make notes and drawings.   He
'may also put off the commencement of the work—though
'not beyond three years—and may suspend it, whenever
'owing to numerous demands coming at the same time it is
'not possible to supervise at once all the excavations, or
'whenever the proper scientific methods for such excavations
'are not being observed.

'Foreign institutes or foreign citizens who, with the consent
'of the government, and under conditions to be from time to
'time laid down, undertake archaeological excavations, must
'hand over as a gift the objects found to one of the public
'collections of the kingdom.

'In all other cases the government has a right to the fourth
'part of the discoveries or the equivalent value.

'The details with regard to the exercise of this right will
be indicated in the regulations for carrying out the present
law.

'Art. 15.

'The manager of an excavation must give immediate
'notice of the discovery of any monument or object of art
'or antiquity. Anyone who makes a discovery by accident is
'bound by the same obligation.

'In both cases care must be taken for the safety of the
'monument that is brought to light, and this must be left
'untouched till it has been inspected by the competent
'authority. The government is bound to have it visited and
'examined as soon as possible.

'In the case of a discovery of monuments or objects of
'ancient art made in connection with any kind of excavation,

'the authorities may adopt any measures of safety and pre-
'caution that they may think necessary or useful for assuring
'the preservation of the remains and preventing their degra-
'dation or ruin.

'Art. 16.

'For public and scientific reasons the government may
'carry out excavations on ground which is not state property.
'The proprietor will have a right to compensation for any
'loss or injury that he may suffer through such excavations.

'The public utility of the work will be declared by decree
'of the Minister of Public Instruction after consultation with
'the Council of State.   The compensation, when it cannot be
'amicably settled, shall be determined according to the scale
'indicated in articles 65 and following of the law of June 25,
'1865, no. 2359, in so far as this is applicable.

'Of the objects discovered in the excavation, or of their
'money equivalent, a fourth part will belong to the proprietor
'of the ground and the remainder to the government.

'Art. 17.

'When remains or monuments are discovered of such
'importance that the public interest demands that they be
'preserved and public access rendered possible to them, the
'government shall be empowered definitely to expropriate the
'ground in which are the remains or the monuments, as well as
'that necessary to enlarge the excavation and construct a
'path of access.

'The declaration of the public utility of such expropriation,
'after taking the opinion of a competent commission, is made
'by Royal Decree on the proposal of the Minister of Public
'Instruction, after the procedure indicated in article 12 of the
'law of June 25, 1865, no. 2359.'

The later articles of the Act, nos. 25 to 35, deal with
penalties for the infringement of the prescriptions with which
we have been dealing.   These are fines from 50 to 10,000 Lire,
or £2 to £400.   Any offender who does not pay his fine can
be dealt with under the Penal Code, art. 19 (Act, 33).

It needs hardly to be said that the chief activity of the officials in charge of monument administration in Italy is not devoted to carrying into force the restrictive measures which have now been indicated. What chiefly occupies them is the supervision of the public museums and collections and the upkeep of the countless ancient buildings over which the state exercises ownership or control. The work is primarily that of needful repair, though artistic 'restoration' is often overdone in the Italy of to-day as it is in most other European countries. A report of what is accomplished year by year is issued by the Minister of Public Instruction under the title *L' Amministrazione delle Antichità e Belle Arti in Italia.* Taking the issue for 1901–2[1] we find that there are several sections in the report. First comes a notice, occupying 160 pages, of all the works of repair or restoration carried out on the artistic and historical monuments of the kingdom. The division is by regions and provinces. A couple of extracts may be taken almost at hazard. 'REGIONE III—VENETO. 'PROVINCIA DI VENEZIA. VENEZIA—*Ex-Scuola di San* '*Marco, ora Ospedale civile.*—Il magnifico soffitto di legno 'intagliato del quattrocento, nella sala di S. Marco, e in 'condizioni pessime, par le corrosioni dei tarli e i danni 'cagionati dal tempo. L' Ufficio regionale si e rivolto al 'Consiglio d' amministrazione per ottenerne le necessarie 'riparazioni. Ha trovato buone disposizioni, e intanto ha 'consigliato un experimento parziale col liquido disinfettante 'del Trois, gia adoperato con buon esito pel risanamento 'd' antichi legni intagliati[2].'

'REGIONE IX—SICILIA. PROVINCIA DI GIRGENTI. 'NARO — *Antico Duomo.* — L' Ufficio regionale ha fatto 'eseguire i lavori di assicurazione provvisoria alle fabbriche

---

[1] Roma, Tipografia Ceccini, 1902.

[2] '*Former School of San Marco, now Civic Hospital.* The splendid ceiling of 'inlaid wood of the fifteenth century in the saloon of St Mark is in a very bad 'condition through the ravages of worms and the injuries caused by time. The 'regional administration applied to the council of management for the purpose of 'securing the necessary repairs. It found every desire to do what was needed, 'and in the meantime has advised a partial experiment with a preservative liquid, 'that has been already used with good effect to arrest decay in inlaid woodwork.'

'dell' antico Duomo. La spesa relativa di L. 1519.73 venne 'sostenuta dal Ministero della Istruzione[1].'

The next section is headed *Scavi Archeologici*, and contains a record of all excavations and their results. Four pages are occupied with a summary of the year's work on the Roman Forum and Palatine. A report on museums and picture galleries follows, with lists of acquisitions. A section of forty pages is devoted to a record of measures proposed or taken or forbidden with regard to movable works of art in the possession of ecclesiastical or civil corporations. Sometimes a demand for permission to alienate a work of art is granted by the authorities, and at other times it is refused. Processes are set on foot against those who have alienated an artistic treasure without leave. The various Uffizi Regionali report on the restoration of works of art or on their removal, and occasionally record the discovery of some hitherto concealed treasure. Special commissions are appointed to go over collections with a view to the purchase of a portion by the state. This was done in 1901–2 in the case of the collection of Prince Chigi. Another commission considered the question of the reparation of the famous Tintorettos in the Scuola di San Rocco at Venice.

In another part the Giunta Superiore di Belle Arti reports on matters concerning modern art and artistic institutions, and the musical and dramatic arts occupy a closing section. The whole book of more than 300 pages forms an interesting record of various labours, the extent of which is a measure of the immensity of the artistic wealth of the country.

There remains to be given a brief notice of the measures in force to secure not so much the protection of ancient artistic monuments, as the proper laying out and ordering of cities and the general amenity of the streets.

Italy is in a very favourable position in these regards, and the authorities of her cities seem to have greater aedilician

---

[1] *'Ancient Cathedral.* The regional administration has caused to be executed 'the works needful to secure the immediate safety of the ancient cathedral. The 'expense involved, amounting to L. 1519.73 (£60), has been borne by the 'Minister of Public Instruction.'

power of an aesthetic kind than those of any other land. It does not of course follow that the most sagacious use is always made of these powers; what we are concerned with at the moment is the existence of these powers and their extent.

Those interested in Italian cities are familiar with the term 'piano regolatore'. This means a general scheme of civic improvement on a large scale to which all rearrangements of frontages and routes of communication, and all rebuildings, must conform. By the Expropriation Law of 1865, Art. 86, Communes with a population of at least 10,000 are authorized to draw up these plans 'on which shall be 'traced the lines which have to be observed in the recon- 'struction of the inhabited area'. Such plans are of course supervised by the central authorities, who give effect to objections which may be raised against them. After due consideration, the 'piano regolatore' will be approved by Royal Decree on the proposition of the Minister of Public Works acting after communication with the Council of State. The carrying of it out will then be a 'work of public utility', and in favour of it the process of expropriation may be resorted to. A limit of time, not greater than twenty five years, will be laid down within which the plan must be executed. Wherever it is in force all reconstructions must accord with it; 'the proprietors of lands and of the buildings upon them, 'if they desire to carry out new constructions or to rebuild or 'modify those that exist, whether by their own will or of 'necessity, must conform to the schemes traced on the plan' (Art. 89); and 'any works executed in contravention of the 'scheme shall be demolished, and the proprietor condemned 'to a fine up to L. 1000' (£40) (Art. 90)[1].

It needs hardly to be pointed out what a power for good this regulation places in the hands of municipal authorities, but all depends on the sagacity and good taste which have presided over the constitution of the plan. The 'piano regolatore' of Rome, to take one conspicuous example, has

---

[1] *Leggi sulle Espropriazioni per causa di Utilità Pubblica*, Roma, Stamperia Reale, 1890.

been criticized from the aesthetic point of view with great freedom and in the writer's opinion with a good deal of justice[1]. The long straight avenues, such as the Via Cavour which has dislocated the topography of the Esquiline, seem quite out of character with the natural configuration of the site of the Eternal City! On the other hand, if the scheme for the treatment of a city that is growing and becoming busier be a thoroughly well considered one, taking into account the proper balance of the new and of the old, and mindful of topography and history as well as of the exigencies of modern business, then the more comprehensive it is the better. The Italian communes, with their 'piani regolatori' providing for the civic improvements of a quarter of a century to come, are in a better position than British urban councils, whose efforts in these directions are too often tentative and accidental. 'There is often pointed out the immense advantage of working on a comprehensive scheme covering a large district, as against our usual piecemeal and hand-to-mouth proceedings. Sir William Emerson, president of the Royal Institute of British Architects, in 1901 even urged that " the whole question of the rebuilding of London ", in spite of its enormous difficulty and the huge expense it would involve, ought at once to be taken in hand[2].' There is in our system no doubt the compensating advantage that a mistaken policy, if only tried on a small scale, can be rectified in the future. In matters of this kind however, so important for the future well-being of our communities, there ought not to be vacillation and doubt. It should not be beyond the capacity of the most sagacious minds in modern societies to evolve principles permanently right on which all such schemes could be framed, and if these principles be followed the widest scheme will be the best.

Another Italian institution, great in its capacity for good when worked with judgement, is the 'regolamento edilizio' or

---

[1] See for example the lecture on the subject by M. Buls, referred to ante, p. 127.

[2] Quoted from a paper by the writer on 'Urban Legislation in the Interests of Amenity at Home and Abroad', in the *Journal of the Royal Institute of British Architects*, Third Series, vol. XII, p. 70.

code of building by-laws, which towns are authorized to draw up and enforce. If the expropriation law of 1865 be the foundation for the system of 'piani regolatori', the charter for the 'regolamenti edilizi' is the Communal and Provincial Law of May 4, 1898, no. 164, which authorizes Communal Councils to frame building by-laws with a view to preventing new buildings from injuring the appearance of city streets and places. Such local by-laws have of course to obtain the sanction of the central authorities, and are under the control of the Ministry of Public Works. The aesthetic powers granted are probably greater than exist anywhere else in civilized states. It is only in Germany, as we have seen (ante, p. 115 f.), that anything of the kind appears to exist, and in Germany the powers are mainly confined to the prevention of injury to the traditional appearance of the older parts of towns[1].

Local building regulations with provisions for aesthetic control exist in various Italian cities, but it will be sufficient to quote from those of Rome. The current Regulations for Civic Works (Regolamento Edilizio) of the Commune of Rome, dating from 1887, contain eleven chapters, of which the third is headed, 'Concerning existing buildings of an artistic and historical character,' and runs as follows :—

Art. 19. 'Existing buildings in the city and suburbs, 'possessed of a distinctive artistic and historical character 'which renders their complete preservation obligatory, shall 'be scheduled in a list appended to these regulations.

'This list shall be drawn up by the direction of the com-'munal authorities with the approval of the Commissions for 'Civic Works and for Archaeology, and of the Minister of 'Public Instruction, within the space of three months after 'the sanctioning of the present regulations.

Art. 20. 'It is absolutely forbidden to execute on any 'building thus scheduled any kind of work tending to modify

---

[1] The Italian municipal authority is not perhaps quite so anxious about this sort of preservation as his Teutonic brother, or he would not change the time-honoured names of his streets and places. The recent transformation of 'Via del Corso', the most famous street in the world, into 'Corso Umberto I' is a revelation of the way some modern Italians regard the sanctities of old association !

'the disposition of its parts or endanger in any degree its
'stability ; as for instance by addition to its height, by closing
'or opening apertures, altering cornices or other architectural
'members, painting over cut-stone ornaments, and the like.

'These provisions are applicable in equal measure to the
'external and to the internal elevations of the said buildings,
'with their courts and adjuncts, in all cases where the artistic
'and historical character above spoken of belongs also to the
'interiors of the structures.

Art. 21. 'Only in exceptional circumstances can the
'communal authority permit the execution of any work of
'the kind on the said buildings ; and in such a case only on
'the special report of the Commission for Civic Works and
'with the assent of the Minister of Public Instruction.'

The Commission for Civic Works (Commissione Edilizia)
is composed of twelve members elected by the Civic Council,
of whom six must be members of the Council, while the rest
may be chosen from outside ; the Syndic of Rome or his
deputy is convener. The Commission is consulted on new
building projects, and sanctions them when they are not
'contrary to the general demands of art and amenity, and to
'the provisions of the present regulations.' The regulations in
other sections give power to the municipal authorities to
order re-painting when buildings are coloured in such fashion
as to injure the aspect of the city, to forbid attic storeys
where aesthetic considerations are opposed to them, and
generally to control the artistic treatment of frontages.

The schedule (Elenco), designed to accompany the regulations, took some years to draw up, and was issued in 1896,
when its authors presented it to the Council with the wish
that it might help 'to preserve intact the artistic patrimony
which the centuries have handed down to our city'. The
monuments are divided into the following classes :—(1) Basi-
licas, Churches, Monastic Buildings, Hospitals and their
adjuncts ; (2) Palaces, Houses, Inns (these are in two classes
according to their greater or less importance); (3) Forts,
Towers, Bastions, Walls and Gates of the city ; (4) Open
Places, Monuments, Fountains, Obelisks, and the like.

CHAPTER IV.

GREAT BRITAIN AND IRELAND.

BIBLIOGRAPHY AND SOURCES OF INFORMATION.

Public General Acts:—The Ancient Monuments Protection Act, 1882,
45 & 46 Vict. ch. 73; The Ancient Monuments Protection (Ireland)
Act, 1892, 55 & 56 Vict. ch. 46; The Ancient Monuments Protection
Act, 1900, 63 & 64 Vict. ch. 34.

Local and Personal Acts:—Chester Improvement Act, 1884, 47 & 48 Vict.
ch. 239; London County Council, General Purposes Act, 1898,
61 & 62 Vict. ch. 221, § 60; Edinburgh Corporation Act, 1899,
62 & 63 Vict. ch. 71, §§ 45–48. Etc., etc.

Information kindly supplied by the Secretary to H.M. First Commissioner
of Works. Returns kindly communicated from the Office of Works,
Dublin. Reports and Papers issued by the London County Council,
and by other County Councils.

C. P. Kains-Jackson, *Our Ancient Monuments and the Land Around
Them*, with a preface by Sir John Lubbock, Bart., M.P. Lond. 1880.

David Murray, LL.D., F.S.A., *An Archaeological Survey of the United
Kingdom: The Preservation and Protection of our Ancient Monuments.* Glasgow, 1896.

Some portions of what follows have already appeared in *The Quarterly
Review* and *The Builder.* For permission to use this matter the
writer's best thanks are offered to the proprietors and editors of the
Review and of the Journal.

THE United Kingdom possesses Ancient Monument Acts,
but, except in Ireland, there is little direct participation by
the State in the work which these Acts are designed to further.
If we judged from the charges to the account of monuments
in our annual budgets, we should say that in Britain government did less for monuments than is done in any other
European country. The same however might be affirmed
about the higher education or about the Church. Government

contributes to these surprisingly little, yet it would be a mistake to conclude from this that Britons are indifferent either to learning or religion. The truth is that in the United Kingdom there are immense endowments, independent of government resources, which are charged with the upkeep of great educational establishments, like the Universities and Colleges of Oxford and Cambridge, as well as with the furtherance of religious agencies and undertakings of every kind. When these endowments fail, what is wanting is made up largely by the private munificence of individuals. Though this last source of revenue for public purposes may not flow quite so freely in Britain as in the United States, yet it serves to supply deficiencies which in other countries of Europe would be met by grants from government.

Let us take for example the case of the most important class of ancient monuments in France and in England, the mediaeval cathedrals. In the former country the cathedrals are state property and the upkeep of them and of the episcopal palaces accounted in the French budget of 1896 for nearly sixty thousand pounds.

In England the cathedrals and their adjuncts are independent of the state, and are administered out of the proceeds of endowments, from some of which the institutions have been benefiting for something like a thousand years. When there is some sudden or special demand, as for repairs or restoration, recourse is had to the freewill offerings of the faithful, and if government add a subsidy this comes rather as a private subscription than as a matter of official routine.

In France again the country churches belong for the most part to the Communes, and the French Monument Act of 1887 supplies machinery which enables the state first to schedule any such building as a historical monument, and then to take it under official protection. In England on the contrary the churches are held by curious tenures, partly private and partly ecclesiastical, which have a good deal of interesting history behind them, and neither the government nor any public administrative body of a secular kind has any responsibility for their upkeep, or any control over their

treatment[1]. In other words, across the Channel government
is officially charged with control, or authorized to exercise
such control if it desire, over practically all the ecclesiastical
monuments of the country, whereas in England the direct
concern of the state in this extensive and important class
of monuments has no effective existence. It must be repeated
however, that, as in the cases of learning and religion, so here
there is no reason to conclude from government inaction in
Britain that French cathedrals and other churches are better
cared for than our own. The point is that with ourselves the
sphere of government interference in the matter of monuments
is far less extended than among our neighbours across the
narrow sea, but the monuments themselves do not necessarily
suffer.

It would be interesting to institute a comparison from the
same point of view between Great Britain and other European
countries besides France, and to ascertain how far our own
specially national way of doing things, or letting things do
themselves, explains the anomaly of our public indifference
to matters which abroad are made the subject of elaborate
arrangements. Such a series of comparisons would however
lead us too much into detail, and it will be sufficient to point
out generally wherein our official machinery, judged by the
continental standard, is defective.

The class of monuments specially contemplated in this
book are ancient architectural monuments, and it is regard
to these that our own arrangements are most to seek. On
museums and galleries and public collections, at any rate in
England and Ireland, there is a large though by no means
excessive expenditure, and art on its educational side has
for a long series of years been fostered with considerable zeal,
though not always in the past with the highest wisdom. In
the case of one particular class of objects included under the
wide sense of the term 'monument' explained in the First
Part (ante, page 16 f.), the British government has set an
example to others. This is the class of Historical Manuscripts,

---

[1] Except of course in those cases where the Crown or a public body happens
to hold the patronage of the living.

on which there is a standing Commission appointed in 1869. The object of the Commission is 'to inquire what papers and manuscripts belonging to private families and institutions are extant which would be of utility in the illustration of history, constitutional law, science, and general literature', and in pursuance of this object the Commission has already examined more than five hundred public and private collections of unpublished documents. In a debate on the Ancient Monuments Protection Act, ultimately passed in 1882, attention was called by Mr Cochran Patrick to 'a remarkable contrast between the way in which we in this country treated our recorded history and our unrecorded history. He believed no country in the world had taken greater care of its written records, or done more to place them within the reach of every historical student; but while that was so, he believed that no country in Europe had done less to preserve the remains and relics of pre-historic ages, which were all the records we could have of a very considerable portion of the history of these Islands[1].' In going on now to show how little we do officially for ancient monuments in the narrower and more usual sense, it is well to remember that there are some departments in which this indifference is not shown.

For the supervision and upkeep of architectural monuments we have no State Commissions, no staff of Inspectors[2] nor Custodians, and (perhaps happily) no official restorers, the presence of whom or of some of whom in most other countries is signalized in these pages. The official inventory cannot be said to exist, and in this matter Great Britain is in an almost isolated position, as there are hardly any European countries that have not set on foot, and partly carried through, schemes of the kind. On the other hand there has been considerable and long-standing activity in Britain on the part of private societies and of individuals, of which some notice has been already given in the First Part, § 7. Ancient monuments and beautiful

---

[1] *Hansard's Debates*, CCLIX, 878.

[2] The late General Pitt Rivers held the post of Inspector of Ancient Monuments under the Act of 1882, presently to be noticed, but upon his death in 1900 no successor was appointed.

natural scenes and sites have found in John Ruskin and in William Morris defenders as eloquent and as able as Victor Hugo or Viollet-le-Duc, and though no one on this side of the Channel has shown all the indefatigable zeal and organizing ability of de Caumont, yet innumerable local antiquaries and officials of antiquarian societies have been actively at work on our loosely compacted British 'Denkmalpflege'.

The credit of initiating direct legislation on the subject in the British Parliament belongs to Sir John Lubbock, now Lord Avebury, and the history of his endeavours to secure the passing of the Act which bears his name is not a little instructive. The Bill was first introduced in the Commons in 1873, Mr Gladstone being then in power. It was read a second time, but as the government refused to promise any money it was withdrawn in Committee. In 1874 under the administration of Mr Disraeli it was again brought in, but, opposed by Mr Cavendish Bentinck as 'a measure of spoliation', it was thrown out on the second reading by a majority of fifty three. In 1875 it did better, and the second reading was voted by a majority of twenty two, though in the debate even 'Historicus', in the person of Sir William Harcourt, opposed it on the ground of its interference with the rights of property[1]. The Bill was withdrawn in Committee. It would be tedious to trace its further progress in detail, but in one of the final debates in 1882 Sir John Lubbock reported that the Bill had been read a first time on nine occasions, it had passed its second reading six times, been steered successfully through a select Committee and a Committee of the whole House, and had even been read a second time in the House of Lords though afterwards dropped for want of time.

In the course of these debates some illuminating items of information were vouchsafed to the House. The mover of the Bill, for example, stated that farmers had a penchant for carting away ancient tumuli, because the bones of the mighty dead which they contained rendered the earth specially good for manure. An eloquent plea for preservation in the interests of future scions of the English-speaking race at large was

[1] *Hansard's Debates*, CCXXIII, 900.

urged in 1875 by Mr Ferguson, some sentences from which were quoted in the First Part, ante, page 31. An instance of a peculiarly Hibernian form of 'Denkmalpflege' is too amusing to be omitted. A certain great Irish nobleman possessed the ruins of a very interesting historical castle, and wishing to preserve these from damage he directed his agent to have a wall built round the field in which they were situated. The agent provided him with a splendid wall, but employed in its construction all the stones of the ruined castle!

The reports of the various debates show that the argument as to interference with rights of property was the main, though not the only, one urged against the measure. Some professed friends of ancient monuments objected to the machinery proposed, or to the constitution or the limitation of the schedule of monuments affixed to the Bill, but the cry of 'spoliation' was continually making itself heard. It was pointed out that the same plea of interference with private rights had been urged against the appointment of the Historical Manuscripts Commission, though as a fact the Commission had had more voluntary applications from owners who wished their MSS examined than they were able to deal with. The opponents of the Act persisted however in regarding it as 'a distinct interference never before attempted with the rights or enjoyment of private property[1]', and before it could be passed the Bill had, on this side of it, to be essentially modified. The Bill, as introduced and fought through Parliament up to 1882, possessed a compulsory clause similar to, though less drastic than, the compulsory clauses of continental Monument Acts. If an owner wished to destroy an ancient monument on the schedule he would be bound under the Act, as drawn, to offer it for purchase at a valuation by the Treasury. As explained by Sir John Lubbock the principle of the Bill was that, after proper notice had been given, an owner of one of the monuments comprised in the Bill, who wished to destroy it, should, at least, give the country the option of purchasing it at a fair price[2].

---

[1] Mr Rodwell, *Hansard's Debates*, CCXXXII, 1550.
[2] ibid., CCXXXVII, 1988.

This provision it was apparently found impossible to carry through. In 1881 at any rate, when Mr Gladstone had returned to power, the author of the Act, instead of again moving it, carried in the House a resolution calling on the government to take the matter up officially, and the result finally was that in 1882 the Act, as modified, was introduced by the Lord Chancellor in the House of Lords and carried rapidly through, the same good fortune attending it in the Commons a fortnight later, so that it received the Royal Assent on August 18, 1882. The Lord Chancellor in introducing the measure expressly stated that the difference between this and the previous measures was, that in this there was no compulsory power of interference with any ancient monument[1], but it is noteworthy that the echo of the old cry still made itself heard. There was a protest in the House of Commons against 'the invasion of the rights of property which was to be carried out under the Bill in order to gratify the antiquarian tastes of the few at the public expense[2]', and in the Lords it was said that the Bill 'interfered very seriously with the rights of property[3]'. The speaker in the Commons was Mr Warton, in the House of Lords the late Marquis of Salisbury.

When we compare the ample machinery for the official and semi-official care of monuments on the Continent, with what has actually been done on similar lines in our own country, we are inclined to describe our own measures as only shy and tentative efforts at arrangements which across the Channel and the North Sea are well-equipped and in full working order. Some of the functions of the continental Minister in charge of the Fine Arts are fulfilled among ourselves by the First Commissioner of Works, and grateful recognition should be accorded to the services rendered to the cause by Ministers in this position. It is work however that is done in a measure *sub rosa*, and often only semi-officially. Of official measures the British Isles now possess the following:—
(1) The Ancient Monuments Protection Act, 1882, 45 & 46 Vict. ch. 73, of which the history has just been given; (2) The

---

[1] *Hansard's Debates*, CCLXXIII, 15.   [2] ibid., 1599.   [3] ibid., 15.

Ancient Monuments Protection (Ireland) Act, 1892, 55 & 56 Vict. ch. 46; (3) The Ancient Monuments Protection Act, 1900, 63 & 64 Vict. ch. 34; (4) One or two provisions in Municipal Acts applying to special towns or districts. The Act of 1882 was based on a schedule of ancient monuments of outstanding importance drawn up by societies or committees of archaeologists in the three kingdoms. This embraced sixty eight monuments or groups of monuments[1] in Great Britain and Ireland, all but about half-a-dozen of which belong to the class generally termed pre-historic. The main provision of the short Act itself was to the effect that the owner of any ancient monument to which the Act applied, might constitute the Commissioners of Works guardians of such monument, and that in such case the Commissioners should be thenceforward responsible for its upkeep, and for the purpose should have reasonable rights of access to it. The cost was to be defrayed 'from moneys to be provided by Parliament'. The Commissioners were, on their side, empowered to prevent any injury being done to the monument, even by the owner thereof. By the third clause the Commissioners, with the consent of the Treasury, were empowered to purchase out of money voted by Parliament any ancient monument to which the Act applied. The purchase was to be arranged in accordance with the Land Clauses Consolidation Acts[2], but the compulsory clauses of these Acts were not to apply. Any purchase therefore must be by agreement. It was further provided that other ancient monuments not in the original schedule might, at the request of their owners, be taken over in similar fashion into guardianship. Up to the present date twenty four of the original sixty eight monuments have been placed under the Commissioners of Works, and eighteen fresh ones not in the original schedule have been added, all in England and

---

[1] Monuments like Stonehenge and other cromlechs, consisting in a number of similar objects closely connected, figure in each case as one monument on the list. The three tumuli at Newgrange, Dowth, and Knowth, by the Boyne in Ireland, are also reckoned together as one, so that the small figure arrived at by counting the entries hardly gives a fair idea of the whole number of protected monuments.

[2] 8 & 9 Vict. ch. 18 (1845), and Amendment Acts thereto of 1860 and 1869.

Scotland, so that there are now in all forty one in Great Britain under the protection of the law. So far as any expenditure is concerned, these Acts have in Britain become almost a dead letter, while since the death in 1900 of the Inspector of Ancient Monuments, General Pitt Rivers, no successor has been appointed to the post.

The case of Ireland has to be dealt with separately from that of Great Britain, though the Act of 1882 applied as much to Ireland as to any other part of the British Isles. As is usual with that much persecuted country, distressful Erin has had far better and more liberal treatment in the matter of monuments than the sister kingdoms. When the Irish Church Act of 1869 was passed[1], many churches had fallen out of use that were at the same time worthy of preservation on artistic or historical grounds. The care of these was accordingly placed in the hands of the Commissioners of Public Works in Ireland, to be preserved as national monuments, and fifty thousand pounds was set apart for their maintenance. At the time of the passing of the Ancient Monuments Act of 1882, a hundred and thirty four old Irish ecclesiastical buildings were in charge of these Commissioners, and under the Act of 1882 they received the guardianship of seven monuments of the pre-historic class. In 1892 a special Act was passed for Ireland, extending the operations of the Act of 1882 to any ancient or mediaeval structure or monument with respect to which the Commissioners of Works are of opinion that its preservation is a matter of public interest by reason of the historic, traditional, or artistic interest attaching thereto. This can only however be done at the request of the owner of the monument. Under this Act of 1892 forty eight monuments, chiefly abbey ruins, ancient churches, round towers, and the like, have been added to the list, so that the whole number under the guardianship of the Board of Public Works in Ireland at the close of the year 1904 amounted to one hundred and eighty nine[2]. There is available for their maintenance a

---

[1] 32 & 33 Vict. ch. 42. See clause 25.

[2] From a return kindly furnished by the Board of Works, Dublin, October 1904.

yearly sum of about a thousand pounds, which contrasts markedly with the niggard supplies which is all the monuments in Britain obtain from public sources.

The English official intelligence, toiling after the nimble Irish wit, achieved in 1900 'An Act to amend the Ancient Monuments Protection Act, 1882', by which the provisions of the Irish Act of 1892 were applied to England and Scotland, but in an amplified form, in accordance with which County Councils have the same powers that were conferred in Ireland in 1882 and 1892 on the Commissioners of Works. This provision is of the utmost importance as introducing the German and Italian system of local organization in place of the centralization of the former Acts. There is another clause to the effect that Commissioners of Works or County Councils may receive voluntary contributions toward the upkeep of any monument under their charge, and enter into agreements with an owner 'or with any other person' 'as to such maintenance and preservation and the cost thereof'. This again is a most promising provision, as it brings official authorities into touch with private societies, such, for example, as the National Trust for Places of Historic Interest and Natural Beauty, as well as with individuals who may take special personal or local interest in some monument or group. This common action of official and private agencies is of the utmost importance for a satisfactory treatment of the monument question, and the want of this in the over-centralized France is specially commented on by Dr Clemen in his work on the subject. A provision for the public access to monuments, of which Commissioners or Councils are guardians under the Act, forms a useful adjunct, as there is no such provision in the original Act of 1882. Such access is however still subject to the good pleasure of the owner.

Under the law of 1900 no action has been taken from the side of the Commissioners of Works, but there is a prospect of some activity among local authorities. As regards London, in the *Report* of the London County Council for 1903–4 it is recognized that 'under the Ancient Monuments Protection Acts, 1882 and 1900, the Council is the authority for preserving any structure, erection, or monument of historical or architectural interest, or any remains of such, in London or any adjacent county', and the *Report* gives some account of its exercise of these powers through its Historical Records and Buildings Committee. The most encouraging feature in this procedure is the fact that, already in 1898, before the passing of the public Act of 1900, the London County Council had obtained the insertion of a clause in its General Powers Act of that year, enabling it to purchase by agreement buildings and places of historical or architectural interest, and to undertake their maintenance, and in April, 1900, the Council purchased for a considerable sum a certain ancient house in Fleet Street, for the purpose of preserving it as a historical monument, while utilizing it at the same time for modern ends[1].

Another function with regard to ancient monuments, which foreign states acknowledge as a duty but to which British governments have not yet, save in the case of MSS., set their hand, has also been undertaken by the London

---

[1] The following is an extract from the London County Council's *Report* for 1903–4: 'Under the powers conferred by its General Powers Act, 1898, the Council on 3rd April, 1900, upon the recommendation of the General Purposes Committee, decided to purchase the freehold of No. 17, Fleet-street, at a total cost of £20,300. This house, which was built in the reign of James I., about the year 1610, for Henry, Prince of Wales, as an office of the Duchy of Cornwall, is an almost unique specimen of the architecture of the period, and contains a remarkably fine ceiling and some good carving. The house is to be partially rebuilt, at an estimated cost of £7,000, and the work connected with the back portion of the house has been completed. The ground floor is to be set back for the purpose of widening the street, while the front room on the first floor, which contains the ceiling alluded to, and which was originally the Council Chamber, will be retained in its present position on cantilevers and opened to the public. The present face of the building, which there is reason to suppose is merely a false screen, is to be removed, and the original front, which is some 20 inches behind the existing front, will thus be exposed to view. These works, however, have had to be deferred for the present pending the completion of an agreement between the Council, the City of London Corporation, and the Society of the Inner Temple, with respect to the land to be thrown into the public way. The City of London Corporation has contributed £2,500 towards the cost of this memorial.' It should be added that the action of the Council in connection with this house has not passed without criticism, and the intrinsic value of the building, as well as the policy of its purchase have been called in question by some of the members.

County Council, and this is the preparation of an inventory or register. The initiative thus shown deserves to be specially signalized, as the inventory is a necessary first step in any procedure designed for preservation, and it is greatly to be hoped that the partial measures set on foot in the metropolis may be followed by a state scheme of inventorization covering the country at large. The importance of the subject justifies the inclusion here of an extract from the Preface to the first published volume of the London register, in which Mr Lawrence Gomme, now Clerk to the Council and formerly its statistical officer, narrates the initial steps taken in the work.

'In 1896, 21st January, on the motion of Sir John Lubbock (now Lord Avebury), the Council resolved—" That the following addition be made to the order of reference of the General Purposes Committee—' To consider and report in the case of the contemplated destruction of any building of historic or architectural interest, what course of action the Council should adopt.'"...The Committee took active steps to carry out the Council's wish, and on the 23rd February, 1897, reported to the Council what they had done with a view to giving effect to the above-mentioned resolution. In the first place the Committee deemed it essential that a list, as complete as possible, should be obtained of all buildings of historic or architectural interest in London, and they appointed a sub-committee to deal with the matter. With a view to obtaining the necessary particulars for such a list, a communication was addressed to certain societies, several of which expressed their willingness to assist the Council. Subsequently it was decided that the best means of arriving at a satisfactory and expeditious mode of procedure would be to hold a conference with the various societies who had been asked kindly to assist the Council in the matter, and accordingly a conference took place at the County Hall on 4th December, 1897. Representatives from the following societies attended, viz.—Architectural Association ; British Archaeological Association ; City Church Preservation Society ; Committee for the Survey of the

Memorials of Greater London; Kent Archaeological Society; Kyrle Society; London and Middlesex Archaeological Society; London Topographical Society; National Trust for Places of Historic Interest and Natural Beauty; Royal Archaeological Institute; Royal Institute of British Architects; Society of Antiquaries; Society of Arts; Society for the Protection of Ancient Buildings; and Surveyors' Institution.

'In the course of an interesting discussion, during which the representatives of the various societies expressed their gratification at the Council taking action in the matter, and the hope that the interest shown by the Council would stimulate greater public interest in ancient buildings, Sir Robert Hunter, representing the National Trust for Places of Historic Interest and Natural Beauty, stated that the members of different societies were all of opinion that some register or list of buildings, interesting by virtue of their antiquity or architectural beauty and associations, should be compiled. In support of this it was contended that at the present time there was considerable ignorance as to what London possessed in the way of buildings of interest, and that frequently it was only realised that a building was of historic interest when that building was in danger of being removed. The Trinity Almshouses were cited as an instance. A list or register would, it was thought, remove in a great measure the risk of losing such buildings. The Committee for the Survey of the Memorials of Greater London having already commenced to prepare such a register, it was thought that a good purpose would be served if that committee were to continue its work in connection with the preparation of the register. In the end the conference passed a series of resolutions...

'The General Purposes Committee of the Council afterwards considered these resolutions, and resolved that they should be adopted, and taken up to the Council.

'The Committee thereupon made known to the Council that the Committee for the Survey of the Memorials of Greater London had already taken steps to compile a register of historic buildings in London, had collected a considerable amount of material, and had generously offered to hand over to the Council the result of its labours, so far as they related to London, if the Council would print the register. On the 27th July, 1897, the Council resolved to print the register, and voted the necessary sums for the purpose.'

The result of this action has been the publication of a volume in quarto, fully illustrated, edited by Mr C. R. Ashbee from materials collected by members of the Committee for the Survey of the Memorials of Greater London, and printed for the London County Council[1]. The editor contributed an instructive Introduction of thirty pages, dealing with questions of preservation as well as of inventorization, and the book runs to fifty pages of print and thirty six of plates. It only however embraces one parish, that of Bromley-by-Bow, out of the four hundred included in Greater London. Hence it is pretty obvious that the whole Survey could hardly be carried out in this form, and as a fact the work is not at the moment advancing, but will probably be carried forward on a somewhat less ample scale. It may be noted that the inventory of the old houses at Lyons mentioned ante, p. 59, is comprised in about sixty pages.

The London County Council has also taken over from the Society of Arts the work of indicating houses in London associated with historical events or distinguished individuals, and within the last couple of years more than a score of fresh tablets have been thus affixed. When a tablet has been erected, it is the Council's practice to have a short account of the house written, and when enough material of the kind has been brought together to publish it in the form of a small booklet. Three of these booklets, entitled *Indication of Houses of Historical Interest in London*, have been issued[2], at the democratic price of one penny each. Furthermore, on the occasion of the opening of any Park or Garden, or the inauguration of any of the numerous public works carried out by the Council, a well printed pamphlet has been

---

[1] *The Survey of London*, etc., Lond., P. S. King & Son, Great Smith Street, Westminster, 1900.

[2] Lond., P. S. King & Son.

prepared, illustrated with plans, reproductions of old maps, etc., and giving besides the information needed at the moment an excellent historical account of the particular locality and its associations. Thus, the opening of the new southern approach to the Tower Bridge in 1902 was the occasion for the drawing up of Historical Notes, containing a valuable disquisition on the antiquities of the district traversed by the new thoroughfare, and beginning with the true and suggestive remark that ' there are no thoroughfares in England, and but few in other countries, which can lay claim to so many and so varied historical associations as the Old Kent Road.' The opening of the Garden of Nelson Square, Southwark, in February 1904, was not allowed to pass without a résumé of the history of the locality from the twelfth century downwards.

All this part of the work of the London County Council, not unconnected with the fact that it possesses in its Clerk a scholar and antiquary of high repute, is on the lines of the broadest and most intelligent policy in the general matter of monument administration. When such things are done abroad, in Paris or Brussels or Vienna, they are quoted against us as putting to shame our own insular utilitarianism. To do them ourselves seems un-British, almost unseemly, and many will hardly believe that this care for the historical associations that cling about even the drearier London streets, this note of idealism struck in the midst of the steady grind of the wheels of civic business, are real facts of the metropolis of to-day !

That County Councils in general will in time take advantage to a fitting extent of the powers conferred on them by the Act of 1900 may be confidently predicted. The example of Northamptonshire may be quoted. The Council of this county had before the passing of the Act taken some steps in the interest of the Queen Eleanor Cross just outside the town, and had been informed, in an official letter, in which anxiety to escape responsibility for a national monument seems the uppermost feeling, that neither the Crown nor the Office of Works had any rights over the structure. No one in fact seemed to own the monument, and the County Council, 'omnium consensu capax imperii', assumed charge of it, and now hold it under the Act of 1900 against all comers, including the iconoclastic youth of the neighbourhood who used to throw stones at the figures.   The Ancient Monuments and County Records Committee of the Council are also taking an interest in the historical bridges of the county and have issued a circular to all Urban and Rural district Councils in the county, calling attention to the Act of 1900 and commending to their care the historical monuments of their districts.

Much may be looked for in the future from the intelligent action of County Councils in the matter of the preservation of their ancient monuments.   The publication of the magnificent *Victoria History of the Counties of England*[1] should give a great impetus to this part of their work.

With respect to official action taken by British towns for the protection of their monuments of artistic and historical interest and of city amenity in general, the cases of Chester and Edinburgh may be briefly referred to.   By the Chester Improvement Act of 1884 the city walls are to some extent protected by a provision that no new structures are to be allowed to come within six feet of them save with consent of the Corporation.   The Town Council of Edinburgh in 1899 obtained from Parliament certain powers for the control of sites upon which advertisements might be posted, and in 1904 a report was issued on the subject of the working of these powers that contains instructive reading.   'These powers had long been felt to be necessary to check the growing evil which was threatening to destroy the amenity of the city. The evil was felt in other places, but Edinburgh was peculiarly vulnerable in its amenity at many points.   The very attractions which it possesses as a resort for visitors from all parts of the world, and as a place of residence, lend themselves

---

[1] Published by Archibald Constable, London.   The work is planned on a gigantic scale and will devote four to six and more quarto volumes to each county, so that a total of more than 150 volumes in all is contemplated.   In most foreign countries such an undertaking would receive a government subsidy.

in a peculiar way to the devices of the advertising agent, which seem to be successful in the degree in which they outrage the sensibilities of the inhabitants. A systematic and deliberate attempt, it was believed, was then being made to exploit the City on a large scale, and sacrifice its amenity and interests for the benefit of outside parties, who cared nothing for the local injury they might inflict. The parties who thus offended were generally companies whose head-quarters were in London or elsewhere, and who merely used Edinburgh as an advertising station. The citizens called for protection, and the proposed clauses showed the best method which occurred to the Corporation for giving this protection. The application to Parliament was opposed by the powerful advertising syndicates whose offices were in Liverpool, London, Glasgow, Manchester, etc. As they said in their Petition, they had a "distinct and separate interest" from the general "body of ratepayers of the City of Edinburgh". The question at issue was this :—whether Parliament would allow the City, against the wishes of its ratepayers and rulers, to be exploited, and its most cherished features destroyed, for the pecuniary advantage of persons whose interests might be inimical to those of the citizens.'

The result of the powers gained from Parliament to oppose these alien foes has been wholly satisfactory. Further details as to municipal and other action in relation to advertisements are given in the publication of the Society for Checking the Abuses of Public Advertising (Scapa)[1], published in 1903, and entitled *A Beautiful World.*

The question of aesthetic control over new buildings in private hands has for some time past formed a frequent subject of discussion in British architectural and artistic circles. Special servitudes apart, no such control can in a legal sense be exercised by any British municipal or public body, but it should be pointed out that Britain is in this respect no worse off than most European countries. Indeed with the exception of what we find in Italy (ante, p. 146 f.) and Germany (ante,

---

[1] 1 Camp View, The Common, Wimbledon, London, is the address of the honorary secretary, Richardson Evans, Esq.

p. 115 f.) aedilician powers of an aesthetic kind can hardly be said to exist. This applies even to France, where as we have seen (ante, p. 93 f.) the only safeguards are moral methods of suasion and the relatively high standard of taste among the members of the public. It is however an open question whether certain powers of aesthetic control over new architectural ventures should not be given, under proper conditions, to urban authorities. Successive Presidents of the Royal Institute of British Architects, and representatives of other artistic bodies, have expressed a keen desire to see something of the kind established, and a First Commissioner of Works has publicly given utterance to sentiments not unfavourable to such a scheme[1]. It is understood that a Memorial to Government is in preparation urging the importance of the subject.

[1] *Journal R. I. B. A.* Third series, vol. XI, p. 11. See also the paper in the *Journal* referred to in the footnote, ante, p. 145.

CHAPTER V.

THE AUSTRIAN EMPIRE.

BIBLIOGRAPHY AND SOURCES OF INFORMATION.

Von Wussow, II, 292 f. (cf. I, 192 f.), prints the Regulations for the work of the Central Commission, and the Hungarian Monument Act of 1881.

Die Denkmalpflege (Zeitschrift) and the Reports of the German Monument Congresses (*Tag für Denkmalpflege*) give more recent information and documents.

The writer thanks Dr Karl Kobald, of the Central Commission, for information conveyed to him in a letter kindly written at the instigation of Ober-Baurath Theodor Hödl of Vienna, to whom he had applied for recent facts about monument administration in the Empire.

ONLY one portion of the Austrian Empire possesses at present an Ancient Monuments Act. This is the Kingdom of Hungary which has an Act dating from the year 1881. For the empire as a whole a draft of a law was prepared some ten years ago but was withdrawn. Again in 1902 a proposal for a law was submitted to the Austrian House of Peers by the President of the Central Commission, and this is still under consideration. The draft specially contemplates architectural monuments, and the first paragraph lays it down that 'Architectural monuments, that is public buildings whether of a religious or secular character and interest, in whosesoever possession they may happen to be, are under the protection of the law.' In the case of purely private buildings, the law is to have no hold on them (§ 7) unless the owner places the monument under its protection.

This special interest in architectural monuments agrees
with the tenor of the Hungarian law of 1881 as well as with
the operations of the Austrian government generally in regard
to these matters. The Hungarian law (printed by von
Wussow, II, 296) is concerned with monuments of art (Kunst-
denkmale) which it defines (Abschnitt I. § 1) rather vaguely as
'every building under or upon the surface of the soil with its
'appurtenances, which possesses the value of a historical or
'artistic monument'. In the case of existing structures, or
those that have newly come to light through excavations, the
Minister of Religion and Education has to decide whether
they are to be kept up as monuments of art. A structure
declared to be of this character may belong (*a*) to a private
proprietor, or (*b*) to a municipality, a commune, or a recognized
religious body. In each case the owner is bound to keep the
monument in repair at his or their own cost (Abschn. I. § 4,
'der Eigenthümer ist verpflichtet, das Denkmal, dessen
'Erhaltung angeordnet worden ist, auf seine eigenen Kosten
'zu erhalten'), and no work is allowed upon it without leave of
the Minister. When these conditions are not, or cannot be,
fulfilled, then the Minister may proceed to effect the compulsory purchase of the monument.

The procedure of expropriation can also be put in force in
cases when excavations on private land seem in the interests
of science to be advisable, and when the proprietor is not
prepared to carry these out (§ 9). It is a special feature of
the Hungarian law that for the above purpose a temporary
expropriation is contemplated, the land passing out of its
owner's control for so long as may be necessary to carry out
the excavations. (Abschn. II. § 11.)

Offences against the law are punished by fines. (Abschn.
III.)

The Minister is assisted by a Council on Monuments
consisting of professional and lay members. (Abschn. IV.)

The general policy of the Imperial Government is also at
present directed rather towards architectural monuments than
movable objects of historical and artistic interest. Certain
earlier measures dating from the end of the eighteenth and

first half of the nineteenth century had for their object the
acquisition for the imperial collections of coins and other
relics of antiquity discovered within the limits of the empire,
and an imperial edict of 1818 forbade the export from those
limits of any objects of artistic or historical interest the loss
of which would be seriously felt. Such objects might however
be freely transferred from one of the crown-lands to another.
In 1850 the care of monuments in Austria entered on a new
phase.   There was then founded by imperial decree the
' Central-Commission zur Erforschung und Erhaltung der
Kunst- und historischen Denkmale ' which is still in active
operation.   Although, as noticed above, there is as yet no
Monument Act for the whole empire, the government has for
fifty years past been fruitfully active in the care of monuments,
and this is enough to show that the interest felt by different
countries in this subject is not to be measured by the formal
Acts passed by their legislatures.

The Central Commission received what is substantially its
present form from a rescript of the Minister of Religion and
Education in 1873, but certain alterations were made in 1899.
Its object is declared to be to excite the interest of the public
in the study and maintenance of monuments and to assist
the efforts in this direction of learned societies and of experts,
so that the different races of the empire may take pride in
preserving the memorials of their past[1].   There are three
departments of its activity, one embracing objects of pre-
historic and of classical antiquity ; a second, artistic monuments of the mediaeval and later periods down to the end of
the eighteenth century (in 1899 the scope of its labours was
extended to embrace the first half of the nineteenth); and a
third, historical monuments especially in the form of archives
and other documents bearing on the history of the arts.   The
Commission consisted at first of a president and twelve or
fifteen members, but the number of the latter was in 1899
increased to twenty.   They are chosen for five years from the
ranks of known experts in art, archaeology, or history, and the

[1] Von Wussow, I, 195.   *Die Denkmalpflege*, 1900, p. 64, gives more recent
details from official sources.

service is an honorary one. To aid them in their work there
is a body of Conservators also appointed for five years, and
serving without salary though receiving their expenses. Since
1899 their number has been increased to 146, while 348
'Correspondents'—individuals known for their knowledge of
and interest in monuments—are distributed about the provinces. These 'Conservators' are the eyes and hands of the
Commission. They work according to districts, of which
there are now 167, covering all the lands of the empire, and
it is their duty to keep in touch with local societies and individuals and to influence public opinion everywhere in favour
of the safeguarding of the memorials of the past. They have
to form inventories of the treasures falling under the three
departments above referred to, in so far as these belong to
the districts under their charge; to secure for the imperial
museums movable objects especially of classical antiquity
that from time to time come to light, and to deal in the best
manner possible with all questions of the restoration and
upkeep of architectural monuments. On these matters they
have to report to the Commission and receive from it their
instructions. One of their duties is to report upon projects
for new railways, roads, and other public works, in view of any
injury that these may threaten to ancient monuments.

It is important to note that there is no compulsion
attempted to be exercised on private owners of monuments.
The Conservators are charged to deal with these by way of
persuasion and management so as to secure as far as possible
that these monuments shall be as well treated as those
actually the property of the state. The right of expropriation
on artistic or antiquarian grounds is not reserved, but this
may be granted in the forthcoming Monument Act for the
empire, the draft of which has been long under consideration.
For ordinary purposes the Commission has a fixed income
but for any special demand an appeal may be made to the
Minister. In the case of one monument—the most important
in the whole empire—the palace of Diocletian at Spalatro
in Dalmatia, there is a project for special legislation, and in
the spring of 1903 a committee of experts spent fourteen

days in examining the building and drawing up a special report on its condition.

The Central Commission issues as its main publication the well-known and valuable *Mittheilungen*, and besides this has published yearly reports on its operations. The lists of monuments on which the Conservators have been engaged are intended to be published in the form of a 'Kunsttopographie' covering the whole extent of the empire.

A recent development of the activity of the Ministry of Religion and Education in the Care of Monuments, is its extension into the field of natural scenes and objects. In view of the project of a law for the protection of these, a request was made a year or so ago to the philosophical faculty of the University of Vienna for a report on the subject. The result has been a communication pointing out the value of certain natural scenes and objects from the five points of view (1) of natural history, (2) of mineralogy, (3) of physiography, (4) of sociology and history, (5) of aesthetics.

In Austria neither the central government nor the self-governing municipalities have any official control over the construction of new buildings from an aesthetic and artistic point of view. The same applies to alterations on and demolitions of old structures in private or corporate possession. Hence the protection of the older features of the towns of the empire is a matter more of private than strictly official concern. The newly founded society for Vienna and Lower Austria has been mentioned above, ante, p. 39. Vienna itself demands very careful treatment, if there is to be preserved that pleasant blending of new and old in which so much of the city's charm consists. There still remain in the inner city, east of the Kärntner Strasse, near the Post Office, and elsewhere, excellent examples of seventeenth century domestic architecture which it will be most important to preserve, and the proceedings of the protective society will be watched with interest by all lovers of the noble capital.

Prague, the capital of Bohemia, one of the finest cities in Europe, has also its local society, and demands all the attention that can be given to its amenity. It possesses, mostly in the main city but to some extent also in the Klein-Seite across the river, mediaeval relics of great picturesqueness and beauty, as well as a fine display of Renaissance palaces and mansions mostly in the neighbourhood of the Royal Schloss. There is considerable danger lest the desire of a section of the population for broad straight streets, like some of the newer thoroughfares, may lead to disastrous clearances in the business centres round the market place, where old streets and houses still preserve to the city its ancient character. Prague needs as much as Edinburgh does the application of some of those salutary civic regulations applicable to the older towns of Germany.

CHAPTER VI.

BELGIUM, HOLLAND, AND SWITZERLAND.

BIBLIOGRAPHY AND SOURCES OF INFORMATION.

BELGIUM.

Royaume de Belgique. Commission Royale des Monuments. *Arrêtés Royaux*, du 7 Janvier 1835, instituant la Commission Royale des Monuments, etc. *Règlement d'ordre des Travaux de la Commission*, Bruxelles, 1898.

Bulletin des Commissions Royales d'Art et d'Archéologie. Yearly Reports, Hayez, Bruxelles.

Communications from M. Charles Buls, ex-burgomaster of Brussels, and from M. A. Massaux, secretary of the Royal Commission.

HOLLAND.

Reports (Eerste, Tweede, Jaarverslag) of the Royal Commission (Rijkscommissie) appointed in 1903 to draw up an inventory of the artistic wealth of the kingdom.

Letter on the Care of Ancient Monuments in Holland, kindly sent by Dr Jan Kalf, secretary to the above Commission.

SWITZERLAND.

Arrêté Fédéral du 30 Juin 1886, concernant la participation de la Confédération à la conservation et à l'acquisition d'antiquités nationales (in *Die Schweizerische Bundesgesetzgebung*, Basel, 1889 f. I. 868).

Loi du 10 Septembre 1898, sur la Conservation des Monuments et des Objets d'Art ayant un intérêt historique ou artistique (for Canton de Vaud). Lausanne, 1898.

Règlement du 21 Avril 1899, pour l'exécution de la loi du 10 Septembre 1898. Lausanne, 1899.

The writer owes the communication of some of these documents to the kindness of M. André Mercier, of the Faculty of Law, Lausanne.

The Monument Act of the Canton of Bern passed in 1902 is given in *Dritter Tag für Denkmalpflege*, Carlsruhe, 1902, p 158.

BELGIUM, Holland, and Switzerland have been grouped together as comparatively small countries, that possess great national treasures in ancient monuments, and from the culture and enlightenment of their citizens may be expected to treat them with all possible piety and judgement. In Belgium the Care of Monuments has had a long history, and in the present day there is most praiseworthy activity both on the part of official agencies and of private bodies and persons. In certain departments of civic administration concerned with ancient buildings Brussels has set a good example, which other towns that combine like her the new and the old would do well to follow. Holland took an important move as recently as 1903 by the appointment of its Royal Monument Commission. In Switzerland there is both Federal and-Cantonal legislation in favour of preservation. In all three countries the important matter of the preparation of inventories of artistic treasures has been provided for by official regulations.

BELGIUM.

Belgium possesses no Monument Act, but the artistic treasures in which it is so exceptionally rich receive due attention both from the side of the state and from that of societies and individuals. Von Wussow prints a royal decree of 1825 on the subject of the churches of the country and their contents, forbidding any reconstructions or alterations of their fabrics without royal consent, and providing that no objects of artistic or historical interest in the churches should be alienated except by leave of the state authorities. In 1835 there was established a 'Commission Royale des Monuments' with functions somewhat similar to those entrusted to the 'Central-Commission zur Erforschung und Erhaltung der Kunst- und historischen Denkmale' of the Austrian Empire. The aim of the Belgian Commission was to secure the maintenance of national monuments that are of importance through their age, their historical associations, or their artistic character; and the method of working, through a small central committee and a large number of local correspondents, is similar to the Austrian. The preparation of an inventory of the artistic treasures of the country was enjoined on the Commission by a Royal decree of 1861. On this the secretary to the Commission, M. Massaux, kindly wrote in September 1904, 'l'inventaire des objets d'art appartenant aux édifices publics du pays n'est pas terminé. On s'en occupe activement, mais il faudra encore beaucoup de temps pour le mener à bonne fin.' The yearly *Bulletin* of the Royal Commission gives a review of the operations it carries on. These consist in considerable measure in works of restoration, which give rise at times to the controversies with which this subject is rife. The Société Nationale pour la Protection des Sites et des Monuments en Belgique breaks a lance from time to time with the official body. See for example the *Bulletin* for 1903.

The last few years have witnessed in Belgium a great revival of public interest in city aesthetics. 1894 saw the establishment of a society entitled 'L'Œuvre Nationale Belge' or 'L'Œuvre Nationale de l'Art Appliqué à la Rue', the main object of which was to improve the artistic character of new work both in buildings and in details such as electric light standards, shop signs, and the like, but its influence extends also to the preservation of excellent work handed down from the past.

The Belgian towns, especially Brussels, have furnished useful object-lessons in connection with the care of monuments. The Grand' Place in the capital is in great part surrounded by old Gild-houses of much picturesque beauty. One of these, called the Maison de l'Étoile, was pulled down in order to enlarge a street running toward the station. The effect was 'like that of the loss of a front tooth from a fine set', and M. Charles Buls, who as burgomaster has done much in this connection for the town, had the house rebuilt with arcades on the ground storey to facilitate circulation. Under the same administration an arrangement was made by the town with the proprietors of all the other fine houses round the Place, by which their preservation was secured. 'La ville s'engageait à restaurer et à entretenir les maisons à charge par le propriétaire de laisser gréver sa maison d'une servitude de maintien intégral. Aujourd'hui la conservation de ces anciennes maisons de gildes est absolument assurée à perpétuité[1].' This is a signal example of success obtained without the pressure of the law by tactful action on individuals. Neither the Belgian state nor the communes or towns have any legal power to prevent a private proprietor of a historical or artistic monument from demolishing or spoiling it, but it is open to them to set on foot the process of expropriation on grounds of public utility. The threat of this will often bring a recalcitrant proprietor to his senses. The state has acquired by this process of compulsory purchase the Abbeys of Villers and of Aulnes; the town of Ghent the Château des Comtes; the town of Brussels the house called that of the Cheval Marin. Free purchase is also resorted to, and a fine house which comes into the market may be acquired by the town and employed for some civic purpose.

HOLLAND.

Holland is, like her neighbour kingdom Belgium, destitute of any formal Monument Act, and no control of an aesthetic kind is exercised by government or municipalities over the designs for new buildings. The country is however by no means indifferent to the historical and artistic treasures with which it is so bountifully endowed. Within the last few years numerous archaeological and historical societies have been formed in the different towns, and it is part of their business to make an inventory of ancient monuments within their district, and to use every means of persuasion to secure their safe preservation. These local societies are united in a federation, the Nederlandsche Oudheidkundige Bond[2], which has several times been successful in calling in the aid of government in the interests of monuments. Every year the burgomasters in the various towns are called on to furnish to the Minister of the Interior a report on any projected alteration, restoration, or demolition of buildings of historical or artistic interest. When these are in the possession of municipalities or of religious bodies the state will assist by

---

[1] From a letter to the writer from M. Ch. Buls.
[2] Secretary, M. J. C. Overvoorde, Leiden.

contributions augmenting local funds. When the owner of the monument is a private person and there is danger of its injury or destruction, government tries to prevent this by offering to pay wholly or in part the expenses of restoration, or in urgent cases it will purchase the building. This only occurs when some suitable public use can be found for the structure.

The state expends on the Care of Monuments some considerable sums, and there is a special department at the Ministry of the Interior in charge of this work. The Roman Catholic hierarchy are reported as assisting actively in the work of preservation, by communicating with the state authorities in cases of restoration, and forbidding their clergy to alienate artistic objects belonging to the churches[1].

The year 1903 saw the establishment of a State Commission (Rijkscommissie) under the presidency of the distinguished architect Dr P. J. H. Cuypers, charged to draw up without delay a summary inventory of all artistic and historical monuments in the country both immovable and movable, which is to be followed by a scientific publication illustrated by photographs and measured drawings, after the pattern of the best German inventories of artistic treasures. Six architects, three archivists, and two archaeologists, assisted by a photographer and draughtsmen, are engaged on the work. 1850 is the limit of time up to which monuments of value may be included, and these are roughly classified as (1) pre-historic and Roman, (2) town walls, gates, etc., (3) castles, (4) civic structures of a public kind, (5) churches and charitable institutions, (6) private buildings, (7) miscellaneous.

The second Report of the operations of the Commission, issued early in 1905, prints at the end a document in 21 sections giving directions for the carrying out in detail of the work of inventorization. This contains matter of much value in connection with this department of the care of monuments.

---

[1] From information kindly furnished by Dr J. Kalf, secretary of the State Commission.

SWITZERLAND.

The arrangements of monument legislation in Switzerland correspond to those in the German Empire, in that the separate Cantons make independent laws on the subject, just as is the case with the German States. Federal legislation on the Care of Monuments also exists, though in a somewhat rudimentary form. Of the Cantons, Vaud, Bern, and Neuchâtel possess Monument Acts, and there is one in advanced preparation in Canton Valais, whose capital is the romantic Sion, and also in Canton Ticino. Freiburg in 1900 adopted certain measures of protection but has not yet proceeded to legislation.

It was reported by the Federal Representative at the third Monument Congress in Germany held at Düsseldorf in 1902 that other Cantons were considering similar measures, and already possessed Commissions on Ancient Monuments which reported on questions of restoration. In some Cantons official inventorization of monuments was also in progress[1].

Under the head of Federal action in favour of monuments the following may be recorded.

On June 30, 1886, the Federal Assembly of the Swiss Confederation passed a resolution (Arrêté Fédéral = Bundesbeschluss[2]) concerning the participation of the Confederation in the maintenance and the acquisition of national antiquities. The following are its main provisions :—

Art. 1. Whenever the Federal finances permit of it, an annual credit of not more than 50,000 francs, or about £2000, is set apart for the preservation and acquisition of national monuments. This sum will be dispensed,

(a) for the purchase of objects of antiquity of an outstanding national interest ;

(b) for expenses of excavations ;

---

[1] *Dritter Tag für Denkmalpflege*, Karlsruhe, 1902, p. 10.

[2] An Arrêté Fédéral, or Bundesbeschluss, is a legislative Act passed by the Federal Assembly consisting of the two Federal Chambers, the Council of State and National Council, and ratified by the executive body or Federal Council. It differs from a Federal law only in the fact that it is not, save in certain cases, the subject of the popular referendum.

(c) for contributions towards the upkeep of monuments of historical and artistic importance ;

(d) for subventions in aid of archaeological collections in the Cantons, on occasions when these desire to obtain objects of historical interest the price of which exceeds their available resources.

Art. 2. Objects acquired by the help of Federal contributions cannot be sold nor alienated without the consent of the Federal Council.

By Art. 3, the Federal Council, as executive authority, was charged with the issue of regulations for the carrying out of this resolution. These regulations were promulgated on February 25, 1887, and comprise the following articles.

Art. 1 puts in the hands of the Federal Council the allocation of the grants, etc., from the credit.

Art. 2 runs as follows : ' The Department of the Interior ' nominates for a period of three years a Commission of ' experts charged,

' (a) to examine and report on questions submitted by the ' Department as regards the expenditure of the credit ;

' (b) to exercise supervision, in accordance with the resolu- ' tion (Arrêté Fédéral), over the preservation and acquisition ' of national antiquities, and to present on its own initiative ' proposals for carrying out the objects in view ;

' (c) to assist the Department of the Interior in the execu- ' tion of resolutions taken by the Federal Council.'

Art. 3. ' This Commission bears the name of " Federal ' Commission for the preservation of the antiquities of Switzer- ' land ".' The rest of Art. 3 and Art. 4 provide for an allowance of 15 francs a day in Switzerland and 25 francs abroad, with travelling expenses, to members of the Commission when on official duty; for the temporary appointment of expert advisers from outside ; and for special allowances to meet exceptional demands.

Art. 5 places in the meantime the functions of the Commission of experts in the hands of the Council of the Swiss Society for the Preservation of Historical Monuments of Art. (Schweizerische Gesellschaft für Erhaltung historischer Kunstdenkmäler.)

Arts. 6 and 7 give conditions under which contributions and subventions will be accorded.

Art. 8. 'The Department of the Interior keeps two 'inventories, one, of the antiquities in regard to which the 'Confederation reserves its right of property and of free 'disposition ; the other, of objects acquired by the aid of 'Federal subventions, which objects cannot be sold nor 'alienated without the consent of the Federal Council.'

Art. 9. 'The Department of the Interior is charged with 'the execution of the present regulations which come im-'mediately into force.'

Under these regulations 'for a long period of years very considerable contributions have been made by the Federal authorities', and the Council of the Swiss Society, still acting as a Commission, has in each case advised and superintended all that has been done. For ten years past the preparation of an inventory, or Monument Archives, has occupied the attention of the Council of the Swiss Society, and been partly paid for out of the credits sanctioned by the resolution of June 30, 1886[1].

In the matter of Cantonal as distinct from Federal legislation, Vaud has taken the lead, and on September 10, 1898, the Grand Council of the Canton passed a law concerning 'the conservation of monuments and objects of art possessing a historical or artistic interest', and this was followed on April 21, 1899, by the issue of administrative regulations for the carrying out of the Act.

The law is obviously framed on the model of the 'Monuments Historiques' Act of France, of 1887, but it is brief and well expressed, and is translated here verbatim as a useful model for an Act of the kind.

---

[1] *Dritter Tag*, pp. 10, 85, reports of Federal Representative at the Monument Congress of 1902.

'Chapter I. General Dispositions.

'Art. 1.   The State of Vaud provides to the fullest extent
'possible for the preservation of monuments and objects of
'art which offer for the country a historical or artistic interest.

'Chapter II. Organization.

'Art. 2.   With a view to the investigation and preserva-
'tion of all that may be of interest to the Canton in
'connection with art, history, and especially antiquities, there
'is hereby instituted, in the Department of Public Instruction
'and of Religion, an administrative post carrying the functions
'of Cantonal Archaeologist, and in addition a Commission
'called " Commission on Historical Monuments ".

'Art. 3.   The Cantonal Archaeologist is nominated by
'the Council of State for a period of four years, on the
'proposal of the Commission on Historical Monuments.   He
'is reeligible.   His annual salary is from £160 to £200.

'Art. 4.   The Commission on Historical Monuments is
'composed of the Head of the Department of Public Instruc-
'tion and Religion, of the Head of the Department of
'Agriculture and Commerce, of the functionary holding the
'office of Cantonal Archaeologist, and of eight other members
'nominated by the Council of State.

'Art. 5.   This Commission is presided over by the Head
'of the Department of Public Instruction and of Religion,
'or in his absence by the Head of the Department of
'Agriculture and Commerce.   The Cantonal Archaeologist
'acts as secretary.

'Art. 6.   The Commission on Historical Monuments holds
'a meeting at least once every six months.   Its members
'receive an honorarium for attendance, the amount of which
'is fixed by the Council of State.

'Art. 7.   The minutes of the meetings, and the reports,
'memorials, accounts, plans, sketches, photographs, etc., pre-
'pared for the Commission constitute its archives.   These
'archives are accessible for purposes of study to the public,
'on a demand addressed to the Department of Public
'Instruction and of Religion.

'CHAPTER III. SCHEDULING ("CLASSEMENT").

'*Immovable Objects.*

'Art. 8.   Immovable objects by nature or by intention[1]
'(fixtures) of which the preservation may have, from the point
'of view of history or of art, a national interest, shall be
'scheduled (classés) in whole or in part, by resolution of the
'Council of State, on the proposal of the Commission on
'Historical Monuments.   The land on which there may be
'discovered monuments or objects of archaeological interest
'is assimilated to historical monuments and treated as such.

'Art. 9.   Every public edifice belonging to the State can
'be scheduled as of right.   In the case of public edifices
'belonging to a Commune, these can be scheduled notwith-
'standing the opposition of the Commune.

'Art. 10.   If the act of scheduling result in depriving the
'Commune of a source of income, or diminishing its enjoy-
'ment of the scheduled monument, an indemnity will be
'allowed.

'Art. 11.   A monument belonging to a private person can
'only be scheduled with the consent of the owner.

'Art. 12.   The State makes a financial contribution
'towards the expense of the upkeep of scheduled monuments,
'and if occasion arise, towards that of their restoration.

'Art. 13.   A scheduled monument cannot be alienated
'nor destroyed, even in part, nor be made the object of any
'work of restoration or repair nor of any alteration whatsoever,
'without the authorization of the Council of State, after
'report by the Commission on Historical Monuments.   The
'effect of the act of scheduling remains the same into
'whosesoever hands the scheduled monument passes.

'Art. 14.   In the case of an infraction of the above article,
'the proprietor of the scheduled object is bound to restore to
'the State, with interest from the day when he received them,
'the subsidies which he has received for the upkeep or the

---

[1] 'Les immeubles par nature ou par destination', a phrase borrowed from the
French law of 1887.   An immovable object by nature is a building such as a
church, or a megalithic monument ; one by intention is a fixture destined to be
permanent, such as an altar, the stained glass of a window, etc.

'restoration of the monument. He is moreover subject to a
'penalty which may amount to £40, in accordance with the
'law of February 15, 1892, on the repression of offences
'against administrative regulations.

'Art. 15. The Council of State is authorized at any time
'in exercise of its powers or on the demand of the proprietor
'to order the total or partial excision from the schedule of
'monuments previously placed thereon. The Commission on
'Historical Monuments should give its opinion on the question
'involved.

'Art. 16. The Council of State is authorized to have
'recourse to compulsory purchase whenever this appears
'necessary in order to ensure the preservation of monuments
'which present in relation to the country at large an interest
'of a historical or artistic kind.

'Megalithic monuments and erratic blocks, together with
'the ground on which they rest, can be in the same way
'expropriated by the State on just and equitable compensa-
'tion being paid.

'Art. 17. In the event of the authorized sale of a
'scheduled monument, the State shall have a right of pre-
'emption at an equal price.

'Movable Objects.

'Art. 18. With due regard to what is said below in
'articles 19 and 20, the provisions of articles 8, 9, and 11–17
'are applicable to movable objects of public interest in
'relation to the history of art.

'Art. 19. Among such objects those that belong to the
'State shall remain inalienable and unassignable, so long as
'they continue on the schedule.

'Art. 20. Scheduled objects belonging to Communes or
'private persons cannot be alienated without the consent
'of the Council of State, after consultation with the Com-
'mission on Historical Monuments.

'CHAPTER IV. EXCAVATIONS.

'Art. 21. The Commission on Historical Monuments,
'with the authorization of the Council of State, can under-

'take excavations wherever it judges it advantageous to
'make them.

'When the excavations have to be undertaken on property
'belonging to a private person, the proprietor is held bound
'to permit them, and he is forbidden to make any changes
'on the locality from the moment when he has received
'notice from the Council of State.   He has however the
'right to an indemnity, the amount of which, in case of
'dispute, is fixed in accordance with the law of December 29,
'1836, on judicial assessments.

'Art. 22.   The State may become owner, on the pay-
'ment of half their value, of the objects found in the
'excavations undertaken by the Commission on Historical
'Monuments.

'The State will favour the development of collections in
'local museums.

'Art. 23.   It is strictly forbidden to any person not
'furnished with a special authorization from government
'to carry on any excavations or searches in the waters of
'the Canton or on the borders of Lakes Léman, Neuchâtel,
'or Morat, with the intention of recovering objects belonging
'to Lake Dwellings.

'It is specially forbidden to take up and appropriate the
'piles which mark the sites of these stations.

'Art. 24.   Every contravention of the preceding article
'shall be punished by a fine up to a thousand francs
'(£40)......

'Art. 25.   The Council of State shall issue regulations
'with regard to the execution of the provisions of the
'present law, which will come into force the first of January,
'1899.'

CHAPTER VII.

THE SCANDINAVIAN KINGDOMS. DENMARK, NORWAY, AND SWEDEN.

BIBLIOGRAPHY AND SOURCES OF INFORMATION.

Von Wussow, *Die Erhaltung der Denkmäler*, Berlin, 1885, I, 215 f.

Reports on the Preservation of Ancient Monuments in Denmark, issued by the Directorate for the Preservation of Ancient Monuments, and by the National Museum, Copenhagen, Kjøbenhavn, Thieles Bog-trykkeri, various years.

Reports to British Foreign Office, 1897 (ante, p. xiii).

Worsaae, *The Preservation of Antiquities and National Monuments in Denmark*, published in the *Memoirs of the Society of Northern Antiquaries*, 1877. English translation in *Reports of the Smithsonian Institution* for 1879, Washington, 1880, p. 299, and in *Proceedings of the Society of Antiquaries of Scotland*, 1879–80, p. 348.

Report on the Inventorization of Swedish Antiquities by the Riksantikvar, Dr Hans Hildebrand, published in the *Månadsblad* of the Royal Academy of History and Antiquities, Stockholm, 1890, Appendix, p. 25.

Communications from Dr Sophus Müller, Director of the National Museum, Copenhagen ; from Dr Harry Fett, Secretary of the Foreningen til Norske Fortidsmindesmærkers Bevaring, Christiania ; and from Professor Oscar Montelius, Stockholm.

THE Scandinavian Kingdoms have been distinguished from an early period by an intelligent care for the ancient monuments, with certain classes of which they are so abundantly supplied. There exist no Monument Acts in the strict sense, but numerous Royal Decrees supply the place of these, and the Royal Rescript issued by the King of Sweden in 1886, on 'The Protection and Preservation of the Monuments of Antiquity', is of the same scope as a regular parliamentary Monument Act. Sweden is in a fortunate position, in that at an early date the state assumed a tutelary position in regard to all the ancient monuments of the country, and the principle was then established that monuments, and objects discovered in excavations, on private lands are not at the disposal of the individual proprietor, but are matters of state concern. In the present day it would be impossible in any advanced country to establish by direct legislation this principle, but when, as in Sweden, it has come down as a matter of traditional prescription, the advantage to the cause of monument preservation is incalculable. In Denmark the authorities in charge of ancient monuments report that, though actual legislation is defective, yet owing to vigilant action through local authorities, and to the high state of popular education, monuments are on the whole treated with care and intelligence. The following gives some idea of the system pursued in these northern kingdoms, it being premised that Denmark and Norway resemble each other in regard to their system for the care of monuments, while Sweden, which has fixed measures of long standing, has a place apart.

DENMARK.

The earlier history of monument administration in Denmark is given in a paper by Professor Worsaae, written in 1875 (see Bibliography). The existence there of an old law, not unlike the English one of treasure-trove, has already been referred to (ante, p. 64). By a Danish royal ordinance of 1737 this was so interpreted as to grant to the Crown[1] 'all treasure or deposit of gold, silver, and precious objects, without an owner, found in the earth ; and the finder was bound, under certain penalties, to turn over his stock to the treasury without any indemnity'.

In 1752 however the necessary modification was made, without which no such law will in practice secure its avowed aim, and it was arranged for the finder who brought in his treasure to receive its full bullion value and something

---

[1] The quotations that follow are from Worsaae's paper.

more. 'It is generally known in Denmark that the finder will obtain from the state (the agents of which examine and appraise the articles found) not only a higher price than private persons would pay, but that the care taken in collecting and preserving the objects will be recompensed by an honorarium added to the price of the metal.' From 'finds' thus secured for the state, the nucleus of a collection had been formed, and at the beginning of the nineteenth century, in 1807, a Royal Commission for the care of antiquities was established, under which gradually grew up the famous Museum of Northern Antiquities at Copenhagen. The funds at the disposal of the commission have enabled it to pay for discovered treasure, called by the Danish term 'Danefae', the 'property of the dead'; and the public spirit of the people has brought in abundant gifts. 'By reason of a strong national sentiment, the people make it a point of honour to collect material for the history of pre-historic times, so that it is no longer necessary to prohibit the exportation of relics of stone, bronze and iron,' and 'it rarely happens that important treasures when found do not come promptly to the knowledge of the museum.'

In regard to immovable objects of antiquarian interest, with which this book is more nearly concerned, the commission of 1807 turned its attention at once to their preservation. This object was greatly furthered by the appointment in 1847 of a salaried Inspector of Ancient Monuments in the person of Professor Worsaae. Soon after, in 1849, the commission was dissolved, and since that date the administration of ancient monuments has been closely connected with the management of the Museum of Northern Antiquities.

The point of chief interest about Danish arrangements is the illustration they afford of rational methods of monument administration, in which reliance upon laws and penalties is at a minimum, and different classes and bodies in the community are approached by way of moral suasion, with a view to securing common action in favour of a national end. Not only, as Worsaae has said, is it not found necessary to prohibit the exportation from the country of movable objects of anti-

quity and art, but the process of expropriation is not relied
on for the protection of immovable monuments on the land of
private or corporate proprietors. In 1848, it is stated that the
government refused to sanction a measure which would have
put this power into the hands of the authorities[1]. There are
various reasons for the effectiveness in Denmark of these
methods of persuasion, on which so much reliance is placed.
For one thing, national feeling is strong, and is nourished by
the consciousness of the possession of a world-famous collection of national antiquities. Then the level of education is
comparatively high; the country is small, and people are
everywhere accessible to influences emanating from the centre
of affairs. Hence it is that the condition of the land in
respect of its ancient monuments can be described in terms as
pleasing as those contained in a letter with which the writer
has been favoured by Dr Sophus Müller, who as Director
of the National Museum is at the centre of monument
administration. 'We have no laws,' he writes, 'preventing
private possessors from injuring monuments of historical or
artistic interest of which they are the owners. Nevertheless
the ancient monuments are not actually exposed to destruction or vandalism, and it is very rarely that a monument of
any value and interest is ruined. The local authorities all
over the country are instructed by regulations and circulars
to assist the National Museum in all matters concerning the
preservation of monuments. The Museum itself is provided
with the pecuniary means that are required, and in most
cases, owing to the high state of popular education, the
personal interest of owners is easily roused. All the ancient
monuments, that are declared inviolate and placed under the
inspection of the National Museum, have been so treated
through the voluntary act of their owners, and it is very
rarely that any compensation has been paid. In this way,
for instance, several thousands of pre-historic tombs and
barrows have been preserved from any future destruction.'

Official reports on the measures taken to carry out this
policy, of more recent date than that of Worsaae, are furnished

---

[1] Worsaae, *Smithsonian Report*, p. 304.

in publications issued by the National Museum (see Biblio-graphy), and some extracts from these will show the manner of procedure in dealing with the various classes and bodies who are to be brought to share in the common work of preservation.

The state itself began with a self-denying ordinance of 1848, to the effect that all forts, sepulchral mounds, runic stones, or ruined structures, existing on the crown domains or in the state forests, should be declared national property, and that, if any part of these domains came to be alienated, those monuments should be expressly reserved in the articles of sale as belonging to the nation. An effort was made at the same time to induce ecclesiastical corporations to establish the same provisions with regard to ancient monuments on their estates, while ' the commission on monuments, and later on the Director of Monuments and of the Museum (November 1849) addressed printed circulars to all the land-holders of the kingdom to induce them to make the same reservations, and many of them submitted thereto with the greatest goodwill. In this way without much expense, a great number of impor-tant and characteristic monuments were placed under the protection of the law....In the numerous excursions made each year by the director of ancient monuments,...and in his personal relations with the people, he acquired for the state a great number of relics, some of which were sold at a reasonable price, others given gratuitously—indeed, by yeomen hardly able to do it[1].'

More recent appeals to ecclesiastical bodies are recorded in the *Report on the Preservation of Monuments in Denmark* issued by the Directorate of Monuments in 1891[2]. The Directorate appealed to the Minister of Public Worship and Instruction to provide for the insertion of a clause in all deeds of sale of church lands securing the preservation of all

---

[1] Worsaae, loc. cit., p. 305.

[2] *Beretning om Fredning af Antikvariske Mindesmaerker i Danmark*, 1886–1891, Kjøbenhavn, 1891, p. 1 f., and *Mindesmaerker fra Oldtiden, Fredlyste i Aarene*, 1897-1902, Kjøbenhavn, 1903, p. 1 f., give the information which follows, to the end of the section on Denmark. For help in the translation of documents in the Scandinavian languages the writer is indebted to Miss C. la Cour.

ancient monuments. Remissness in the matter of the care of monuments on glebe lands, especially in cases where the glebe was let to tenants, had been a cause of anxiety to the authorities, and on February 19, 1886, a schedule was sent from the Minister through the Bishops to all the clergy, requiring their signature to an undertaking that they would in the meantime preserve intact all monuments on their glebes, till these should have been officially inspected. Fifty six stone cairns, three hundred and eighteen tumuli, and five earthworks were in this way protected.

In the case of railway works, the Directorate made a successful appeal to the Minister to incorporate in all new concessions granted to railway projectors certain clauses forbidding any tampering with ancient barrows before inspection by the Museum authorities, and requiring the delivery to the Museum of any antiquities found in the course of the railway excavations. In February 1890 the Government was again approached with a complaint about the destruction of monuments by those engaged in making roads. The result was that the Minister of the Interior in June 1890 issued a circular to the Sheriffs instructing them to make known to the communal authorities that persons in charge of road-making operations were to observe the same rules as those laid down in the case of railways.

The reclamation for purposes of cultivation of heathland, carried on by a private company, was involving the levelling of barrows and similar injury to other ancient remains, and an appeal was successfully made to those responsible for carrying on the work. An article in the periodical organ of the moorland association, in 1889, acknowledged the value of these memorials, which are specially numerous on the heaths of Jutland. 'Their presence is witness that these barren regions were in the middle ages the seat of a population. From about 1200 A.D. till the middle of the nineteenth century the inland part of Jutland degenerated, and the barrows alone still speak of the better times of old. Now again life begins on the moors in the form of serious work to conquer the soil. Let us hold these memorials of the olden time in constant honour, as they form an eloquent chapter in the remarkable history of the heath country.'

The chief object of these protective operations has been to secure the safety of ancient monuments on the ordinary estates and farms in private hands in all parts of the kingdom. One of the latest reports, issued by the Museum in 1903, gives a satisfactory account of progress in this respect, especially during the decade 1892–1902. Two thousand five hundred monuments were during these years put under protection, and of these, two thousand two hundred and twenty were freely given over, while in the case of the remainder compensation was paid. Diplomas of honour and gifts of plate have been presented as a recognition of the public spirit displayed. Any proprietor, who is willing to place ancient monuments on his land under the protection of the law, executes a legal document by which he binds himself to preserve the monuments in question on behalf of the state, in accordance with the regulations of the National Museum. 'I pledge myself and the succeeding owners and occupiers of the property to protect and preserve the monuments so that they shall be in no wise harmed by digging, ploughing, removal, heaping on them of stones, or in any other manner. No planting shall be allowed. A notice of protection may be put up on the spot.' (This takes the form of a stone with the initials F. M., 'Fredet Mindesmaerke' 'Protected Monument'). An acknowledgement is also given of liability to a fine in case of any wilful or careless injury to the monument, and the Museum is authorized periodically to inspect the objects and to make the fact of protection public.

The greatest damage which these monuments incur is said to arise when property changes hands through compulsory sale or foreclosure of a mortgage. The Directorate of Monuments has however approached the companies which lend on mortgage asking them to recognize in every case the position of the protected monuments on estates which may fall into their hands, and in the year 1889 this arrangement was ratified with the principal companies concerned. It is pleasant to find commercial associations, like these loan and reclamation companies, prepared to evince some of the same patriotism and public spirit which is shown by other sections of the community.

NORWAY.

Like Denmark, Norway is not provided with a body of monument legislation, but exercises superintendence over this department of the national treasures through an official custodian of antiquities, who holds the title of 'State-Antiquary', and through the council of a subsidized society, which has its headquarters in Christiania and branches at Bergen, Trondhjem, Lillehammer, Larvik and Fredrikstad. This society is entitled Foreningen til Norske Fortidsmindesmærkers Bevaring, and it issues a periodical report of its operations. It was founded in 1844 as a private association, but after 1860 it received an official character, and obtained a subvention to be employed for a proper investigation into the sepulchral and other monuments of the country, the repair of old structures of interest, and where practicable, their purchase. The Society has become possessed in this way of twenty four properties in the form of ecclesiastical and civil buildings, as well as some runic stones. The state subsidy amounted in 1904 to nearly £700. The arrangement is somewhat similar to that which prevails in Switzerland, where the Council of the Swiss Society for the Preservation of Historical Monuments is entrusted by the Federal Government with the functions of a monument commission. The Norse Society forms the advisory council for the State-Antiquary, and deliberates on all proposals for alterations in the older churches and their fittings.

A new and comparatively stringent measure in regard to ancient monuments is now before the Norwegian Storting, and if it pass very little will be left to private arbitrament.

SWEDEN.

It has been already noticed that in Sweden the attention of the governing powers was at an early date directed to the question of the preservation of ancient monuments. The famous Gustavus Adolphus, 1611–1632, appointed official custodians of these national treasures, and instituted the office of Antiquary of the Kingdom, Riksantikvar, a post now filled by the veteran archaeologist, Dr Hans Hildebrand. In 1666 Charles XI issued a Royal Edict declaring that the ancient monuments of the kingdom, whether on royal domains or on the lands of the yeomanry, were under the royal protection and must be preserved from all injury. This measure applied to all old forts, castles, cairns, standing stones, tumuli, and barrows. The same protection was extended to ecclesiastical structures with all their fittings, ornaments and adjuncts, while the nobles were exhorted to give due attention to all ancient monuments and works of art in their own possession. Further rescripts of the seventeenth century forbade the alienation of ecclesiastical treasures to private individuals, and the sale or melting down of coins or objects of gold or silver found in the earth. Such objects were claimed as Crown property, though the finder was indemnified by the payment of part of their value. The concealment of a 'find' was visited by a penalty. By a later ordinance of 1736 the finder of treasure was to be recompensed with the bullion value plus one-eighth, and this is the arrangement which at present prevails.

These early rescripts established the rule which has been acted on ever since, that the state is, as a general principle, the proprietor of all the ancient monuments in the country, while before the close of the eighteenth century there was established the machinery through which the administration of monuments is still carried on. In 1786 there was organized the Royal Academy of Science, History, and Antiquities, which fills the place occupied in other countries by monument commissions, and, with the Riksantikvar for chief of the executive, carries out the provisions of the laws and rescripts bearing on the subject of monument administration.

These laws and rescripts are conveniently summed up in an elaborate Royal Decree promulgated first in 1867, but reissued with substantially the same content in 1873 and finally in 1886. The following gives in a corrected form the translation of this decree which was communicated to the

British Foreign Office in 1896 and is printed among the *Reports* of the subsequent year (see Bibliography, p. xiii)[1].

'His Majesty's gracious Decree respecting the Preservation of Ancient Monuments.

'(Given at Stockholm Palace November 29, 1867, 'May 30, 1873, and April 21, 1886.)

'§ 1. ALL monuments which preserve the memory of 'the ancient inhabitants of the country are placed under the 'protection of the law, and accordingly may not be injured 'nor destroyed by the owner or occupier of the land, nor by 'any other person save under the conditions set forth in 'Articles 3, 4, and 5.

'§ 2. Monuments include mounds of earth or stone (grave 'mounds or stone tumuli) raised by hand ; tombs of stone 'with their mounds of earth or stone, where such occur ; other 'ancient graves or burying places ; stones, recumbent or 'upright, isolated or in rows or groups, whether arranged in a 'systematic order or no ; stones or faces of cliffs with inscrip-'tions and figures ; crosses of stone and other signs ; remains 'of dwellings abandoned since ancient times, and of deposits 'indicating old dwelling-places ; remains of long-since aban-'doned burghs, castles, churches, chapels, monasteries, 'oratories, or other public buildings or constructions, likewise 'other like monuments of such an age that they can now no 'longer be held to be private property.

'§ 3. The Royal Archaeological Academy has the right, 'through the State Antiquary, or other specially appointed 'person, to cause ancient stones or other remains of antiquity 'which have fallen down to be raised and repaired, after 'formally notifying the fact to the owner or occupier of the 'land, and also to sketch and examine, by excavating or 'other means, monuments, on the condition that the owner 'or occupier of the land shall receive compensation for any 'damage or expense which he may thereby incur.

'§ 4. (*a*) Monuments which are already used as arable

---

[1] For a revision of this translation, which was printed in 1897 in a faulty form, the writer is indebted to the great kindness of Professor Oscar Montelius.

' soil, marsh land, or pasture, may continue to be cultivated
' as such, but not to a greater depth than hitherto.

' (*b*) If the owner or occupier of such land wish to cultivate
' or make use of it for building or other purposes to a greater
' extent than is allowed under paragraph (*a*), or should he
' desire to otherwise employ, alter, or remove any permanent
' remains, he must notify his intention with a precise descrip-
' tion of the monument, if in the country, to the nearest
' government official, and if in the town, to the Magistrate,
' and it shall be their duty to report the fact without delay to
' the Governor of the Province, who shall send in a report on
' the subject to the Royal Academy.

' The Royal Academy has then the right to decide whether
' the application can be granted, and if so, whether conditions
' will be imposed or no.

' Their decision shall be communicated to the applicant
' through the Governor, together with a notification that
' should he not be satisfied with it, he may appeal to the
' Ecclesiastical Department within the time fixed by the
' Decree of the 14th November, 1866.

' In the latter case the decision shall be communicated to
' him free of charge.

' (*c*) The Royal Academy has the right, in cases where
' consent is given to the alteration or removal of such an
' ancient monument, to cause the same to be inspected and
' sketched beforehand, or to send some person in the Academy's
' employ to be present at its alteration or removal, but he
' may not cause the owner or occupier of the land any
' unnecessary delay or discomfort. If in such remains anti-
' quities be found, these should be offered to His Majesty and
' the Crown.

' (*d*) Should any one else for scientific investigation wish
' to open up any specially mentioned monument, he may ask
' permission from the Academy, which has the power to
' determine exactly how the above shall be effected, should
' they grant the leave.

' § 5. When during the construction of roads, railways,
' canals, or in any other public works, remarkable monuments

' are found in the way of the road or canal, or obstructing the
' execution of the works, and when the destruction of these
' remains can only be avoided with great difficulty, then,
' before the destruction takes place, drawings of the remains
' shall be forwarded to the Royal Academy, and an opportunity
' given to the Academy to inspect the same through some
' specially commissioned person, should they consider it
' necessary; yet the work must not thereby be retarded.

'§ 6. In the parcelling of any ground where there are
' monuments, the space occupied by these monuments is to
' remain unparcelled, if possible.

' When such an agreement cannot be arrived at by friendly
' negotiation, the Regulations cited above as to the pre-
' servation of ancient monuments remain in force.

'§ 7. Any one who by blasting, demolishing, digging,
' ploughing, or other means damages, demolishes, or destroys,
' or in any way disturbs monuments, shall be fined according
' to the circumstances from 5 to 500 kroner (5s. 6d. to £27),
' should it be found that he knew or ought to have known
' that they were antique remains, and shall be obliged to
' restore the same, if possible, to their former state.

' If he neglect to do this the restoration may be effected
' at his expense.

' If antiquities be found these should be handed over to the
' Royal Academy, and on examination it will be decided
' what compensation is due.

'§ 8. (a) Any one finding in the earth or water, in old
' buildings or elsewhere, ancient coins, weapons, tools, orna-
' ments, vessels, or other antiquities of gold, silver, or copper,
' shall by law offer them to the State, without breaking, filing,
' cleaning, or damaging them in other ways, and either to
' the nearest officer of the Crown or else to the Governor
' immediately report where and how the remains were found,
' whether there are remains in the neighbourhood, and any
' other information which may be of service in the matter.

' The Governor shall, without delay, see that the antiquities
' are sent in, or, if this cannot be conveniently done by the
' post, forward a written notice to the Royal Academy.

'If the latter consider that the find or any part thereof
'ought to be included in the collections of the State, the full
'metal value of gold and silver finds with an eighth part extra
'shall be paid to the owner, and in the case of copper, what-
'ever amount above the metal worth, which may be considered
'equivalent to the scientific value of the find.   Should the
'Academy be unable to meet this expense with its grant from
'the State for this purpose, a report to this effect shall be sent
'in to His Majesty the King, who will decide whether the find
'may be bought in from other funds or be returned to the
'owner.

'(b)   When the owner of other antiquities of lesser material
'value, which have been found by chance, wishes to offer the
'same to the King and the Crown, he may do this in the
'same manner through the Governor ; and the Academy shall
'pay compensation for whatever portion of the find offered
'they consider should be reserved to the State's Archaeo-
'logical Collections ;   this remuneration shall be greater or
'less according to the state of preservation of the objects and
'their value to the museum and to science.

'(c)   Any one destroying, melting down, dispersing or
'giving away such a find mentioned in (a) before it has been
'offered to the King and the Crown, forfeits without com-
'pensation whatever part of the find he still has in his
'possession, and pays a fine double the value of what he has
'destroyed, &c.

'§ 9.   Old churches distinguished by unusual architecture
'or ancient ornaments or any to which historical memories
'cling, or which have paintings or inscriptions on their vaults,
'roofs, or walls, may not be demolished, altered, or turned to
'other uses until notice has been given in appropriate terms
'to the King, so that His Majesty, after considering the case,
'may decide what must be retained or be handed down to
'posterity by drawings and descriptions, before the demolition
'or alteration takes place.

'The same Law also applies to other buildings connected
'with churches, such as old tombs, and other monuments
'which are found in churches or churchyards, but the rights

' of private persons or families to such monuments are pre-
' served to them intact.

'§ 10. Should there in a church or elsewhere within an
' ecclesiastical building be found movable articles which serve
' to perpetuate the memory of the customs or art of olden
' times and which do not belong to a private person or family,
' such as old vestments, pictures, altar paintings, crosses and
' crucifixes, jewels, vessels, baptismal fonts, censers, hand-
' bells, indulgence caskets, poor boxes, pictures not fixed to
' the wall or other works of art, relics or grave-stones, epitaphs,
' standards, escutcheons, mourning banners, weapons, and
' armour, old letters and writings, these may not be given to
' any private person, nor to any collections at home or
' abroad without first being offered to the King and the
' Crown, and those whose duty it is to keep them shall be
' responsible that this is done.

' When Runic stones are set in the pavement of a church
' and liable to be damaged, these shall be taken out and set
' up in some open and suitable place. Should the parish not
' be willing to meet the expense incurred thereby, representa-
' tions should be made on the subject to the Royal Academy.

' When a parish wishes to have a bell recast on which
' inscriptions are found, these should be copied and com-
' municated to the Royal Academy. If the inscriptions are
' in Runic or other middle-age letters, or if on the bell drawings
' or figures of unusual nature are found, an exact reproduction
' of these shall be forwarded to the Academy to enable the
' Academy to examine and take a cast of the inscriptions and
' figures before the bell is recast. If the parish wishes to sell
' the bell which they intend to recast, it shall first be offered
' to the King and the Crown in its original state.

'§ 11. The inventory which by law is to be found in
' every church of its movable property must include also the
' articles mentioned in the preceding paragraph (§ 10), and
' at every change of incumbent and at every visitation it shall
' be carefully examined to see that everything is in good order
' according to the inventory. The Royal Academy has the
' right to have such an inventory made out after due noti-

' fication to the clergyman of the parish or the legal
' representative.

' The incumbent and the vestry must see that such
' movable property of the church is not destroyed by wear
' and tear, and shall provide for such articles as are no longer
' used for the service of the church a suitable room in the
' church or its precincts.

' § 12. The Royal Governor and Consistory, the officiating
' clergy, and the officials of the Crown are instructed to see,
' in so far as lies in their power, that this Decree is strictly
' observed.

' The Royal Governor has the right, after notice from the
' State Antiquary, or request from a private landowner, or on
' other grounds, to cause certain monuments or those of
' certain places to be publicly placed under the protection of
' the law, and when damage is nevertheless done to such a
' protected monument, this fact shall be considered as an
' aggravating circumstance in judging the offence.

' The State Antiquary has also the right, when he dis-
' covers that this Decree has been violated in any particular,
' to prosecute the person concerned.'

Amongst other questions connected with monument
administration, that of inventorization has received attention
in Sweden. On this the Riksantikvar issued in 1891 a
report[1] of which the following is a summary. The Academy
disposed of a government grant for the investigation and
description of ancient monuments, the object in view being a
complete record of the possessions in this department of
the fatherland. 'When I entered on my post,' writes Dr
Hildebrand, ' I saw that the time had come to begin the
systematic arrangement of the material already obtained, and
to work continuously for its completion. In this way the
" Antiquarian Topographical Archives " were instituted.
They consist of two divisions, (a) text, and (b) illustrations.
The text-section is arranged according to provinces, districts,
and parishes, with a portfolio for each parish (where the

---

[1] *Kongl. Vitterhets Historie och Antiquitets Akademiens Månadsblad*, Stockholm, 1890-92, Appendix, p. 25 f.

monuments are few two or three parishes have a portfolio among them). In these portfolios are contained separate sheets for separate parishes, for churches, for hamlets and farms in the parish, and on these sheets are gradually entered in order all descriptive details as they are ascertained. Illustrations of monuments of heathen times find their place also in these portfolios.

'The illustration-section consists of two series, one for ecclesiastical and the other for secular buildings, each arranged according to provinces. In the ecclesiastical series are to be found 4,092 drawings and photographs; in the secular series 375.

'From the experience which I have of such matters abroad, I venture to assert that no state in the world can boast of such a collection as the Swedish Antiquarian Topographical Archives.'

CHAPTER VIII.

RUSSIA AND FINLAND.

BIBLIOGRAPHY AND SOURCES OF INFORMATION.

GENERAL REGULATIONS for the Constitution and Work of the Imperial Archaeological Commission, issued by command of the Emperor through the Ministry of the Imperial Court, February 2, 1859.

IMPERIAL DECREE, as to the operations of the Imperial Archaeological Commission and the Imperial Academy of the Fine Arts, in the matter of excavations and restorations, March 16, 1889.

Further DECREE on the same subject, October 31, 1890.

Circular issued in 1901 by the Minister of the Interior with regard to the Protection of Ancient Monuments.

Communications from the President of the Imperial Archaeological Commission, and the Secretary of the Academy of Fine Arts, January and March, 1905.

IMPERIAL DECREES relating to the establishment of an Archaeological Commission in Finland, the appointment and functions of a State Antiquary for Finland, etc., etc.; Helsingfors, June 19, 1884; December 17, 1885; September 22, 1892.

Letter from the State Antiquary of Finland, January, 1905.

RUSSIA.

THERE is no elaborate legal machinery for monument administration in Russia, but the subject is by no means neglected. In the *Reports* to the British Foreign Office in 1896–7 it is stated that 'the legal Adviser of Her Majesty's Embassy having been consulted respecting the laws in Russia concerning the preservation of ancient monuments, etc., states that there are no statutable provisions with regard to this matter at all.' This may be strictly true, yet in 1859 there had been constituted, under the Ministry of the Imperial

Court an Imperial Archaeological Commission for this very purpose, and this commission, together with the Imperial Academy of the Fine Arts, has been in charge of ancient monuments ever since.   According to the present constitution, 'every project for the restoration or the destruction of an 'ancient edifice must be previously laid before the Imperial 'Archaeological Commission, in the hands of which the project 'is submitted to a detailed examination by specialists in 'ancient architecture and representatives of the Academy of 'Fine Arts, the Clergy, and Ministries interested.

'In regard to excavations, it is necessary to obtain special 'permission to carry on archaeological researches on lands 'belonging to the State, to churches and convents, to towns 'and rural communes[1].'   Russia is of course a country where matters of this kind are not managed by statutory provisions so much as by Decrees and Circulars of the Autocrat and his representatives.   The degree of effectiveness of the measures thus set on foot depends on the same causes which make for the success or inefficiency of all such proceedings in bureaucratically governed countries.

The administration of ancient monuments in Russia belongs to the Ministry of the Imperial Court, rather than to any department of the executive government.   In 1901 however the Minister of the Interior issued a circular[2] to the provincial governors, municipalities, and heads of police, calling attention to the duties of local authorities with regard to monuments of art and antiquity.   In order to secure the proper performance of these duties the Minister gives directions for the compilation of an inventory of the artistic and antiquarian treasures of the Empire.   All local authorities are accordingly ordered to draw up accurate lists of the monuments within their jurisdiction, with descriptions, drawings, and plans; and to accompany these with historical notes, and with a report on the present condition of the monuments, including estimates for requisite repairs, etc.

[1] Extract from a letter kindly sent by the President of the Archaeological Commission, Count A. Bobrinski.
[2] Summarized in *Die Denkmalpflege*, 1901, p. 104.

The lists were all to be sent in by April 1, 1902! This would mean the complete and scientific inventorization of the monuments of the vast Russian dominions within a space of about one year, and the reader may speculate as to the likelihood of the work being satisfactorily accomplished at quite so early a date.

The Russian press hailed the issue of the circular with cordial satisfaction. The *Novoe Vremya* pointed out that the government had for a long time past given attention to this subject but without much result. The Academy of Arts and the Archaeological Commission had been charged with the task of protecting ancient monuments from vandalism, but neither of these bodies possessed local representatives in different parts of the country so as to be able effectively to carry on their operations. The Minister of the Interior on the other hand had relations with local bodies in every part, and what was impracticable to societies and academies in St Petersburg was for the Ministry of the Interior quite within the bounds of possibility. *There would be at last at any rate an inventory of all objects of value, and that was the first step to a really effective activity in the domain of the preservation and restoration of historical monuments.*

The establishment of the Imperial Archaeological Commission dates back, it has been mentioned, to 1859. The following is an abstract of the Decree for its constitution and working[1].

There are twenty seven articles in the Decree, which is divided into three parts (1) 'General Regulations', (2) 'Activities of the Commission', and (3) 'Internal organization of the Commission'. Article 1 runs as follows:—' The Imperial 'Archaeological Commission constitutes a separate depart-'ment in the Ministry of the Imperial Court, and has for its 'objects, 1st, the search for objects of antiquity, especially 'those relating to the national history and the history of those 'people who once lived in territories now occupied by Russia; '2nd, the collection of information on those monuments of

[1] The acknowledgements of the writer are due to his colleague Dr Charles Sarolea for help kindly given by the translation of the Russian documents quoted in the text.

'antiquity to be found within the Empire ; 3rd, the scientific 'investigation of objects discovered in excavations.' Articles 2, 3, and 4 provide that the commission is to have an authoritative President who is in immediate touch with the Minister of the Court ; is to have the cooperation of honorary and corresponding members ; and is to take superintendence of the Museum of antiquities at Kertch in the Crimea.

Under the heading 'Activities of the Commission' we read, Article 5, 'With a view to the discovery of objects of 'antiquity the Commission will carry on excavations on 'ancient burial mounds, and in other localities which are 'remarkable from a historical point of view and appear to 'promise archaeological discoveries.' Article 6, 'It appertains 'to the Commission to keep under observation all discoveries 'of objects of antiquity made throughout the Empire, and 'local authorities are instructed to send in information of these. 'If practicable, antiquities which come to light are to be sent 'by the local authorities for the inspection of the Commission.' Article 7 provides for the supervision of all work connected with ancient monuments. In important cases the commission may be represented by its inspector. According to Article 8 'The Commission is to follow with attention the progress of 'all great public works, such as the construction of railways, 'the laying out of roads, etc., in order to take advantage of 'any opportunities that may be offered for archaeological 'research.' Articles 9 and 10 run as follows :—'For the at-'tainment of the objects of Articles 5, 6, 7, and 8, the President 'of the Commission will enter into preliminary relations with 'persons whose cooperation will be required in the various 'localities.' 'To encourage the handing over of objects of 'antiquity to the Archaeological Commission there will be 'granted in each case a monetary gratification corresponding 'not only to the actual or bullion value of the gold or silver 'or other material of which the object may be composed, but 'also to its archaeological worth and rarity.'

The remaining articles of the Decree are occupied for the most part with provisions for administration, status of officials, etc., and are not of general interest.

In an Imperial Decree of March 1889 it is laid down that the archaeological commission has exclusive right to the control of all excavations on Crown lands, or lands belonging to public or religious institutions[1]. All institutions or persons desiring to undertake such excavations, independently of their relations with the local authorities of the district, must make a preliminary agreement with the archaeological commission. All objects of value that come to light, especially those important from a scientific point of view, must be sent to the commission for submission to the Emperor.

All projects for the repair or restoration of the monumental remains of antiquity must be submitted to the commission, which will confer with the Imperial Academy of the Fine Arts. A further decree of October 31, 1890, gives directions for the joint action of these two bodies in connection with all such projects. Every scheme for restoration must be submitted in detail and considered by the two bodies, who will appoint inspectors of the work. After the completion of the operations all the plans and drawings employed are to be deposited in the archives of the archaeological commission.

FINLAND.

The Grand-Duchy of Finland possesses a somewhat elaborate monument administration, which it owes to the memory of its long political connection with Sweden[2]. Until the dissolution in 1809 of this connection, the older Swedish laws and dispositions in the matter of monuments, dating from the days of Gustavus Adolphus and Charles XI, were in force in the Province, while even after 1809 the ordinance of 1666 (see ante, p. 192), and

---

[1] 'Quant aux fouilles, il est obligatoire de se munir d'une permission spéciale pour faire des recherches archéologiques sur les terres appartenant à l'État, aux églises et couvents, aux villes et aux communes rurales.' Extract from a letter from the President of the Imperial Commission.

[2] The following is an account of the Care of Monuments in Finland kindly furnished by Professor Aspelin, State Antiquary of Finland, through the good offices of Professor Vrjö Hirn, of the University of Helsingfors. To both these gentlemen the writer desires to return his best thanks, as well for private information, as for the communication of the text of the Imperial Decrees relating to Finland noticed in the Bibliography.

that of 1736 about 'treasure-trove' (ibid.), with other such regulations, remained legally valid. After the separation however, there was in Finland no authority charged with superintending their administration. At the diet of 1867 the Estates of Finland presented a petition to the Czar of Russia expressing the need not only of an ordinance protecting the monuments of the country, but also of an authority superintending the observance of this. This petition resulted at last in the Imperial Ordinance of April 2, 1883, on the protection and preservation of ancient monuments. ' By this ordinance, ' all fixed remains, i.e., ruins of castles, palaces, fortifications, ' churches, and other important public buildings, stone-barrows, ' cemeteries, cairns, grave-stones, rocks and stones with engraved ' inscriptions, are put under the protection of the law and may ' not be removed nor destroyed without permission. Trans- ' gression is punished with fines from 10 to 200 marks [1 mark ' = 1 franc], and the transgressor has to stand the cost of re- ' establishing the monument in its original condition. Local ' authorities must not—at the risk of being accused of breach ' of duty—make any changes in churches or other public ' buildings, which are decorated with ancient paintings, in- ' scriptions, or architectonic ornaments, before the authorities ' have had the opportunity of examining them and making ' drawings. Old fittings and other movable objects, which ' illustrate ancient customs or ancient technical methods, must ' not be removed from churches or other public buildings ' before the authorities have had the opportunity of taking ' copies of them, or eventually purchasing them for the state. ' Ancient coins and other archaeological finds are to be offered ' to the state, when they will be paid for with their full value ' plus one quarter, or, if the object have no market-price, with ' a sum that has been fixed by valuation. Embezzlement of ' the finds is punished with the loss of the price and fines ' of from 10 to 300 marks.

' By an ordinance of 19 June 1884 there was instituted an ' Archaeological Commission for the care of the ancient monu- ' ments of the country. The Commission consists of seven

'members, of whom only the archaeologist of the state, the
'active member, is permanent and salaried.   The other mem-
'bers are elected for three years by several learned societies.
'The commission, which meets as a rule twelve times a year,
'has under its care the ancient monuments as well as the
'historical museum of the state.'

The ordinance of 1884, Art. 6, foreshadowed the establishment of this museum which however was not actually founded
till 1893.

A later ordinance of December 17, 1885, defines more in
detail the functions of the state antiquary or archaeologist.
Thus, Article 2 runs as follows :—' The state archaeologist, by
'means of a knowledge of the country, gathered partly on his
'official journeys, partly through salaried officers sent out by
'the Archaeological Commission, and by the utilization of
'previously amassed antiquarian material, shall by degrees
'draw up a systematic description or inventory of the archaeo-
'logical treasures of the country.'......The last paragraph of
Article 2 is worthy of special attention and of imitation :—

'All information received concerning discoveries and an-
'cient remains is to be arranged by the state archaeologist in
'order of parishes, and preserved in the archives of the
'archaeological commission.   As soon as a considerable area
'has been systematically investigated the state archaeologist
'shall draw up a brief account of its antiquarian remains, in
'order that it may be published by the commission and dis-
'tributed free of cost to the municipal authorities of the place
'concerned, and to the clergy, local officials, and other persons
'whose cooperation can be looked for in the work of protecting
'ancient monuments.'

According to Article 5, 'For the protection of important
'monuments standing on private ground, the state archaeolo-
'gist shall endeavour to obtain their transference by gift or
'by deed of purchase to the state or to the commune.   In
'other cases he is to take steps to ensure that clauses be
'appended to terms of lease or of transference of property for
'securing the protection of such monuments.'   The authorities

of the district are to be apprised of all these proceedings, and notice will be given to them when any infringement of regulations has been reported.

Article 6 introduces the vexed question of restoration. ' The state archaeologist shall seek to restore to their original ' condition monuments which have been disturbed or injured, ' if this can be done without great expense. Concerning ' more considerable and costly works of protection, the state ' archaeologist must bring the proposals before the Com- ' mission. In the repairs or alterations made in old churches ' or other remarkable buildings, he must use all care that the ' original style of the structure be retained, and that any ' important remains from ancient times found in the excavation ' be preserved.'

Professor Aspelin reports that the yearly budget of the commission amounts at present to about 80,000 marks (£3200). Finland is not specially remarkable for its ancient monuments, but the arrangements made for their upkeep and supervision are, as will have been seen, of a very thorough and enlightened kind.

CHAPTER IX.

SPAIN AND PORTUGAL.

BIBLIOGRAPHY AND SOURCES OF INFORMATION.

SPAIN.

GOVERNMENTAL DECREES on the subject of ancient monuments, especially of November 15, 1844 ; of November 24, 1865, with modifications of December 30, 1881 ; of December 16, 1873 (issued under the Republic by the President Emilio Castelar) ; of December 26, 1890 ; and of June 1, 1900. The texts of these decrees were given in the relative issues of the *Gaceta de Madrid* ; that of 1865 is given in substance in an English translation in the *Reports to the British Foreign Office* of 1897, p. 33.

The writer is greatly indebted to Señor Luis Mª Cabello y Lapiedra, who acted as general secretary to the International Congress of Architects at Madrid in 1904, and who has been good enough to furnish for the purpose of this book the texts of most of the decrees mentioned above, and to accompany them by a valuable letter of explanation.

'Los monumentos nacionales', by Señor Rodrigo Amador de los Rios in *La España Moderna*, Madrid, April 1903.

Monumentos Declarados Nacionales, list drawn up by the Academy of Fine Arts of San Fernando, 1904.

PORTUGAL.

Conselho dos Monumentos Nacionaes ; *Decreto Organico, e Mais Legislação Correlativa*, Lisboa, 1902.

Señor A. R. Adães Bermudes, of Lisbon, Hon. Corresponding Member of the Royal Institute of British Architects, has been so kind as to furnish the writer with the text of the above and with a translation of it in French.

SPAIN.

SPAIN, as befits the magnificence of the land and its wealth in noble memorials, possesses a somewhat elaborate system for the care of the national treasures in architecture and the decorative arts. There is no formal Monument Act, though a project of one was introduced into the Senate on December 7, 1900, and presently withdrawn. A succession of Royal and Republican Decrees, and an apparatus of Commissions and Inventories, comprise the official machinery available for monument administration.

In 1844 a Royal Decree called into being Monument Commissions both central and provincial, and the important code of regulations for the working of these, drawn up in 1865, gives the system as it at present exists. It consists of five chapters with forty seven articles. The chapters are headed 'Of the Organization, Object, and Functions of the Provincial Commissions for Historical and Artistic Monuments'; 'Of the Duties of the Provincial Commissions for Monuments'; 'Of the Academic Work of the Provincial Commissions for Monuments'; 'Of the Provincial Museums' and 'General Dispositions'. In each of the forty nine provinces of the kingdom there is a provincial commission composed of corresponding members of the Royal Academies of San Fernando and of History, the councils of which form a central commission on monuments in the capital. The general duties of the commissions are to safeguard and restore historical and artistic monuments the property of the state; to create, encourage, and supervise provincial museums both of the fine arts and of antiquities; to acquire for these pictures, statues, medals and other artistic objects, as well as MSS and historical documents; to take the direction of archaeological excavations; to preserve the tombs of royal persons and men of renown, and to safeguard public buildings generally so as to secure them against decay and incongruous restorations; and finally to intervene in all public works, undertaken with municipal or provincial funds or at the expense of the state, on ancient sites, in the neighbourhood of the great Roman roads, or in any other place where the existence of ancient constructions is suspected, in order to prevent the loss or abstraction of such objects of artistic or archaeological interest as may be discovered.

The practical operations of the commissions for carrying out these objects are prescribed in Chapter II. They are to act as councils for the provincial governors in all proposed restorations, excavations, etc., and are empowered to take the initiative in their dealings with him in various circumstances detailed in the sub-sections of Article 21. Thus they are to protest against any works being carried out on public buildings until the Royal Academy of Fine Arts of San Fernando has inquired into the case, and against any proposed demolition or alienation of monuments of real value or of national interest whatever pretext be alleged for the same. They are to propose prompt repair when any artistic monument in public hands is falling into dilapidation, to oppose the sale abroad of monuments or documents of national interest, and to acquire artistic objects for public collections. On the other side the obligations of the provincial commissions towards the Academies of Fine Art and History are similarly detailed in Articles 22 to 26. The cost of these various operations of repair, acquisition, excavation, etc., is to be borne by sums provided partly in the provincial estimates and partly in those of the state, augmented on occasions by special grants.

Under the heading of the academic labours of the commissions, comes first of all the preparation of a catalogue raisonné of those buildings in the various provinces, the artistic merit and historical importance of which make them worthy of a place in the Statistical Account of Monuments projected by the central commission. Ancient sites are to be inventoried, monographs prepared on objects of special interest, investigations carried out, biographies of local artists compiled, etc. Visits of inspection are to be paid to places where immovable objects of value are situated.

The chapter on provincial museums contains nothing of special interest, and the 'general dispositions' provide that all local officials and public bodies are to aid the commissions in the carrying out of their operations.

It is provided in Article 10 that the provincial commissions are to meet regularly once a week[1], and oftener if needful— a provision which implies a lively faith on the part of the authors of the decree in the energy of provincial antiquaries. The financial provisions, noticed above, sound very liberal, but it is to be feared that both the personal energy and the material funds available have not sufficed for the carrying out of the excellent programme of the decree. A number of later rescripts testify however to the continued interest of the central authorities in the question of protecting the national treasures. Under the Republic, President Castelar, in 1873, noting that 'a blind spirit of destruction seemed to have seized on the minds of certain popular authorities, that, moved by a misconceived zeal and driven on by a strange political fanaticism, had not hesitated to sow with ruins the soil of the fatherland, to the discredit of the national honour', reasserted the provisions of the decree of 1865 as to the destruction without the consent of the central authorities of any public edifice of value, and exhorted the provincial commissions and other bodies to fresh vigilance in the performance of their duties[2].

The important matter of inventorization, which had been put into the hands of the provincial commissions, had not proceeded satisfactorily, and was taken up again in 1900 when it was made the subject of a Royal Decree[3]. In the preamble it is stated that the need for such an artistic inventory had been recognized since the beginning of the nineteenth century, and that it had been put in the forefront of the measure that created the provincial commissions in 1844, but that the work had languished. It was now to be resumed with the view of forming 'a complete catalogue of everything to which belonged a recognized value for history or for art'. The work is to be done province by province,

[1] 'Las Comisiones provinciales de Monumentos celebrarán cada semana y en dia determinado sesion ordinaria.'
[2] *Gaceta de Madrid*, December 18, 1873.
[3] ibid., June 2, 1900.

a commencement being made with the province of Avila. The Royal Academy of Fine Arts of San Fernando has the direction of the whole undertaking, and a commissioner has been appointed 'to catalogue all the historical and artistic monuments, as well as any other objects of acknowledged merit, existing in the province of Avila'. The work is to be completed within eight months, and about thirty pounds a month are allowed for remuneration and expenses.

An excellent review of the national wealth in architectural monuments is given in the paper by Señor Amador de los Rios mentioned in the bibliography, and a succinct provisional list has been drawn up by the Academy, embracing certain monuments of national importance—monumentos declarados nacionales. It will naturally be a long time, even in the most favourable circumstances, before a complete inventory can be made of the almost inexhaustible treasures architectural and artistic of which Spain is the possessor. The withdrawal of the Monument Act of 1900 was a disappointment for those interested in these treasures. They remain under the charge of the Minister of Public Instruction and of the Fine Arts, assisted by the two academies and by the provincial commissions so far as these are actively efficient. For practical work there is a body of official architects, charged, as in France, with the upkeep and the restoration of the national monuments. This is termed the Servicio de Construcciones Civiles, and works under a Reglamento of December 1890[1].

PORTUGAL.

Reference has already been made to a decree of King John V of Portugal, of the year 1721, which gave evidence of an enlightened interest in historical memorials not unnatural in a country that had made itself a world-power through its commerce and discoveries. The works over which the royal aegis was then thrown were the memorials of the Phoenicians, Greeks, Carthaginians, Romans, Goths and Arabs, and the care for those relics of older races, that had

---

[1] *Gaceta de Madrid*, December 27, 1890.

once touched the Lusitanian shores, exhibited an elevation of view that was beyond the ordinary level of thought of the early eighteenth century. All such relics, in whosesoever possession they might be, were to be protected and the interest in them of the state was to be recognized by the private owner. In the opening years of the nineteenth century the provisions of this edict were reinforced, and again in 1840, in connection with the suppression of the monasteries, measures were taken to secure the safe preservation of the national treasures in the form of mediaeval buildings.

In 1880 a Ministerial Decree brought Portugal into line with so many other European states by setting on foot the preparation of an inventory of national monuments, which was entrusted to the Royal Society of Architects and Archaeologists. A provisional inventory was after a very brief interval actually drawn up.

The Portuguese care of monuments has however entered on a new phase by the promulgation at the close of 1901 of a Royal Decree and Code of Administrative Regulations, which have the scope and force of a regular Monument Act. The following are extracts from these documents, of which a French translation has been obligingly furnished by Señor Adães Bermudes of Lisbon.

The decree in question, dated October 24, 1901, establishes certain councils or boards to assist the operations of the Ministry of Public Works, Commerce, and Industry. One of these is a 'Council on National Monuments', consisting of twenty members, nominated by the Minister, that is to fulfil in the main the same functions as the Royal Commission on Monuments in Belgium, the Central Commission of Austria, and other similar bodies. The Council is formed for deliberation and control, and its operations are defined in clauses which may be quoted in full as giving the modern view of the duty of the state in regard to national memorials. It is within the competence of the Council:—

'I. To schedule ("classer") the national monuments, 'according to rules adopted by the Council and duly ap-'proved by the Minister, from the points of view of

'archaeology, history, and architecture, and to exercise
'supervision over their upkeep, whether they belong to the
'state, to private individuals, or to corporations.

'2. To study and pass judgement on projects for conser-
'vation, repair, or restoration, which may be submitted to it.

'3. To propose such projects on its own initiative.

'4. To supervise the exact execution of all works that
'have received official sanction.

'5. To deliberate on all subjects placed before it by the
'Minister in accordance with the terms and scope of this
'decree.

'6. To proceed to take all the technical measures
'necessary for a restoration in graphic form of the national
'monuments.

'7. To draw up monographs, historical, descriptive, and
'artistic, of the more important national monuments.

'8. To bring together, arrange, and classify, all the
'notices and documents which may have a bearing on the
'history of Portuguese art.

'9. To form collections of copies and models to serve as
'aids to study and instruction in schools and in the national
'museums.

'10. To make special regulations for carrying out its work.

'11. To offer proposals for the disposition of the funds
'which for the purposes of this decree may be inserted in
'the national budget, and to superintend the actual adminis-
'tration of the grants.'

Other articles of the decree provide that the classification
(scheduling) of the national monuments shall be determined
by decree, counter-signed by the Minister of Public Works,
etc., and published in the official journal; and that on
monuments thus scheduled no work of any kind shall be
carried out on any pretext, without previous sanction of
the Council ratified by Ministerial decree. Proposals for
expropriations on ground of public utility, in the interests of
the national monuments scheduled in the terms of the decree,
are to be prepared in accordance with the advice of the
Council.

It is also provided by Art. 31 of the decree that, as a complement to it, the government shall present to the Chambers proposals for measures facilitating the process of expropriation in the interests of national monuments 'when circumstances call imperiously for it'; and also for arranging the legal procedure and the scale of fines in cases of resistance to the exact fulfilment of the decree.

It will be noticed that in the decree the question of 'classement', or scheduling, is treated in general terms, as if the process presented no elements of difficulty or complication. We have already seen however, in the case of many projects of legislation, that this process, especially when applied to monuments in private hands, is not easy to carry through ; nor is it a simple matter to fix the legal effect of the 'classement', or to decide what penalties are to be inflicted on those that contravene the arrangements which it involves. Hence we find the Minister of Public Works in Portugal addressing a memorial to the King, pointing out the necessity of 'establishing the fundamental rules on which classification must be based, and defining in a precise fashion the consequences of this classification, that is to say, the conditions of the protection which the scheduled monuments will enjoy'. With this in view, a supplementary decree was drawn up and received Royal Assent on December 30, 1901, the object of which was to fix 'the basis for the classification of immovable objects worthy of being considered national monuments, as well as the classification of movable objects of recognized intrinsic or extrinsic value, belonging to the state, to administrative corporations or other public institutions'.

The text of this supplementary decree follows almost exactly the provisions of the French 'Monuments Historiques' Act of 1887, and on that account need not be analysed here in detail. The main point of difference concerns the question of penal sanction. As this is a Royal Decree and not an Act formally passed by the legislature, fixed penalties are not threatened in it, and the question of these, as was noticed above, has to be referred to the Chambers.

CHAPTER X.

GREECE AND TURKEY.

BIBLIOGRAPHY AND SOURCES OF INFORMATION.

GREECE.

ΣΥΛΛΟΓΗ ΑΡΧΑΙΟΛΟΓΙΚΩΝ ΝΟΜΩΝ, ΔΙΑΤΑΓΜΑΤΩΝ ΚΑΙ ΕΓΚΥΚΛΙΩΝ, ΕΝ ΑΘΗΝΑΙΣ, 1892. Contains the text of the law of 1834 together with Royal and Ministerial Rescripts from 1833 to 1892. The law of 1834 is given in a German translation in von Wussow, II, 252 f.

Ο ΠΕΡΙ ΑΡΧΑΙΟΤΗΤΩΝ ΝΟΜΟΣ ΤΗΣ 24 ΙΟΥΛΙΟΥ 1899 κ.τ.λ. ΕΝ ΑΘΗΝΑΙΣ, 1899.

The writer has to thank M. P. Kavvadias, Ephor-General of Antiquities, for his kindness in sending the above prints for the purpose of this book.

Die Denkmalpflege, 1902, p. 47.

TURKEY.

Imperial Iradé of February 21, 1884, on the subject of archaeological excavations, etc.

For a translation of this, the effective Turkish law on the subject of ancient monuments, the writer is indebted to the kindness of his friend Professor Alexander van Millingen of Robert College, Constantinople.

GREECE.

SOON after the establishment of the modern kingdom of Greece, while the seat of government was still at Nauplia, there was drawn up a somewhat elaborate monument law, prepared by the German advisers of the Crown. The early date of this enactment, promulgated in May 1834 ; its fulness, for it runs to 114 articles ; and the exceptionally interesting nature of its subject matter, give this Hellenic law a very distinguished place among enactments of the kind. As an effective instrument it was superseded by the more recent Monument Act of 1899, with the Decrees for its administration, which itself has since received modifications; but in the main the general scheme drawn up by the framers of the Act of 1834 lies at the foundation of the existing arrangements for the care of the national antiquities.

The Act had to establish the whole apparatus of scientific and artistic as well as archaeological study, and the first section provides for the foundation at Athens of more than a dozen institutions of the kind including a central museum of antiquities, while local museums, libraries, etc., were, as conditions allowed, to be gradually established in the different nomarchies. The magnificent Central or National Museum in the Patisia Street at Athens carries out one of the purposes contemplated in the Act, while the local museums in different parts, such as those at Eleusis, Argos, Mykonos, and other places, also go back to the original scheme.

Section II provides for the personnel. There was to be established a body of Conservators and central and local Commissions composed of scientific and artistic experts, at whose head was to be placed the Ephor-General of Antiquities. This official, acting under the Minister of Religion and Education, was to be at the head of all the scientific and artistic collections of the state and of local bodies, and to exercise an almost despotic control over all operations of the conservators and commissions.

In Section III we come to the subject of the monuments themselves, and Article 61 contains the often quoted declaration, embodying the most extensive claim that any state has ever put forward in the matter of monuments, to the effect that 'all objects of antiquity in Greece, as the productions of the ancestors of the Hellenic people, are regarded as the common national possession of all Hellenes[1].' The remainder of the Act is for the most part taken up with enactments designed to carry into effect this principle, and as these have

---

[1] Ὅλαι αἱ ἐντὸς τῆς Ἑλλάδος ἀρχαιότητες, ὡς ἔργα τῶν προγόνων τοῦ Ἑλληνικοῦ λαοῦ, θεωροῦνται ὡς κτῆμα ἐθνικὸν ὅλων τῶν Ἑλλήνων ἐν γένει.

been superseded by the provisions of the more recent Act we
need not go through them here. It should be noted however,
that just at the end of the Act, introduced by what looks like
an afterthought, there comes a declaration that 'those objects
also which have been handed down from the earlier epochs
of Christian art, and from the so-called middle ages, are not
exempt from the provisions of the present law.' It is obvious
that what the framers of the Act had almost entirely in view
were antiques, whereas as we shall see presently the tendency
of the most recent Hellenic legislation is in the direction of
securing full protection for mediaeval relics as well as those
of classical times.

The Monument Act of 1899 is introduced by a preamble,
in which the principle just laid down is again recited, and the
people are told that ALL ANTIQUITIES, AS THE WORK OF
THE FOREFATHERS OF THE HELLENIC PEOPLE, ARE A
COMMON NATIONAL POSSESSION OF ALL HELLENES. The
older law based on this principle was however faulty, and
must be now replaced by one which shall absolutely prevent
all loss or injury in the case of immovable monuments, as
well as clandestine sales out of the country of portable
objects of art and antiquity. To secure these ends somewhat
severe penalties are threatened, up to five years' imprisonment and the loss of civic rights. Private citizens are
warned in this same preliminary discourse that if they possess
antiquities they must forthwith declare them to the authorities, and must give immediate notice if any fresh discoveries
are made on their property. The old things of Hellas are
the eternal witnesses of the past glory of the land, to which
the neo-Hellenes owe so much. Wherefore let all Hellenes
love these monuments of antiquity and prize them as the
apple of their eye, and lend practical aid to the authorities to
secure their safe preservation.

The Act itself falls into nine chapters headed respectively
'On Antiquities in General'; 'On Immovable Monuments';
'On Movable Monuments'; 'On Excavations'; 'On the
Import and Export of Antiquities'; 'On the Disposition of
Antiquities and on Private Collections'; 'On Copies of

Antiquities'; 'Temporary Arrangements'; 'General Arrangements'; and the first articles reassert the claim of the state over the national monuments in general. 'All the objects 'of antiquity, whether movable or immovable, to be found in 'Greece; in or on any land belonging to the state, in rivers 'or lakes or at the bottom of the sea; on property moreover 'belonging to towns, communes, monasteries, or individuals; 'from the remotest period downwards, are the property of 'the state. As a consequence, to the state belongs the care 'of all investigations or searches and all preservative measures 'regarding such objects, as well as their collection and deposit 'in public museums.'

'Objects that have come down from the earliest days of 'Christianity or from the middle ages are not excluded from 'the operations of the present law.'

'All operations under the Act fall within the Department 'of the Ministry of Religion and Public Instruction.'

Chapter II, on immovable antiquities, contains important provisions. 'Ancient buildings and all other immovable 'monuments that have been discovered or may come to light 'on the ground of individual proprietors are considered public 'property. In cases where it is decided that the building or 'monument thus brought to light should be preserved, the 'proprietor receives compensation according to the provisions 'of the law for Public Works of January 4, 1888' (Art. 5).

By Article 6 any discovery of antiquities must be at once reported to the Ephor-General, who will decide if it be worth preservation in accordance with Art. 5. If not the proprietor will have the disposal of it.

Article 7 forbids damage of any kind to ancient remains movable or immovable. No quarrying or burning of lime is allowed within 300 metres of such remains, or is anything to be done either to them or near them that can by any possibility cause them injury.

In Chapter III it is laid down that all movable works of antique art or objects bearing on the history of the land have their proper place in the museums and archaeological collections of the state. When valuable objects of the kind come

to light on a private estate, either accidentally or as a result
of authorized excavations carried out by the proprietor, the
latter receives one half of the worth of such objects as are
taken for the museums.   Any discovery of the kind must be
at once reported.   In cases where the authorities pronounce
the objects not worthy of a place in the museums, they are
left at the disposal of the proprietor, though they are entered
at the same time in a state register.

Chapter IV, on excavations, begins again with the
annunciation of a sweeping general principle, i.e. ' The
' Ministry of Public Instruction is authorized to undertake
' excavations in search of antiquities not only on land
' belonging to the state or to municipalities, communes and
' monasteries, but also on private estates.   For this purpose
' the compulsory purchase of the land required for the
' excavations can be resorted to ' in accordance with a law
of which the date is given.   Tentative excavations may be
made without previous expropriation, the proprietor receiving
a suitable indemnity.   Such tentative diggings are not to be
such as would endanger his house or other such property.
When excavations are made on private land by agreement,
without expropriation, compensation is to be given, and a
third part of the value of any movable objects obtained for
museums is to be given to the proprietor (Art. 14).

Proprietors are forbidden to excavate on their land without permission (Art. 15).

The fifth chapter concerns the import of antiquities into
Greece, to which there is no hindrance, and their export from
the country, which is strictly forbidden save on permission
obtained.   The infringement of this rule carries a heavy
penalty.   Passing over certain provisions relating to the
traffic in antiquities within the limits of the kingdom, etc., we
come in chapter seven to the curious provision that no dealer
in genuine antiquities is at the same time to traffic in reproductions, under penalty of fine and imprisonment.

There are various provisions relating to private collections
of antiquities.   Within six months of the passing of the law
all owners of such had to furnish an accurate catalogue in

duplicate to the Ephor-General. After due notice to the authorities, such antiquities may be bought and sold within the limits of the kingdom according to the provisions of the older law, but must not be sold beyond its borders. Any objects not declared as above, will, when attention is subsequently directed to them, be regarded as newly discovered, and subjected to the provisions of Chapter III of the present law.

It is a noteworthy feature of this new Greek Monument Act that the penalties for infraction of its provisions are severe. The mild 'action for damages', which under the French Act the authorities can bring against a recalcitrant private owner, is replaced here by fines up to 10,000 drachmae (£400), and by imprisonment. Thus the penalty of neglecting to declare a find (Art. 6) may amount to imprisonment for a year. Unauthorized excavators are threatened with two years' confinement (Art. 15), while any official that connives at infractions of the law may be imprisoned for five years.

It has been already mentioned that an increased care for the early Christian and mediaeval monuments of the country, as distinct from antique remains, has been observable in recent Greek procedure. The fact that the Monument Act applies to the former as well as the latter is emphasized in the very forefront of the Act of 1899, but only comes in as an afterthought in that of 1834. The fact is that Greece is rich in interesting early Christian and Byzantine relics, and possesses moreover very grand remains of Venetian fortifications, such as those that guard the harbour of Candia. The winged Lion of St Mark still claims as his own many a stretch of noble walling washed by Aegean waves, or fanned by the hill breezes on some Acropolis summit. These are well worthy of preservation side by side with the older relics, and on the proposition of the Ephor-General, M. Kavvadias, a Ministerial Rescript was issued in 1902 calling attention to the necessity for scrupulous care in the preservation of this part of the national treasure in monuments, of which the Acts of 1834 and 1899 took account.

TURKEY.

The traditional custom of exploiting the antique remains in the Ottoman dominions for the benefit of the museums of Europe is supposed now to be abrogated, and the administration of Turkish antiquities has been placed on a regular footing. Lord Elgin and J. T. Wood, Carl Humann and Heinrich Schliemann, enriched the collections of London and Berlin with some of the masterpieces of ancient art, the provenance of which was in each case part of the Turkish dominions, but with the close of the century that had seen these treasures successively shipped to Europe, there came about a change of policy, and the whole system of dealing with the antiquities of the Empire was regulated by Imperial Decree. The development of the collections of antiques at Constantinople has been a feature of the last quarter of a century, and the New Museum opposite the Tschinili Kiosk, that contains now a host of fine objects apart from the overpraised 'Alexander' sarcophagus, is intended to be the place of reception for the best artistic results of new discoveries. In view of the vast extent of the Empire, and its almost incredible wealth in remains from all the artistic periods of the past, arrangements will no doubt continue to be made for the export of antiquities. Thus the collections at Vienna have been enriched, not only by the reliefs from Gjölbaschi (Trysa) in Asia Minor sent home by Benndorf in 1882–3, but quite recently by numerous sculptures from the Austrian excavations at Ephesus, including some late-Roman high-reliefs on a monumental scale. Again, the Sultan has presented to his friend the German Emperor the interesting and decoratively beautiful sculptured façade from Mschatta, now in the new Kaiser-Friedrich Museum at Berlin. These are to be regarded however as exceptional cases, and the control of excavations and of the export of antiquities is in theory at any rate as severely exercised in Turkey as in Greece or Italy.

The centre of the monument administration of the Empire is the Museum at Constantinople, now under the direction of

Hamdi Bey, who may be regarded as the official Conservator of Ancient Monuments for the Sultan's dominions. The upkeep of the religious monuments such as the Mosques, or of the Tombs of the Sultans, is of course provided for in other ways.

As regards antiquities, an Imperial Iradé of February 21, 1884, gives the provisions for monument administration which are now in force. It contains thirty seven articles, and its subject matter comprises 'all the remains left by the ancient 'populations of the states which now form the dominions of 'the Ottoman Empire'. A sweeping claim is made in Art. 3, which states that 'all objects of antiquity within the Ottoman 'Empire that are already known or may in the future be 'discovered in excavations or be found in the bed of the sea, 'in lakes, rivers or water-courses, are the absolute property 'of the state.' When these objects of antiquity exist on private land the proprietor of the soil cannot dispose of them, and must avoid anything which might do them injury. If government desire to excavate in private ground and the proprietor object, the land in question may be expropriated.

No excavations may be undertaken without leave and control, and (Art. 8) 'it is absolutely forbidden to export 'antiquities found within the Ottoman Empire', while an- 'tiquities discovered in excavations made after leave obtained 'belong to the Imperial Museum, the excavator being only 'allowed the right of taking drawings or casts' (Art. 12). By a more recent emendation on this regulation however, the discoverer is entitled to receive a twentieth part of the value of what is found. No permit will be given for more than two years, with a possible extension to three, and will not embrace a larger area than ten square kilometres. A certain rent is paid for a permit, the proceeds of which go for the benefit of the Museum. The salary of the government official who watches the excavations must also be paid by the holder of the permit.

The accidental discoverer of an object of antiquity is treated more generously, of course with a view to encouraging him to give notice of the 'find'. Art. 14, 'The antiquities

'which may be discovered by accident in digging the founda-
'tions of a building, making a drain, etc., shall be divided in
'equal parts between the owner of the land and the govern-
'ment.' The latter may take any special object required into
its own share. There is a penalty for the failure to report
a 'find'. Persons who injure or destroy monuments declared
in Art. 3 to be state property come under the operations of
the penal code, and may be imprisoned for a year.

CHAPTER XI.

THE DANUBIAN PROVINCES. ROUMANIA, SERVIA, BULGARIA, BOSNIA, HERZGOVINA.

BIBLIOGRAPHY AND SOURCES OF INFORMATION.

Roumanian Monument Acts, November 1892, text analysed in *Annuaire de Législation Étrangère*, vol. XXII, p. 819 f. Commentary in Tétreau, *Législation Relative aux Monuments et Objets d'Art*, Paris, 1896, p. 262 f.
Bulgarian *Law relating to the Exploration of Antiquities and Encouragement of Scientific and Literary Enterprises*, November 1889. Text published in Sofia, 1890.
Bosnian *Verordnung der Landesregierung für Bosnien und die Hercegovina*, June 1892. Sarajevo, Landesmuseum, 1900.

Information kindly furnished by Dr Paul Leverkuhn of the Museum, Sofia, Bulgaria ; Dr Truhelka, of the Landesmuseum, Sarajevo, Bosnia; and the Bulgarian Diplomatic Agent, London, to whom the writer is much indebted for his kindness in furnishing a translation of the Bulgarian monument law.

THE Danubian Provinces possess recent monument legislation of a somewhat drastic kind, in which the state claim to control all dealings with ancient monuments is pushed to the fullest extent. As has been remarked already more than once, such legislation is generally more severe in countries of which the population is on the whole in a comparatively low state of civilization. This description, it must be confessed, is rapidly ceasing to have application to Bulgaria, the people of which are showing a devotion to the cause of education which make them the Japanese of that part of Europe.

The monument legislation of ROUMANIA is contained in two Acts promulgated in November 1892, one of which refers to the preservation and repair of public monuments, the other to excavations and 'finds' and movable objects of antiquity and art in general.

A commission for the care of public monuments is constituted under the first of the Acts, and its first task was to draw up an inventory of all historical monuments worthy of preservation. It is a provision worthy of notice that this list is to be revised every five years. No scheduled monument can be destroyed, repaired, or altered without leave of the Minister of Religion and Public Instruction. Offences against this provision may be punished by fines of 100 to 5,000 francs, and destruction of or injury to a public monument may involve imprisonment for a period of six months. If the obligations of a proprietor towards a monument on his land involve too great a burden, he may demand the purchase of it by the state.

The second Act provides that no one shall excavate without the sanction of the Minister. If leave be given, the work is officially inspected, and all discoveries must be at once reported to the authorities. When objects are discovered in excavations on lands belonging to the state, or to a department, a commune, or public establishment, they are declared the property of the state, but the finder has a right to an honorarium to be fixed by the Minister. If the objects come to light on private land they belong half to the proprietor and half to the finder. The corollary is that where a proprietor excavates on his own land he retains the objects found, but his power of dealing with them is limited by succeeding provisions of the Act. Thus, the sale of objects of historical or artistic value can only take place within the limits of Roumania after notice is given to the Minister, while for a sale beyond the borders his authorization is necessary. Such objects cannot be repaired or restored without his leave, and then only under the directions of the monument commission. If a sale be made in Roumania without notice, or a work of repair carried out without authorization, the penalty is confiscation of the object by the state, while if it have been destroyed or exported, the offender may be imprisoned. Any accidental discovery of objects of value must be at once reported. The state may excavate on private property, but the owner may demand the expropriation of the land required for the purpose.

In SERVIA the National Museum at Belgrade has charge of the department of Servian antiquities, and receives a yearly subvention from the state. Its custodian is at the same time Professor of Archaeology in the neighbouring University or High School. In 1883 there was founded a Servian archaeological society for the investigation, preservation, and acquisition of historical and artistic monuments from all periods of the pre-history and history of the land. A project of a monument law brought forward by the then custodian of the Museum in 1882 is not yet ratified[1].

The Monument Act of BULGARIA is headed 'Law relating to the Exploration of Antiquities and Encouragement of Scientific and Literary Enterprises', and it was passed in November 1889. It consists of three sections of which only the first relates to monuments. The second is concerned with the collection of popular songs, traditions, records of customs, and all the other material of the folklorist; and the third with state encouragement for literary enterprises.

The first article of the first section lays down the principle that 'All undiscovered material of an antiquarian character, 'wherever it may come to light, is the property of the state.'

The Act goes on to provide that any one who discovers objects of value accidentally or as the result of search will be allowed half their value, while the owner of the land on which the discovery is made receives one quarter their value. When proprietor and finder are the same person he will have three quarters of the value, and this will be appraised by commissioners appointed by the Minister of Public Instruction.

Articles 7 to 9 run as follows :—

'Any person who proposes to search for objects of an- 'tiquity must apply for the necessary authorization from the 'Minister of Public Instruction.

---

[1] von Helfert, *Denkmalpflege*, p. 34.

'Immovable objects that may come to light, such as ruins
'of temples, forts, etc., wherever they may be found, are state
'property, and remain under the supervision of the local
'authorities.

'Excavations without preliminary authorization are for-
'bidden. Any objects that may have been discovered in such
'unauthorized excavations are confiscated by the government.'

Articles 10 to 16 contain various provisions safeguarding
the conduct of excavations.

Art. 17. 'Any movable objects of antiquity that come
'to light are to be inventoried and described and if possible
'forwarded, by the local authorities to the Minister of Public
'Instruction.

Art. 18. 'The exportation out of the Principality of
'antiquarian objects, without the authorization of the Minister
'of Public Instruction, is forbidden. Such authorization will
'be granted on the presentation of a list of the objects of
'which the exportation is desired. The government reserves
'the right of purchasing for the National Museum a specimen
'of each kind of object in question.

Art. 19. 'Objects of antiquity, which are being exported
'secretly, are, on discovery, confiscated by the government
'without compensation.

Art. 20. 'Persons engaged in searching for antiquities
'must conform strictly to the directions issued by the Minister
'of Public Instruction.'

The second section of the Act contains provisions designed
to encourage the people to communicate material for the
social history of the country, and Art. 31 reads as follows:—

'Private persons who offer notes of popular songs, popular
'sayings, riddles, customs, stories, traditions, etc., as well as
'persons who in accordance with Article 17 of the Act give
'descriptions of tombs, shrines, statues, forts, sarcophagi,
'altars, monuments, arms, utensils, costumes, and the like,
'will receive a pecuniary recompense proportionate to the
'importance and extent of their communications, if these be
'favourably regarded.'

The outcome of the measures thus indicated has been the

establishment at Sofia of a very promising National Museum, that Professor Conze has pronounced to be one of the best of its class. A considerable number of classical monuments have been collected in the department of antiquities.

The provisions applicable to BOSNIA and HERZGOVINA are contained in an Ordinance (Verordnung) 'concerning the preservation of historical monuments, and proceedings with regard to antiquities or other objects of historical or social importance[1]'.

With the view of keeping such objects within the Provinces and securing their due preservation, it is decreed that even when belonging to private owners they are under state care to the extent provided for in the Ordinance.

Fixed objects of antiquarian or artistic value are under the direct control of the authorities, and it is forbidden to destroy, remove, or injure them. No investigation of such monuments and no excavations can be undertaken without official leave.

No movable object of the kind contemplated may be exported beyond the limits of Bosnia and Herzgovina, but a sale within the Provinces is allowed under the proviso that the state has the right of pre-emption. Special permission for exportation can however be granted.

The possessor or the discoverer of any such object must give information about it to the authorities. If he desire to sell it he must name a price, and if the government be not willing to pay this he may dispose of it at the same price to another purchaser, though only within the Provinces.

The finder of any valuable object of antiquity receives a premium on his discovery.

Offences, especially against the provisions about exportation, are punishable by fines of 5 to 500 florins.

Finally all officials are charged to use all care and tact in the administration of the Ordinance, so that the public may feel confidence in the sense and justice of its provisions, and not be tempted to conceal the treasures they may possess or discover.

[1] Bosnia is of course under Austrian administration, and the Ordinance was issued on the Imperial authority in May 1892.

CHAPTER XII.

INDIA, EGYPT, ALGERIA, TUNIS.

Bibliography and Sources of Information.

India.

The Ancient Monuments Preservation Act, 1904 (India). Act No. VII of 1904.

'Archaeological Research in India', by James Burgess, LL.D., C. I. E., from the *Transactions of the 8th International Congress of Orientalists*, Stockholm, 1889.

'Some notes on Past and Future Archaeological Explorations in India', by G. Buhler, in *Journal of the Royal Asiatic Society*, for 1895.

Archaeological Survey of India, *Annual Report*, 1902–3, Calcutta, 1904. Introduction, pp. 1–30.

Egypt.

Bulletin des Lois et Décrets (Egyptian). Various years, especially Decrees of May 16th, 1883; January 31st, 1889; November 17th, 1891. Règlement of March 1889.

Copies of these documents have been kindly furnished by Mr Malcolm McIlwraith, Judicial Adviser to the Khedive, to whom the best thanks of the writer are here tendered.

Von Wussow, *Erhaltung der Denkmäler*, I, 235.

Algeria.

Loi du 30 Mars 1887, Monuments Historiques (France), Chap. IV.

Tétreau, *Législation Relative aux Monuments et Objets d'Art*, Paris, 1896, p. 211 f.

Tunis.

Tétreau, *Législation*, p. 244 f.

THE countries noticed in this chapter, though not in Europe, are to a great extent both administered and inhabited by Europeans, and are particularly rich in ancient monuments, for the care of which Europeans are largely responsible. Hence a brief reference to monument administration in these lands is an almost necessary corollary to an account of what is done in Europe itself.

INDIA.

The story of archaeological work under British rule in India is in the main what a student of our national idiosyncrasies would have expected. Efforts have been spasmodic, and have depended largely on the personal initiative of individual administrators. There has been little continuity in policy, because the objects to be aimed at have not been clearly defined, and the centre of interest has shifted backwards and forwards between the rival aims of research and conservation. No one well-considered system of publication has been adopted and maintained, and publications which have cost much labour and money[1] have appeared with faults that have considerably marred their usefulness. That so much has actually been accomplished is due in part to the initiative of certain Indian Secretaries of State and Viceroys such as Lord Canning, Lord Lytton, and Lord Curzon, but still more to the devoted labour which has been bestowed on various departments of the work by men like Prinsep and Mackenzie in past generations, and Cunningham, Dr Burgess, and above all James Fergusson in our own.

The foundation of the Asiatic Society of Bengal by Sir William Jones, in 1784, is held to mark the beginning of the scientific study of Indian antiquities, but for nearly a century government allowed almost all of the work to remain in the hands of private associations and individuals. In 1862 Lord Canning expressed himself as follows in an official minute[2]. ' It will not be to our credit as an enlightened ruling power, if we continue to allow such fields of investigation...to remain

---

[1] A long list of official publications of an archaeological character embracing 211 items is given at the end of the *Annual Report of the Archaeological Survey* for 1902–3.

[2] Quoted by Dr Burgess on p. 32 of his paper, see Bibliography.

without more examination than they have hitherto received. Everything that has hitherto been done in this way has been done by private persons, imperfectly and without system. It is impossible not to feel that there are European Governments, which, if they had held our rule in India, would not have allowed this to be said.' In accordance with this view there was established at this time the Archaeological Survey of Upper India, and this was carried on for a few years by Colonel, afterwards Sir Alexander, Cunningham. Owing to certain difficulties that arose, the work was in 1865 suspended, but was resumed and placed on a much better footing in 1870, when General Cunningham was re-appointed Director General of the Archaeological Survey of India, with a commission 'to superintend a complete search over the whole country and a systematic record and description of all architectural and other remains that are remarkable alike for their antiquity, or their beauty, or their historical interest'. His work was however practically confined to Northern India, other Surveys being formed about the same time for the Presidencies of Bombay and Madras. Sir Alexander Cunningham remained in office till 1885 and issued in all twenty three volumes of Reports. These were however to a considerable extent the work of native assistants who were imperfectly trained, and the volumes thus lost much of their usefulness.

The idea in the minds of the authorities who set the Survey officers to work, was, as the name of the organization implies, inventorization. The existing monuments were to be looked over, classified, and described, and when the results were duly entered and published nothing more remained to be done. 'An archaeological survey was regarded as something which once done was done for ever[1]' and it was thought that in a measurable time the task would be accomplished and the Survey cease to have any function. No provision was made for carrying out excavations to learn more about the monuments than appeared on the exterior, and the important question of their treatment in the way

---

[1] *Annual Report*, 1902–3, p. 5.

of preservation or repair was left in the background. In fact, as the present Director General of the Survey remarks, 'many of the greatest buildings and monuments of ancient India were steadily sinking into a deplorable condition[1],' when in 1878 Lord Lytton, who was then Viceroy, issued a minute in which he recognized that the conservation of the national antiquities was an 'essentially imperial' duty of the central government. The result was the appointment of a Curator of Ancient Monuments, to report specially on questions of repair and maintenance, and this office was held by Major Cole for a period of three years from 1881. During this period the Curator issued, besides other publications, three annual reports with a programme of future work of conservation, and we are told that 'his reports are to this day the sole works of permanent value dealing with conservation as distinct from research among all the bibliography representing 32 years archaeological activity in India[2].'

In 1885, Dr Burgess, who had been carrying on extensive labours while in charge of the Archaeological Survey in Madras and Bombay, succeeded Sir Alexander Cunningham as Director General, but retired in 1889, and there then ensued a period of reaction, during which the care of ancient monuments in India whether as regards conservation or research sank to its lowest ebb. No new Director General was appointed and there was no official charged with preservation. All that was accomplished for the cause of the monuments was due to local efforts in the various provinces. This period of stagnation came to an end near the close of the century, and a new order of things was inaugurated with the coming to India of Lord Curzon as Viceroy. A new Director General has been appointed, and the work of the archaeological department placed on a more satisfactory footing. Adequate funds are now provided for excavations, repairs, and also for schemes of restoration, which last may very easily be carried too far. It is a promising sign of the times that the native princes are following the example of the central government in instituting Surveys and caring for

---

[1] ibid., p. 4.   [2] ibid., p. 5.

the preservation of the older monuments of their territories. The Viceroy has personally visited the chief monuments of interest and expressed publicly his sense of the duty towards them of the government.

The following sentences from a speech made by Lord Curzon in 1900, before the Asiatic Society of Calcutta, sum up the history of Indian monument administration. 'There has been, during the last 40 years, some sort of sustained effort on the part of Government to recognize its responsibilities and to purge itself of a well merited reproach. This attempt has been accompanied, and sometimes delayed, by disputes as to the rival claims of research and of conservation, and by discussion over the legitimate spheres of action of the Central and the Local Governments. There have been periods of supineness as well as of activity. There have been moments when it has been argued that the State had exhausted its duty or that it possessed no duty at all. There have been persons who thought that, when all the chief monuments were indexed and classified, one might sit with folded arms and allow them slowly and gracefully to crumble into ruin. There have been others who argued that railways and irrigation did not leave a modest half-lakh of rupees per annum for the requisite establishment to supervise the most glorious galaxy of monuments in the world. Nevertheless, with these interruptions and exceptions, which I hope may never again occur, the progress has been positive and on the whole continuous.'

The bright promise which the immediate future seems to offer for Indian archaeology, should not blind us to the fact that the real work has been done by men who have toiled on year after year with no official sunshine on their path, and have in the face of immense difficulties placed the science of that archaeology on a sound basis. Without the energy and patience of men like James Fergusson and many others living or deceased who might be mentioned, the study and care of the monuments of our great eastern possession would not reflect credit on those who administer it.

The seal has been set on this new order of things by

the promulgation in 1904 of a complete and well drawn Monument Act for India, to which some attention must be paid. It is noteworthy that it is fully equipped with the compulsory clauses, prohibitions, and penal sanctions, of which people in the mother country are so shy. This illustrates once again the fact already noticed, that in less advanced communities it is more easy to pass stringent monument laws than in states where the individual citizen is accustomed to stand stiffly by his rights.

The Indian Act has twenty four sections, some of which are conditioned by the special character of the country, especially its numerous religions, while others are of a kind that would suit European circumstances. The preamble runs, 'Whereas it is expedient to provide for the preservation of 'ancient monuments, for the exercise of control over traffic 'in antiquities, and over excavation in certain places, and for 'the protection and acquisition in certain cases of ancient 'monuments and of objects of archaeological, historical or 'artistic interest.' In furtherance of these laudable purposes the Act authorizes the Local Government (Section 3) to declare any ancient monument to be 'a protected monument within the meaning of this Act'. This is equivalent to the French 'classement', or to insertion in the schedule affixed to the British Ancient Monuments Act of 1882. It is not however, like the operation of 'classement' in France, dependent in any case in the first instance on the consent of a proprietor, but proceeds from the independent initiative of the authorities. Objections may however be raised against the notification of the protection within a period of one month, at the expiry of which period 'the Local Government, 'after considering the objections if any, shall confirm or 'withdraw the notification'.

What now is the effect of this notification that a monument is 'protected'?

The mere act of declaring a monument protected carries with it the consequence indicated in Section 16, that no one other than the owner may destroy, remove, injure, alter, deface or imperil it, under the risk of being visited with the

somewhat severe penalty of a 'fine which may extend to
five thousand rupees, or with imprisonment which may
extend to three months, or with both'.

Anything further must be the subject of special arrangements, that are explained in full detail and with satisfactory
clearness in Sections 4 to 14. By § 4 the government may
purchase (by arrangement) or take on lease, or receive as
a gift or bequest, any protected monument; may accept its
guardianship on a written covenant from the owner, or may
assume guardianship of it when there is no owner forthcoming.
In any of these cases the government undertakes an obligation
to maintain the monument in question (§ 11), while on his
part the owner comes under the operation of § 16 noticed
above, and may not destroy, etc., the monument under the
penalties therein laid down. Furthermore § 15 provides that
under certain conditions 'the public shall have a right of
access to any monument, maintained by the government
under the Act', but it seems that when the government has
only been entrusted with the *guardianship* of the monument
the right of public access must be a matter of special agreement (§ 5 [2 d]). On the other hand, the owner is bound
unconditionally by § 11 (2) to allow the authorities access for
purposes of inspection and repair.

The question of guardianship is indeed one of agreement,
and falls properly under § 5, which deals at length with
agreements between owners and the government in favour
of protected monuments. Under this section the government
may propose to the owner of any protected monument to
enter into an agreement for its preservation. The conditions
will depend on what seems in each case expedient, and the
sub-sections of the section indicate what may be included
under such an agreement. It may provide for the maintenance and custody of the monument; for facilities of access
on the part of the public and of official inspectors; for a
right of pre-emption, if the land on which the monument
stands be up for sale. The covenant may also restrict the
owner from destroying or altering the monument or erecting
new buildings near it, though this is in part at any rate

specially provided against in § 16, by which an owner who
has executed such an agreement is prohibited under the
penal sanctions of the section from destroying, altering, etc.
Either party may terminate an agreement on six months'
notice. Due performance of its conditions can be enforced
on the owner (§ 7). Other provisions are of local rather than
general significance.

Sections 9 and 10 contemplate the case when 'any owner
'or other person, competent to enter into an agreement under
'Section 5 for the preservation of a protected monument,
'refuses or fails to enter into such an agreement when pro-
'posed to him'. The government may in such a case enforce
the application to its proper purpose of any endowment
which may exist for the benefit of the monument (§ 9 [1]),
or (§ 10) if it be apprehended that 'a protected monument
'is in danger of being destroyed, injured or allowed to fall
'into decay, the Local Government may proceed to acquire
'it under the provisions of the Land Acquisition Act, 1894
'as if the preservation of a protected monument were a
'"public purpose" within the meaning of that Act'. This
power of compulsory purchase cannot be exercised over any
monument used for religious purposes, or one that is already
the subject of an existing agreement; and must always be
preceded by the offer of an agreement. The conferring of
the power of expropriation at all is very significant for
British monument legislation. It is an avowed recognition
of the principle that the Care of Ancient Monuments is a
'public purpose', and this brings the Indian Act into line
with French legislation, which, as noticed above (ante, p. 74),
is distinguished for its breadth of view on this important
question. When the time comes for British legislation to
face the institution of compulsory purchase on aesthetic
grounds, the precedent of the Indian Act will be a useful
one to cite.

Section 17 regulates traffic in antiquities, by giving the
Governor General in Council power to 'prohibit or restrict
'the bringing or taking by sea or by land of any antiquities
'or class of antiquities......into or out of British India or any

'specified part of British India'. A fine up to five hundred rupees and confiscation of the objects concerned follow any infringement of a prohibition of the kind.

Section 18 gives power to the Local Government to prohibit the removal from the place where they are of 'any sculpture, carvings, images, bas-reliefs, inscriptions or other like objects' without official permission. If an owner of such property consider himself aggrieved by the prohibition of removal, and make out a good case before the authorities, the Local Government may (a) rescind the prohibition, or (b) purchase such property if it be movable, at its market value, or (c) if the property be immovable pay compensation. In cases where the object in question appears to be in danger compulsory purchase 'at its market price' is allowed, but the object cannot be so acquired if it be actually used for religious purposes, or have any traditional or family sanctities.

Section 20 refers to excavations, which can be controlled in the interests of any ancient monument within their area. The owner or occupier of the land may receive compensation.

EGYPT.

The general subject of Egyptian monuments, and the treatment meted out to them at successive periods of a history the longest recorded in human annals, is far too large to be entered on here. It will suffice to give some idea of the actual legislation under which these monuments are at present administered.

There are two departments of this administration, one concerned with Arab monuments the other with the older Egyptian antiquities. A 'Comité de Conservation des Monuments de l'Art Arabe' has existed since 1881, and its object is the inventorization of Arab monuments of interest for history or art, and their due inspection and preservation. The other department, under the 'Comité permanent d'Égyptologie', is of greater importance and has been administered throughout the last century mainly by French agency. The charter of this department is the Khedival Decree of May 16, 1883, which is supplemented by a Règlement, or code of rules

for procedure, issued in March 1889. Article 9 of this
Règlement states that the Committee is to study the general
measures which should be taken for the conservation of the
ancient monuments of Egypt, for the arrestation of the decay
of the objects of antiquity, and for the prevention of excavations irregularly carried out or unauthorized. According to
the Decree, the Bulak Museum of Egyptian antiquities prior
to the Arab conquest, with all the objects it contained or
might contain in the future, was declared the property of
the state and inalienable and unassignable, while the same
was to apply to any future collections that might be formed.

Article 3 runs as follows : 'Sont également déclarés
' propriétés du Domaine public de l'État, tous les monuments
' et objets d'antiquité reconnus tels par le Règlement qui
' régira la matière.' This Règlement (not the same as that of
March 1889) has never yet been promulgated, and the
Decree is left as it stands, claiming the general sovereignty
of the state over all the antiquities of the lands of the Nile.
This vague assertion of state control over all monuments is
practically useful, as it can be appealed to by the executive
to save any threatened object from danger. A Khedival
Decree of August 12, 1897, menaces with penalties 'any who
' appropriate, or remove with a view to appropriation, an
' antiquity belonging to the government, apart from the
' objects in the museums or monuments of the state ;

'Any who by their act injure or reduce in value an
' ancient monument, or cause the ruin of the whole or part
' of an ancient construction, or mutilate the bas-reliefs, statues,
' or inscriptions on any such construction, or who write their
' names or anything else on the monuments.'

There is a third Khedival Decree, of November 17, 1891,
that with the one just quoted appears to make up all the
formal legislation that exists on the subject. It concerns the
question, so important in Egypt, of excavations. The chief
provisions of this Decree of 1891 run as follows. 'Art. 1.
' Excavations can only be carried on by private persons in
' virtue of an authorization granted on the proposal of the
' Director-General of museums and excavations, after delibera-

'tion by the permanent Committee of Egyptology in the
'terms of the sixth article of its regulations of March 9, 1889.'

'Art. 2. All the objects found in the excavations belong
'of right to the state and should be deposited in the Museum
'of Ghizeh (Bulak).

'Art. 3. Nevertheless, in consideration of the expense
'incurred by the excavator the government will yield to him
'a part of the antiquities discovered, in accordance with the
'following regulations.'

These regulations provide for a partition into equal lots,
but the administration reserves its right to any object of
special value. 'In all cases, the administration can appro-
'priate the objects it desires to retain, on recompensing the
'excavator with a sum that can never exceed the cost of the
'excavation which resulted in their discovery' (Art. 5, last
clause).

It is expected that before long a new Decree on the
subject of Egyptian monuments will be promulgated, for the
purpose of codifying and rendering more clear and effective
these regulations.

ALGERIA AND TUNIS.

'The territory of Algeria contains an extraordinary
quantity of ruins and of ancient monuments. Everywhere
the Romans have left traces of their passage, and the works
accomplished by the legions excite still the admiration of
the traveller and the archaeologist. Triumphal arches,
aqueducts, inscriptions, meet us at every step in the Algerian
departments of France, and their abundance is equally great
in Tunis. Unfortunately, these precious relics of the past,
that had survived down to our own time, have during the
course of the nineteenth century been the object of deplorable
mutilations and destructions[1].' The acts of vandalism here
referred to were committed in great part by local officials
who carried out public works after the completion of the

---

[1] Tétreau, *Législation*, p. 211. Gsell, *Les Monuments Antiques de l'Algérie*, Paris, 1901, gives the best account of all these North African monuments.

French conquest. The French home government was urged repeatedly by archaeologists to put a stop to this by legal enactment, and the result was the inclusion of Algeria by a special clause, Article 16, in the Historical Monuments Act of 1887. The article runs as follows. 'The present law is 'applicable to Algeria.'

'In this part of France the state reserves to itself pro-'prietary rights in objects of art or of archaeology, buildings, 'mosaics, bas-reliefs, statues, medals, vases, columns, inscrip-'tions, which may exist upon or in the soil of estates belonging 'to the government or conceded by it to public institutions 'or private persons, and upon or in ground in military 'occupation.'

In view of the large amount of land in the newly settled colony that is government freehold, this provision secures state control over a large field. The terms of it are not so absolute as those of the Turkish Decree of 1884, according to which all antiquities discovered in the territory of the Ottoman Empire, whether above ground or underground, in the sea, lakes, rivers or watercourses, are the absolute property of the state. (See ante, p. 223.)

Algeria, as the wording of the Act just quoted shows, is regarded as a part of France. In the case of Tunis France only exercises a protectorate. Art. 17 of the Act of 1887 states that the provisions applicable to Algeria shall be extended to all countries placed under French protectorate, in which there does not already exist special legislation on the subject. Such legislation exists in Tunis, where there is in force a Decree of the Bey promulgated in 1886. The provisions of this Decree are modelled on those of the French Monument Act, which was at the time under consideration, but its sanctions are much more severe[1]. In analysing the French Act, ante, p. 88 f., it was pointed out that the sanctions were very mild, and disobedience to the main injunction of the Act only involved an action for damages. Furthermore, classification of a monument in private hands depended on the consent of the proprietor. The alienation or sale abroad

---

[1] The Tunisian legislation is analysed by Tétreau, p. 245 f.

of an enrolled movable object only involved the cancelling of the transaction and an action for damages.   In virtue of the Tunisian Decree on the other hand, the government of the Bey can schedule monuments against the will of their owners, and there is a provision that every monument scheduled as classé ' is to have a mark affixed to it which the proprietor is bound under penal sanctions to respect.   Any mutilation of a scheduled monument may be visited by the penalties of Art. 257 of the French penal code, amounting to imprisonment up to two years and a fine of twenty pounds. The illegal exportation of a scheduled object carries with it also penal consequences.   The Tunisian restrictions in the matter of excavations and ' finds' are also more severe than those of the French Monument Act.   A comparison of the Decree with the Act again shows how much more free is the hand of the protector of monuments in the less advanced countries.

APPENDIX.

A NOTE ON THE CARE OF MONUMENTS, AESTHETIC CONTROL IN CITIES, PROTECTION OF NATURAL SCENERY, ETC., IN THE UNITED STATES.

The design of this book, as the sub-title declares, is to take account only of the countries of Europe, but there has been added a chapter on monument legislation in certain non-European lands of old renown, such as India and Egypt, the abundant monuments of which are largely under European care. The inclusion of the United States would on many grounds have been advisable, but would have logically involved a great and undue extension of the limits of the work. A word or two may however here be introduced on the subject of American arrangements in the matters treated of in the foregoing chapters. There is indeed no part of the world in which more interest is taken in certain aspects of the subject before us than America. The problems in a comparatively new country are however different from those that confront the denizen of the older historic lands. There are of course regions of the New World where interesting monuments of great antiquity are to be found, and for the care of these practical measures are taken both by the States and by societies. The *Reports of the Smithsonian Institution*[1], to name only one publication of the kind, are sufficient to show the keen interest that American archaeologists take in the older relics of their land, while certain of the States forming the Union possess provisions in their laws for the protection of ancient monuments. Thus it is stated in the Reports to the British Foreign Office in 1896 that the State of Ohio has a ' Law designed to preserve ' the ancient earthworks in Warren County ' and ' exercises control

---

[1] Washington, U.S.A., yearly from 1847.

'over several places of historic interest'. Furthermore, 'the State 'maintains partially an Archaeological and Historical Society, the 'purpose of which is the preservation of historical material and 'evidences of ancient occupation. This Archaeological and His-'torical Society has recently attempted to afford better care and 'protection to the tumuli of the pre-historic people, and to the relics 'of the pioneers. The State has a museum, and the Archaeological 'Society participates in the management of it. Ohio being one of 'the richest fields in the world for archaeological work, there has 'been vast opportunity for obtaining collections which are interest-'ing from an historical standpoint.... The people of Ohio now 'contribute substantial sums annually for the collection and pre-'servation of historical objects, and there is a probability that the 'State will do much more in the way of appropriating money for 'the purpose of maintaining control and insuring the preservation of 'all objects of public interest[1].'

In the case of many States on the other hand, there are few or no monuments of the kind specially called 'ancient', but there exist in many parts numerous memorials, buildings, and sites commemorating events in the War of Independence or the Civil War, which are safeguarded by state or municipal authorities or by trustees and incorporations. Let us hope that the Report of 1896 from Illinois, with regard to the preservation of these memorials, applies to the country at large. 'The State of Illinois has no 'legislation on this subject. We have a monument in this State, 'at the capital, dedicated to the memory of Abraham Lincoln, and 'we have statues dedicated to General Grant and other heroes. 'No legislation is necessary to preserve them, because there is in 'our State no hand so villainous as to attempt their dispoliation[2].'

Some of the older cities of the Union, as is the case too in Canada, contain public and domestic buildings of historical and artistic value. Considerable interest is taken in some regions in the older colonial architecture, corresponding to the Georgian period in Britain; and in Nova Scotia and Canada, as well as in many cities especially in the southern parts of the United States, buildings of this character are studied and prized. The pressing questions however on the other side of the Atlantic concern rather the proper

---

[1] *Reports*, etc. (see General Bibliography), p. 50.
[2] *Reports*, p. 48.

development of new cities than the preservation of what is old. Intelligent consideration is given to the laying out of parks and open spaces in some of the leading American cities, while as regards the country at large, natural scenery, both in the States and in Canada, has been safeguarded on a magnificent scale. In 1893 a Board of Metropolitan Park Commissioners was constituted for the purpose of acquiring beautiful tracts of country in the neighbourhood of Boston, and the Boston building laws contemplate the laying out of extensive suburban districts on a regular and carefully considered plan. For the whole nation there was reserved by Act of Congress in 1872 the Yellowstone Park, a tract of over three thousand square miles in Montana and Wyoming, which has been 'dedicated and 'set apart as a public park or pleasuring ground for the benefit 'and enjoyment of the people'' Another great reservation of the kind concerns Canada as well as the United States. This is the land on either side of the Niagara river at the Falls. The first idea of preserving the amenity of this was due to the late Lord Dufferin, who, when Governor General of Canada, suggested the measure to the Governor of the State of New York. In both cases the necessary land has been acquired by the public authorities, and its management vested in Commissioners. In the State of New York some three hundred thousand pounds were voted out of public moneys for the original purchase, and there is a heavy annual charge over and above receipts[2].

The most interesting recent development in the American Care of Monuments is the establishment of Municipal Art Commissions in official connection with civic governments. Cities are now authorized to appoint commissions composed of persons who are experts in art matters, and to expend public money on the encouragement of decorative art as applied to public buildings and open spaces. Such commissions exist both in Boston and in New York, and the following is an abstract of some of the provisions for their working[3]. The art department of the City of Boston is under the charge of a board of five members appointed by the mayor from

[1] ibid., p. 43.
[2] *Report* by Sir Robert Hunter to the National Trust. See General Bibliography.
[3] *An Act to Establish a Board of Art Commissioners for the City of Boston,* 1898. *Statutes relating to the organization and powers of the Art Commission of the City of New York,* 1902.

lists furnished by bodies such as the trustees of the Museum of Fine
Arts and of the Boston Public Library. At New York the members
of the commission are to be the mayor of New York and the
presidents of certain museums and libraries *ex officio*, with ' one
' painter, one sculptor and one architect, all residents of the city of
' New York ; and three other residents of said city, none of whom
' shall be a painter, sculptor or architect or member of any other
' profession in the fine arts. All of the six last mentioned shall be
' appointed by the mayor from a list of not less than three times
' the number to be appointed proposed by the Fine Arts Federation
' of New York.' The composition of this commission is worthy of
note. The civic, the professional, and the lay elements are all
represented, and are expected to work together in harmony. The
arrangement is similar to that which prevails in some German towns,
where, as at Hildesheim, the burgomaster is at the same time the
president of the local association for the preservation of the beauty
of the city. In our own country, unfortunately, the attitude of
town councils and local protection societies is too often one of open
or veiled antagonism, and for a self-respecting British mayor or
provost to serve on a commission the avowed interests of which
are artistic, would seem to the average ratepayer almost an im-
propriety. This point is touched on in an interesting paper
embodying a report to this very Art Commission of New York by
its assistant secretary in 1903[1]. The report describes a visit to
various European capitals paid with a view of acquiring information
as to civic aesthetics in general. At the conclusion it is remarked
that America has the advantage over Europe in the relation of the
citizen to the town :—' In Europe the attitude of the citizen toward
' the city is that of dependence. The attitude of the city toward
' the citizen is that of independence. But in American cities the
' attitude of each toward the other is that of interdependence. The
' highest results can only be attained by mutual cooperation, city
' officials with citizens and citizens with city officials. This is
' generally lacking in Europe. It is a most promising sign in
' America.' In presence of many elements in American municipal
life of which that country can hardly be proud, it is gratifying to
come across signs of healthy action in the important domain of city

---

[1] *Civic Art in Northern Europe*, a Report to the Art Commission of the City
of New York, by Milo Roy Maltbie, October 12, 1903.

aesthetics. It may be rather soon to judge of the practical results of these civic art commissions, but their establishment is a fact of no small importance, and one of which in this country we shall do well to take note.

The regulations for the activity of the commissions in Boston and New York are very similar, and those of the latter city are evidently framed on the somewhat earlier regulations at Boston. The New York provisions, which it will be sufficient to quote, are contained in a long section headed 'All works of art to be submitted to and approved by the commission'. No work of art is to become the property of the city unless the work itself and its professed location have been approved by the commission. 'No existing ' work of art in the possession of the city shall be removed, re-located ' or altered in any way without the similar approval of the com- ' mission. When so requested by the mayor or the board of ' aldermen the commission shall act in a similar capacity, with ' similar powers, in respect of the designs of municipal buildings, ' bridges, approaches, gates, fences, lamps or other structures, erected ' or to be erected upon land belonging to the city, and in respect to ' the lines, grades and plotting of public ways and grounds, and in ' respect of arches, bridges, structures and approaches which are the ' property of any corporation or private individual, and which shall ' extend over or upon any street, avenue, highway, park or public ' place belonging to the city, and said commission shall so act ' and its approval shall be required for every such structure which ' shall hereafter be erected or contracted for at an expense exceeding ' one million dollars ' (£200,000).

Putting aside the question of the actual and prospective results on the aesthetic aspect of New York of the operations of this commission, it is important to note how extensive a scope is contemplated for them. Powers of the same kind are sighed for in vain by the dwellers on the Thames or beneath the shadow of Arthur's Seat! The regular building laws of the various American cities do not seem to contain provisions for direct aesthetic control over new designs for private structures, any more than do similar laws in the cities of the Old World, but American public opinion is in this matter perhaps in advance of that of Europe generally. Some of the States and cities in the Union have laws regulating advertisements. It is stated for example that 'The City of Phila-delphia does not allow anything to be erected that will interfere with the beauty of the streets, and therefore does not permit any unsightly or improper advertisements[1].'

Independently of what is done in the towns, there are in parts of the United States Village Improvement Societies that do good in the best of all ways, by interesting the dwellers in a particular locality in their surroundings.

---

[1] Extract from a letter from the Chief of the Bureau of City Property, Philadelphia, U.S.A.

INDEX.

Academy; Royal Irish, 43, 63; of Fine Arts of Parma, 131; Imperial, of the Fine Arts (Russia), 200 ff.; Royal, of San Fernando (Spain), 208 ff.; Royal Archaeological (Sweden), 192 ff.

Act, Acts, advertisement regulation; in America, 247; at Augsburg, 121; at Edinburgh, 45 f., 163 f.; in Hesse-Darmstadt, 112 f.; at Lübeck, 124; in Prussia, 102.

Act, Acts, ancient monuments; their scope, 8 f.;

  ,,   ,,   ,,   in Bulgaria, 45, 64, 227 f.;

  ,,   ,,   ,,   in Canton Bern, 45, 58, 172, 177;

  ,,   ,,   ,,   in Canton Neuchâtel, 45, 177;

  ,,   ,,   ,,   in Canton Vaud, 45, 90, 177, 179 ff.;

  ,,   ,,   ,,   in France, 9, 10, 20, 22, 45, 66, 68, 73 ff., 149, 179, 215, 241;

  ,,   ,,   ,,   in Great Britain and Ireland, 4, 7, 18, 31, 44, 45, 60, 68, 148, 151, 152 ff., 235;

  ,,   ,,   ,,   in Greece, 18, 44, 65, 216 ff.;

  ,,   ,,   ,,   in Hesse-Darmstadt, 9, 10, 19, 20, 44, 45, 66, 69, 101, 107 ff., 118;

  ,,   ,,   ,,   in Hungary, 20, 44, 66, 167;

  ,,   ,,   ,,   in India, 235 ff.;

  ,,   ,,   ,,   in Italy, 9, 10, 19, 45, 66, 132, 133 ff.;

  ,,   ,,   ,,   in Portugal, 45, 90, 213 ff.;

  ,,   ,,   ,,   in Roumania, 45, 64, 225 f.;

  ,,   ,,   ,,   in Switzerland, see 'Canton Bern', etc.;

  ,,   ,,   ,,   in Turkey, 45, 65, 222 f., 241.

Act, Acts, building, local, see 'Building regulations, local'.

Act, Communal and Provincial, of Italy, 146.

Act, Acts, draft monument; general, 9, 44, 107, 133; in Austria, 45, 166, 169; in Baden, 17, 45, 106; in Bavaria, 45, 103; in France, 92; in Great Britain and Ireland, 7, 152 ff.; in Italy, 5, 6, 131 ff.; in Norway, 191; in Portugal, 14; in Prussia, 45, 102; in Saxony, 105; in Servia, 227; in Spain, 45, 209, 212; in Switzerland (Valais) (Ticino), 177.

Act, English treasure-trove, 62 ff.

Act, Acts, exportation, see 'Exportation'.

  ,,   ,,   expropriation, see 'Expropriation'.

Act, Greek, for Public Works, 219.

Act, Irish Church, 156.

Act, Acts, Land Acquisition (India), 237.

Act, Acts, Lands Clauses Consolidation, 68, 155.

Act, Acts, Local and Personal; Chester, 45, 148, 163; Edinburgh, 45, 148, 163 f.; London County Council, 148, 158.

Act, Acts, Local-Government, 115. (See also 'Building regulations, local'.)

Advertising; control of, 38, 45 f., 92, 102, 112 f., 121, 124, 247;

,, Society for Checking Abuses of Public, 38, 164.

Aesthetic control, see Buildings, new, aesthetic control over .

Algeria, treatment of monuments in, 61, 240 f.

Almshouses, Trinity, 160.

Amberg, treatment of monuments at, 123.

Amenity, civic, care for; 17, 23, 25 ff., 28 ff., 45, 117; in America, 244 ff.; in Austria, (Prague) 171, (Vienna) 170; in Bavaria, 103; in Belgium, 174 f.; in France, 93 ff.; in Germany, 45, 93, 115 ff.; in Great Britain and Ireland, 45 f.; in Hesse-Darmstadt, 113; in Italy, 143 ff.

America, treatment of monuments in, 22, 243 ff.

Ami des Monuments, L', quoted, 94;

,, ,, referred to, 33, 38, 46, 53, 75, 92.

Amis des Monuments Parisiens, Les, 94.

Amis des Monuments Rouennais, Les, 94.

Anhalt, treatment of monuments in, 106.

Antiquaries, Society of, 14, 60; of Scotland, 61.

Antiquary, State; in Finland, 204 ff.; in Norway, 191; in Sweden, 192, 198. (See also 'Conservator', 'Director', 'Ephor-general', 'Inspector general', 'Rijksantikvar'.)

Archaeologia, referred to, 14.

Archaeological Survey of India, 232 ff.

Archaeologist; Cantonal, in Vaud, 180.

,, State, see 'Antiquary, State'.

Archives; de la Commission des Monuments Historiques, 84; Swedish Antiquarian Topographical, 198 f.

'Art nouveau, L',' 56

Arts, Fine, Minister of, 8, 79.

Asiatic Society; of Bengal, 231; of Calcutta, 234.

Associations; architectural, 35; interested in London monuments, 159; protective and antiquarian; abroad, 36 ff., 91, 99, 175, 191; at home, 34 ff., 46. (See also 'Societies'.)

Augsburg, treatment of monuments at, 119 f.

Austria, treatment of monuments in, 11, 15, 65, 166 ff.

Avignon, vandalism at, 33. (See also 'Fortifications'.)

Babylonia, ancient, care of monuments in, 13.

Baden, treatment of monuments in, 17, 106 f.

Bamberg, treatment of monuments at, 117.

Baupolizei, see 'Buildings, new, aesthetic control over', and 'Building regulations, local, in Germany'.

Bavaria, treatment of monuments in, 45, 103, 116 ff.

Bayreuth, Markgraf of, 14.

Beauties of Nature, care for; see 'Nature, beauties of'.

Belgium, treatment of monuments in, 39, 173 f.

Bern, see 'Act, Acts, ancient monuments, in Canton Bern'.

Berwick-on-Tweed, vandalism at, 33. (See also 'Fortifications'.)

Border Counties Advertizer, The, referred to, 64.
Bosnia, treatment of monuments in, 64, 229.
Boston, U.S.A., treatment of monuments at, 245.
Bridges, ancient, in Northamptonshire, 163.
Britain, Great, treatment of monuments in, see 'Great Britain'.
Brussels, treatment of monuments at, 174.
Builder, The, 148.
Building regulations, local;
    ,,   in America, 244 ff., (Boston, 245, New York, 245 f., Philadelphia, 247);
    ,,   in Austria, 170;
    ,,   in Belgium, 174 f., (Brussels, 174);
    ,,   in France, 93 ff.;
    ,,   in Germany, 45, 97, 115 ff.,
        Bavaria, 103, 116 ff., (Amberg, 123, Augsburg, 120 f., Bamberg, 117, Lindau, 119, Nürnberg, 118 f., Rothenburg, 121 ff., Würzburg, 119);
        Hannover, 115 f., (Hildesheim, 119 f., Lüneburg, 123 f.);
        Hesse-Darmstadt, 116, (Wimpfen, 119);
        Lübeck, 124;
        Nassau, 115;
        Prussia, 115, (Danzig, 119, Frankfurt, 124 f.);
        Saxony, 116;
        Würtemberg, 116;
    ,,   in Great Britain and Ireland, 163, (Chester, 45, 163);
    ,,   in Italy, 145 ff., (Rome, 146 f.).
Buildings, new, aesthetic control over; in America, 244 ff.; in Austria, 170; in Belgium, 174 f.; in France, 96, 164 f.; in Great Britain, 96, 145, 164 f.; in Italy, 143 ff.; in Saxony, 116.
Bulgaria, 225; treatment of monuments in, 64, 65, 227 f. (See also 'Act, Acts, ancient monuments'.)
Bulletin Monumental, 77.
Bulletins of Societies; 34 ff., 174.

Canada, treatment of monuments in, 244.
Canova, 128.
Canterbury, Chapter House at, its restoration, 50.
Cassiodorus, 13.
Castelar, President, his care for monuments, 211.
Castiglione, Baldassare, 12.
Catalogue of monuments, see 'Elenco', 'Inventory'.
Cathedrals; English, 83, 149; French, 80, 149.
Caumont, Arcisse de, 36, 77 f.
Charles XI of Sweden, 14, 192.
Chateaubriand, 74.
Chester, building regulations at, 45, 163.
Civic Art in Northern Europe, American Report on, 246.
'Classement'; as principle of monument administration, 10, 57 ff., 215; German criticism of, 58, 100; in France, 57 f., 80 ff., 242; in Great Britain, 58, 155 f.; in Hesse-Darmstadt, 109, 111; in India, 235; in Ireland, 156, in Italy, 138 f.; in Portugal, 213 f., 215; in Roumania, 58, 226; in Spain, 208, 212; in Switzerland, (Canton Bern) 58, (Canton Vaud) 181 f.; in Tunis, 242.

Cluny, vandalism at, 75.

Collections, private, see 'Private collections'.

Cologne, 59.

Colonial architecture, 244.

Colonies, the, 3, 31, 244 f.

Comité; de Conservation des Monuments de l'Art Arabe, 238; des Travaux Historiques, 36, 76, 79; Permanent d'Égyptologie, 238, 240.

Commission on Historical Manuscripts, 11, 60, 150 f., 153.

Commissioner of Works, First, 154, 165.

Commissioners of Works, in England and Ireland, 155 f.

Commissions, art, municipal, American, 245; at Boston, 245; at New York, 245 ff.

Commissions, monument, civic; at Frankfurt, 125; at Lyons, 94; at Paris (Commission du Vieux Paris), 59, 94; at Rome, 146 f.

Commissions, monument, national, 8, 32;

,,   in Austria (Central-Commission), 11, 19, 168 f.;

,,   in Belgium, 173 f.;

,,   in Denmark, 15, 186;

,,   in Finland, 205 ff.;

,,   in France (Commission des Monuments Historiques), 76, 79 ff.;

,,   for Great Britain and Ireland (proposed), 11;

,,   in Greece, 217;

,,   in Hesse (Council on Monuments), 109;

,,   in Holland, 58, 176;

,,   in Hungary (Council on Monuments), 167;

,,   in Italy, 130, 133, 135 f.;

,,   in Norway, 191;

,,   in Portugal (Council on National Monuments), 213 f.;

,,   in Prussia, 102;

,,   in Roumania, 226;

,,   in Russia, 201 ff.;

,,   in Saxony, 105;

,,   in Spain, 209 ff.;

,,   in Switzerland; federal, 177 f.; cantonal, 177, (Vaud) 180 ff.;

,,   in Würtemberg, 104.

Commissions, monument, provincial; in France (proposed), 93; in Germany, 102; in Greece, 217; in Italy, 135; in Spain, 209 ff.

Committee for the Survey of Memorials of Greater London, 160 f.

Compulsory Purchase, see 'Expropriation'.

Congrès archéologique de France, 77.

Congress; architectural, at Madrid, 46, 48, 56, 83; of German Historical and Artistic Societies, at Strassburg, 98 f.; international, for the History of Art, (Lübeck) 100.

Congress, congresses, monument, in Germany, 27, 100;

,,   first (Dresden, 1900), 46, 52 ff., 58, 107;

,,   second (Freiburg-i.-Br., 1901), 59, 103, 104, 107, 108, 116, 118;

,,   third (Düsseldorf, 1902), 29, 108, 109, 115, 177, 179;

,,   fourth (Erfurt, 1903), 69, 108;

,,   fifth (Mainz, 1904), 100, 113, 114.

Conseil d'Architecture (in Prefecture of the Seine), 96.

Conseil général des Bâtiments Civils, 95.

Conservators, monument, 8, 32, 41.

Conservators, monument, general, (Anhalt) 106; (Baden) 106; (Bavaria) 103; (Hesse-Darmstadt) 109; (Prussia) 102; (Turkey) 223; (Würtemberg) 104.

Conservators, monument, provincial, (Austria) 169; (Prussia) 102; (Greece) 217. (See also 'Curator', 'Director', 'Inspectors'.)

Corporate ownership of monuments, 9.

Correspondents, provincial, (Austria) 169; (France) 78.

Corso, via del, 146.

Council on Monuments, (Hesse-Darmstadt) 109, 113, (Hungary) 167; on National Monuments (Portugal), 213.

County Council, London, 26, 28, 157 ff.

County Councils, 157, 162, 163.

Cross, Queen Eleanor, by Northampton, 162.

Crusades, the, 13.

Cunningham, Sir Alexander, his work in India, 231 ff.

Curator of Ancient Monuments (India), 233.

'Danefae', 186.

Danubian Provinces, treatment of monuments in, 225 ff.

Danzig, treatment of monuments at, 119.

'Dead monuments', 48.

Dean of Guild (Edinburgh), 96.

Decrees, Papal, Imperial, Royal, Khedival, and Ministerial, see 'Rescripts'.

Denkmalpflege, Tag für, see 'Congress, congresses, monument, in Germany'.

Denkmalpflege, Die (Zeitschrift), quoted, 17, 53, 58, 112, 116, 118.

,, referred to, 14, 15, 19, 38, 100, 103, 105, 109, 119, 168, 201.

Denkmalrat (Hesse), 109, 113.

Denmark, treatment of monuments in, 185 ff.

Diocletian, Palace of, at Spalatro, 169.

Director, Directorate, of monuments (Denmark), 188 ff.; of museums (Egypt), 239.

Domestic work, its value, 23, 30.

Doria Pamphilj edict, 128 f.

Draft Acts, see 'Act, Acts, draft'.

Dunblane Abbey, restoration of church, 49.

Durham Cathedral, treatment of, 55.

Edicts, protective; in Germany, 101; Doria Pamphilj, 128 f.; Pacca, 130. (See also 'Rescripts'.)

Edinburgh, 33, 45, 163 f., 171.

Eginhard, 13.

Egypt, treatment of monuments in; (Ancient) 13; (Modern) 61, 238 ff.

Elenco, 126, 139, 147. (See also 'Inventory', 'Schedule'.)

Emilia, the, treatment of monuments in, 131.

England, treatment of monuments in, 62 ff., 157 ff. (See also 'Great Britain and Ireland'.)

Ephesus, export of sculpture from, 222.

Ephor-General of Antiquities (Greece), 217 ff., 221.

Excavations, control of; 6, 8, 61 ff., 99, 113; in Algeria, 241; in Baden, 107; in Bosnia, 229; in Bulgaria, 227 f.; in Egypt, 239 f.; in Finland, 207; in France, 85, 89 f.; in Greece, 218 ff.; in Hesse-Darmstadt, 111, 113; in Hungary, 167;

in India, 235, 238; in Italy, 128 f., 130, 133, 134, 140 f., 143; in Roumania, 226 f.; in Russia, 201 ff.; in Spain, 209 f.; in Sweden, 193 f.; in Switzerland (Vaud), 182 f.; in Tunis, 242; in Turkey, 222 f.

Exportation (or alienation) of works of art; 6, 13, 66 f., 99; regulations on the subject; in Austria, 168; in Baden, 107; in Bosnia, 229; in Bulgaria, 228; in Denmark, 186; in Egypt, 239 f.; in Finland, 205; in France, 89; in Greece, 218, 220; in Hesse-Darmstadt, 108; in India, 237 f.; in Italy, 67, 128 f., 130, 131, 132 f., 134, 136 ff., 139, 143; in Roumania, 226; in Russia, 203 f.; in Spain, 210; in Sweden, 192, 196 f.; in Switzerland, 179, (Vaud) 182; in Tunis, 242; in Turkey, 222 f.

Expropriation, or compulsory purchase, on artistic or historical grounds; its principle, 9 f., 66, 67 ff., 99, 237;
established; in Belgium, 175; in France, 9, 84 f., 87, 88, 90, 93; in Greece, 220; in Hesse-Darmstadt, 9, 110, 111, 118 f.; in Hungary (also temporary), 167; in India, 237; in Italy, 9, 132 f., 136 f., 141, 144, 146; in Portugal, 214; in Roumania, 227; in Switzerland (Vaud), 182; in Turkey, 223.
inoperative or doubtful; in Austria, 169; in Denmark, 187; in Great Britain and Ireland, 7, 10, 68, 153 ff.; in Prussia, 68.

Fergusson, James, his work for Indian monuments, 231, 234.
'Finds', see 'Excavations, control of'.
Fines, for breaches of monument regulations, see 'Penalties'.
Finland, treatment of monuments in, 204 ff.
Foreigners and excavations in Italy, 66, 140.
Foreningen til Norske Fortidsmindesmærkers Bevaring, 191.
Fortifications, ancient, care for; 6, 17, 23, 74; in Bavaria, 116, (Rothenburg) 122 f.; in Finland, 205; in France (Avignon), 33; in Great Britain and Ireland, (Berwick) 33, (Chester) 45, 163; in Greece (Venetian), 221; in Italy (Rome), 147; in Prussia, 17, 101; in Sweden, 192.
France, museums in, 42 f., 75, 83.
France, treatment of monuments in, 9 f., 29, 33, 58, 66, 73 ff., 165. (See also 'Act, Acts, ancient monuments'.)
Frankfurt, treatment of monuments at, 124 f.
Freiburg (Switzerland), treatment of monuments in, 177.

Gaceta de Madrid, quoted, 211; referred to, 208.
Gentleman's Magazine, referred to, 14, 76.
Germany, treatment of monuments in, 15, 26 f., 31, 44, 45, 59, 98, 164. (See also 'Act, Acts, ancient monuments, in Hesse-Darmstadt'.)
Giles', St, Edinburgh, 19, 55.
Gjölbaschi, sculptures from, 222.
Giunta Superiore di Belle Arti, 136, 143.
Goethe, quoted, 21.
Gothic Revival, the, 15.
Grand' Place, Brussels, its treatment, 174.
Great Britain and Ireland, treatment of monuments in, 4 f., 7, 10, 14 f., 19, 24, 31, 34 f., 38, 40 f., 43, 46 ff. (restoration), 58, 60, 62 ff. (treasure-trove), 66, 148 ff., 235, 237. (See also 'Act, Acts, ancient monuments', and 'Berwick', 'Chester', 'Edinburgh', 'London', 'Northamptonshire'.)
Greece, treatment of monuments in, 15, 65, 216 ff. (See also 'Act, Acts, ancient monuments'.)

Guizot, 57, 74, 76.
Gustavus Adolphus, 14, 192.

Hansard's Debates, quoted, 31, 151, 153; referred to, 152, 153.
Harcourt, Sir William, on Ancient Monuments Act, 152.
Hebrews, the, and monuments, 13.
'Heimatschutz' Society, 27.
Herzgovina, treatment of monuments in, 229.
Hesse-Darmstadt, treatment of monuments in, 44 f., 66, 69, 106, 108 ff. (See also
    'Act, Acts, ancient monuments'.)
Hexham, restoration at, 49.
Hildesheim, treatment of monuments at, 29, 59, 118, 119 f.
History, Victoria, of the Counties of England, 163.
Holland, treatment of monuments in, 58, 173, 175 f.
Houses of Parliament, British, their attitude towards the care of ancient monu-
    ments, 7, 18, 44, 151, 152 ff., 164, 237.
Hugo, Victor, 15, 74, 75, 152.
Hungary, treatment of monuments in, 66, 166 f. (See also 'Act, Acts,
    ancient monuments'.)

Illinois, treatment of monuments in, 244.
Importation of works of art, (Greece) 220; (India) 237.
India, treatment of monuments in, 91, 231 ff.
Insignia on Tuscan palaces, 130.
Inspector, Inspectors, of monuments, 8, 41, 74, 76, 81 f., 103, 128, 129, 135, 151,
    156, 186. (See also 'Conservators', 'Director', 'Curator'.)
Institut des Provinces, 78.
Institutes, foreign, and excavations in Italy, 140.
Inventaire Général du Vieux Lyon, 59, 161.
Inventorization, Inventory, of monuments; its meaning and importance, 11, 35,
                58, 60;
    ,,   in Austria, 169 f., (Vienna) 59;
    ,,   in Baden, 106;
    ,,   in Bavaria, 103;
    ,,   in Belgium, 173;
    ,,   in Finland, 206;
    ,,   in France, 58, (Lyons) 59, 161, (Paris) 59;
    ,,   in Germany (general) (Cologne) (Hildesheim), 59;
    ,,   in Great Britain, 35, 60, 151, (London) 158 ff., (Scotland) 60 f.;
    ,,   in Greece, 220 f.;
    ,,   in Hesse-Darmstadt, 108 f.;
    ,,   in Holland, 58, 176;
    ,,   in Italy, 58, 129 f., 133, 138, (Rome) 147;
    ,,   in Lübeck, 60;
    ,,   in Mecklenburg-Schwerin, 106;
    ,,   in Portugal, 213;
    ,,   in Prussia, 101;
    ,,   in Roumania, 226;
    ,,   in Russia, 201 f.;
    ,,   in Saxony, 105;
    ,,   in Spain, 210, 211;

Inventorization, in Sweden, 198;
    ,,   in Switzerland, 177 ff.;
    ,,   in Würtemberg, 105.
Iona, restoration at, 50.
Ireland, gold objects found in, 63.
Ireland, treatment of monuments in, 156 f.
Italy, treatment of monuments in, 5 f., 15, 45, 58, 66, 67, 68, 126 ff., 164.
    (See also 'Act, Acts, ancient monuments'.)

John V of Portugal and monuments, 14.
Johnson, Dr, referred to, 12.
Journal, R.I.B.A., see 'Royal Institute of British Architects'.
Journals of societies, at home and abroad, 34 ff.
Journal of the Society of Arts, quoted, 91.
Juridical Review, The, referred to, 63.
Jutland, treatment of monuments in, 189.

Korrespondenzblatt, etc., quoted, 55, 58.
Kunsthandbuch für Deutschland, 37, 59.
Kunsttopographie for Austria, 170.

'Laissez-faire', British policy of, 5, 8.
Landscape beauty, see 'Nature, beauties of'.
Law, laws, monument, etc., see 'Act, Acts'.
Legislation, monument, etc., see 'Act, Acts'.
Leo X, Pope, 11, 127.
Lindau, treatment of monuments at, 119.
List, see 'Inventory', 'Schedule'.
'Living monuments', 48.
Local enactments, see 'Building regulations, local'.
Lombardy, treatment of monuments in, 131.
London; Committee for Survey of Memorials of Greater, 160 f. ; monuments in, 26; question of rebuilding, 145.
London County Council, see 'County Council, London'.
Lucca, treatment of monuments in, 131.
Lübeck, international congress in, 100; treatment of monuments in, 60, 119, 124.
Lüneburg, treatment of monuments at, 123 f.
Lyons, treatment of monuments at, 59, 161.

Madrid, Congress of Architects at, 46, 48, 56, 83.
Månadsblad, etc., quoted, 198.
Manuscripts, Historical, commission on, 11, 60, 150 f., 153.
Mark's, St, at Venice, its pavement, 55.
Marks on protected monuments, 107, 190, 242.
Martin, M., on public utility, quoted, 74.
Mecklenburg-Schwerin, treatment of monuments in, 106.
Memoirs, of societies, 34 ff.
Memorial to Government, proposed, on aesthetic control, 165.
Mérimée, Prosper, 76.
Minister of Public Works, France, circular by, 91 f.
Ministers of the Fine Arts, 8, 79.

Minutes, Ministerial, etc., see 'Rescripts'.
Mittheilungen of the Central-Commission, 170.
Modena, treatment of monuments in, 131.
Montalembert; quoted, 75; referred to, 29, 74, 76.
Monument Acts, Commissions, Congresses, laws, legislation, protective Associa-
tions, etc., see 'Acts', 'Commissions', etc., etc.
Morris, William, 38, 53, 117, 152.
Movable works of art, treatment of, 6, 15, 17, 19, 22, 24, 42, 58, 60, 61 ff.
67, 75, 81, 85, 89, 99, 108, 129, 136, 143, 167, 169, 182, 197, 205, 219, 228.
Museums, 24, 42f., 75, 83, 142 f., 150, 186 ff., 203, 206, 209 f., 217, 222, 22',
229, 239, 240, 244, 245.

Naples, treatment of monuments in, 132.
Nassauer Haus, Nürnberg, 118.
National Trust, The, 21, 28, 38, 157, 160.
Native princes in India, their care for monuments, 233.
Naturdenkmäler, 20, 111.
Nature, beauties of, care for; its importance, 20 f., 25 ff.; in America, 244 f
in Austria, 170; in Bavaria, 103 f.; in France, 90 ff.; in Hesse, 111 f., 113;
Lübeck, 124.
Nederlandsche Oudheidkundige Bond, 175.
Niagara Falls, 21; reservations at, 28, 245.
Northamptonshire, action of County Council of, 162.
Norway, treatment of monuments in, 191.
Novoe Vremya, The, quoted, 202.
Nürnberg, treatment of monuments at, 118 f.

Œuvre Nationale Belge, L', 174.
Ohio, treatment of monuments in, 243 f.
Orange, Roman Theatre at, expropriations out of, 85.
Ordinances, Imperial, Royal, etc., see 'Rescripts'.
Oswestry, case of treasure-trove at, 64.

Pacca edict, 130.
Palace of the Popes at Avignon, 84.
Parma, treatment of monuments in, 131.
Penalties, for breach of monument regulations, Baden (draft Act), 107; Bosnia,
229; Egypt, 239; Finland, 205; France, 10, 88 f.; Germany, (Hildesheim) 120,
(Rothenburg) 123; Greece, 218, 221; Hesse-Darmstadt, 10, 113; Hungary,
167; India, 235 f., 238; Italy, (Doria Pamphilj edict) 129, (draft Act of 1872)
132, (Act of 1902) 10, 134, 141; Portugal, 215; Roumania, 226; Sweden,
(edicts of 17th century) 192, (decree of 1886) 195 f., 198; Switzerland (Vaud),
182, 183; Tunis, 241 f.; Turkey, 224.
Periodicals; monument, 38; with interest in monuments, 34 ff.
Peter's, St, its baleful influence on Roman monuments, 11, 14, 128.
Petrarch, 13.
Piano regolatore, 144 f.
Pius II, Pope, 128; Pius VII, Pope, 128, 130.
Place des Vosges; Place Vendôme, 95.
'Ponts et Chaussées', Service of, its care for natural beauty, 91.
Popes, Roman, and ancient monuments, 11, 14, 128, 129, 130.

Posters, see 'Advertising'.
Prague, 170.
Prell's House, Bamberg, 117.
Private property, proprietors, rights of, 5, 7, 9, 10, 61 f., 67 f., 87, 98, 113 f., 132, 134, 152 ff. (See also 'Expropriation'.)
Private collections, state dealings with; in Bulgaria, 228; in Bosnia, 229; in Greece, 220 f.; in India, 237 f.; in Italy, 67, 128 f., 130, 133, 137 ff.; in Roumania, 226; in Tunis, 242; in Turkey, 222.
Proceedings of antiquarian and protective societies, 34 ff., 61.
Proust, M. Antonin, quoted, 74.
Prussia, treatment of monuments in, 15, 17, 19, 44, 68, 98, 101 f., 118.
Purchase, compulsory, see 'Expropriation'.

Quarterly Review, The, 148.
Quast, von, 102.
'Questionnaire', of the Comité Historique des Arts et Monuments, 76.

R. I. B. A., see 'Royal Institute of British Architects'.
Railways and monument preservation, 88, 92, 111, 169, 189, 194, 203.
Raphael, his interest in Roman monuments, 11 ff., 74, 127.
Regolamento Edilizio, see 'Building regulations, local, in Italy'.
Report; to Art Commission of New York, 246; on the Preservation of Monuments in Denmark, 188 ff ; by Raphael (?) on Roman monuments, 11 ff., 127; by the Rijksantikvar of Sweden, 198; by Schinkel to Prussian government, 15, 19, 101.
Reports of antiquarian and protective societies, 34 ff.
Reports; of Archaeological Survey of India, 232 f.; of Austrian Central-Commission, 170; to British Foreign Office in 1897, 98, 193, 200, 208, 243 f.; on Italian monument administration, 142 f.; from localities in Holland, 175; of London County Council, 157 ff.; of Norse Society, 191; of Rijkscommissie on monuments of Holland, 176; of Smithsonian Institution, 243, (Worsaae) 184, 187.
Rescripts on monuments, Papal, Imperial, Royal, Khedival, Ministerial; their scope, 44, 45; in Bavaria, 103, 104, 116, (Bayreuth) 14; in Bosnia, 229; in Denmark, 185 ff.; in Egypt, 238 f.; in Finland, 205 f.; in Greece, 19, 221; in India, 231, 233; in Italy, 128 ff., 135; in Portugal, 14, 212, 213 f.; in Prussia, 17, 101; in Russia, 200 f., 202 f.; in Sweden, 14, 184, 192 ff.; in Tunis, 241 f.; in Turkey, 222 f.
Restoration, 6, 8, 13, 42, 46 ff., 80, 81 f., 105, 127, 142, 169, 174, 175, 207, 233.
Revue de l'Art Chrétien, referred to, 46.
Revue des Deux Mondes, referred to, 76.
Rights of private property, see 'Private property, rights of'.
Rijksantikvar, of Sweden, 192, 198.
Rijkscommissie, in Holland, 176.
Road, the Old Kent, 162.
Romantic movement, the, 15.
Rome; ancient monuments at, 11, 13, 127, 146 f.; treatment of the modern city, 40, 127, 144 f., 146 f.
Rothenburg, treatment of monuments at, 121 f.
Roumania, treatment of monuments in, 58, 64, 225 f. (See also 'Act, Acts, ancient monuments'.)

Royal Institute of British Architects, 40, 52 ; *Journal* of; quoted, 8, 145; referred to, 48, 165.
Ruskin, John; quoted, 28; referred to, 53, 152.

Salisbury, Marquis of, his opinion of the Monument Act quoted, 154.
Sanctions, see ' Penalties'.
Saxony, treatment of monuments in, 105, 116.
Scandinavian Kingdoms, the, treatment of monuments in, 184.
' Scapa ', 164.
Schedule, Scheduling, see 'Classement'.
Schinkel, his report to the Prussian government, 15, 19, 101.
Scotland, treatment of monuments in, 60, 62 f.
Scotsman, The, referred to, 63.
Scott, Sir Gilbert, 51, 83.
Servia, treatment of monuments in, 227.
Servitudes, building, in Paris, etc., 95.
Sicily, treatment of monuments in, 132.
Sixtus IV, Pope, 128.
Sketch Books of architectural associations, 35.
Smithsonian Institution, its *Reports* referred to, 184, 187, 243.
Société; Française d'Archeologie, 77; Nationale pour la Protection des Sites, etc., en Belgique, 174; pour la Protection des Paysages (France), 92.
Societies; antiquarian and protective, abroad, 36 ff.; at home, 34 ff. (see also 'Associations'); Village Improvement, in America, 247.
Society; of Antiquaries, 14, 60; of Antiquaries of Scotland, 61; Archaeological, of Servia, 227; Archaeological and Historical, of Ohio, 243 f.; Royal, of Architects and Archaeologists of Portugal, 213; Swiss, for the Preservation of Historical Monuments of Art, 178 f.
Southwark, Nelson Square, 162.
Spalatro, Diocletian's Palace at, 169.
Stadtbild, das, 23, 28, 45, 117.
State, the, its interest in monuments, *passim*.
States of the Church, treatment of monuments in, 128, 130, 132.
Statute, statutes, see ' Act, Acts'.
Stonehenge, 4, 21.
Survey; of London, 161; Archaeological, of India, 232 f.
Sweden, treatment of monuments in, 14, 185, 191 ff.
Switzerland, treatment of monuments in, 173, 177 ff.

Tablets, on London houses, 161.
Tag für Denkmalpflege, see 'Congress, congresses, monument, in Germany'.
Touring Club, of France, its work for monuments, 91.
Traffic in antiquities, 220, 237. (See also 'Exportation', 'Private collections, state dealings with'.)
Transactions of antiquarian and protective societies, 34 ff.
Treasure-trove, 62 ff., 185.
Trees, protection for, in Hesse, 112.
Trocadéro, casts from sculpture in, 83.
Tunis, treatment of monuments in, 61, 241 f.
Turkey, treatment of monuments in, 61, 65, 222 ff. (See also 'Act, Acts, ancient monuments'.)

Tuscany, treatment of monuments in, 130, 131.

Uffizi regionali, 135, 142.
Utilitarianism and the care of monuments, 25.

Venetia, treatment of monuments in, 131.
Vienna, treatment of monuments at, 59, 170.
Village Improvement Societies, American, 247.
Viollet-le-Duc, 51, 82, 152; his *Dictionnaire de l'Architecture Francaise* referred to, 46.
Vitet, Louis, first General Inspector of Historical Monuments in France, 76.

Walls, city, ancient, see 'Fortifications'.
Wimpfen-am-Berg, treatment of monuments at, 119.
Wordsworth, referred to, 27.
Worsaae, on ancient monuments in Denmark, 185 ff.
Würtemberg, treatment of monuments in, 104, 116.
Würzburg, treatment of monuments at, 119.
Wussow, von, his work on monument preservation referred to, 14, 15, 98, 101, 104, 168, 173.

Yearbook of Learned Societies, referred to, 34.
Yellowstone Park, 21, 28, 245.

CAMBRIDGE: PRINTED BY JOHN CLAY, M.A. AT THE UNIVERSITY PRESS.

For EU product safety concerns, contact us at Calle de José Abascal, 56-1°, 28003 Madrid, Spain or eugpsr@cambridge.org.

www.ingramcontent.com/pod-product-compliance
Ingram Content Group UK Ltd.
Pitfield, Milton Keynes, MK11 3LW, UK
UKHW010344140625
459647UK00010B/822